Radegund

The Trials and Triumphs of a Merovingian Queen

E. T. DAILEY

OXFORD
UNIVERSITY PRESS

OXFORD
UNIVERSITY PRESS

Oxford University Press is a department of the University of Oxford. It furthers
the University's objective of excellence in research, scholarship, and education
by publishing worldwide. Oxford is a registered trade mark of Oxford University
Press in the UK and certain other countries.

Published in the United States of America by Oxford University Press
198 Madison Avenue, New York, NY 10016, United States of America.

Library of Congress Cataloging-in-Publication Data
Names: Dailey, E. T. (Erin T.) author.
Title: Radegund : the trials and triumphs of a Merovingian queen / E. T. Dailey
Description: New York, NY : Oxford University Press, [2023] |
Series: Women in antiquity | Includes bibliographical references and index.
Identifiers: LCCN 2023007350 (print) | LCCN 2023007351 (ebook) |
ISBN 9780197699201 (paperback) | ISBN 9780197656105 (hardback) |
ISBN 9780197656129 (epub) | ISBN 9780197656136 | ISBN 9780197656112
Subjects: LCSH: Radegunda, Queen, consort of Clotaire I, King of the Franks, -587. |
Christian women saints—Gaul—Biography. |
Women ascetics—Gaul—Biography. | Franks—Queens—Biography. |
Merovingians—Queens—Biography. | Abbaye Sainte-Croix de Poitiers. |
France—History—To 987.
Classification: LCC BX4700 .R3 D35 2023 (print) | LCC BX4700 .R3 (ebook) |
DDC 270 .2092 [B]—dc23/eng/20230421
LC record available at https://lccn.loc.gov/2023007350
LC ebook record available at https://lccn.loc.gov/2023007351

DOI: 10.1093/oso/9780197656105.001.0001

Paperback printed by Marquis Book Printing, Canada
Hardback printed by Bridgeport National Bindery, Inc., United States of America

for Henna

pectore perspicuo sapientia provida fulget
Wisdom and foresight flow from a pure heart

Fortunatus, Poems, 7.6, line 19

Contents

Map 1: Gaul in the Sixth Century

Canterbury•

English Channel

Tournai•
Vitry-en-Artois •
•Baralle
Péronne
Biaches• •Vermand
Athies
Noyon• •Laon
Rouen • Cuise-la-Motte• ••Soissons
Berny-Rivière •Reims
Paris • •Chelles

Scheldt

Meuse

Andernach• •Koblenz

•Trier

•Metz

Rhine

Moselle

Seine

Orléans
Neuvy-le-Roi•
Tours•
Saix • •Chinon
Vouillé • •Poitiers

•Auxerre
•Langres

•Dijon

Autun •
•Chalon-sur-Saône

Rhine

Loire

Clermont •
Lyon•
Vienne•

Vienne

Seine

• Saint-Maurice
d'Agaune

Milan•
Pavia•

Po

Bobbio•

• Blaye
• Bordeaux

Garonne

Rhône

Toulouse•

Arles •

• Lérins

THE WORLD OF RADEGUND

0   100   200 km

© 2022, Mappa Mundi Cartography

Narbonne• •Agde

Mediterranean Sea

Map 2: Poitiers in the Time of Radegund

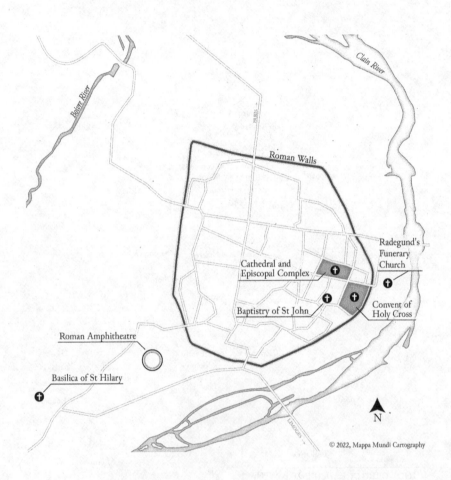

Clain River

Boivre River

PARIS

Roman Walls

Radegund's
Funerary
Church

Cathedral and
Episcopal Complex

Baptistry of St John

Convent of
Holy Cross

Roman Amphitheatre

Basilica of St Hilary

LIMOGES

N

© 2022, Mappa Mundi Cartography

Illustrations

Figures

Acknowledgements

Books are written by authors, but they come into being through the kindness of others. I am very grateful that Helmut Reimitz put my name forward to Oxford University Press as a potential contributor for the series 'Women in Antiquity'. It is my sincere hope that I have done justice to his recommendation. Stefan Vranka commissioned the project and challenged me to write material suitable for a wide audience. If I have come close to achieving this goal, it is only through his insights and advice. He showed remarkable patience as my work was interrupted by the pandemic and the vagaries of my career, through which I have been helped by many colleagues, regretfully too many to mention by name. But I cannot fail to thank Jo Story and Emilia Jamroziak, who have provided me with their steadfast support in my efforts to find a place for myself in academia. I am also ever grateful to Ian Wood, who has continued to guide me through this long journey since I first began my MA and then PhD under his supervision, and who graciously commented on this manuscript.

I am eager to thank four early career scholars, Kent Navalesi, Hope Williard, Shachar Orlinski, and Calum Platts, for permitting me to read their unpublished work on subjects related to this book. I must also hasten to acknowledge two doctoral researchers, Teresa Porciani and Jess Hodgkinson, for so openly sharing their expertise with me. I also found it a privilege to have my ideas sharpened through my conversations with Shelley Puhak as she wrote her recent book, *The Dark Queens: The Bloody Rivalry that Forged the Medieval World*, which brings to life the remarkable story of Brunhild and Fredegund. I also wish to thank Erik Goosmann, who produced the beautifully rendered maps and floorplans that appear here, and who provided me with his expertise—not merely as a talented cartographer, but also as a scholar of the early medieval period. In every instance, the mistakes that appear within this book are entirely my own, and they would surely be more numerous if I had not enjoyed such assistance.

No one read more versions of the draft, or engaged in more discussion about Radegund, than my wife Henna, whose many insights appear in too many places to credit. I fear that she has been made to share far too much of these past many months with a woman who died fourteen centuries ago. My two young daughters, Ayah Mihrimah and Maha Aurelia, also endured my absence with an abundance of patience greater than their years. They were not yet here in 2015 to grace my previous book with their love and laughter. The kindness shown to me by my children makes much more than books, but it makes the books as well. *Haec ornamenta mea.*

E. T. Dailey
Leicester, East Midlands, 2022

Introduction

Touching the Heavens

A great serpent, a winged beast with an enormous mouth, lurked in the cellars of Poitiers. The *Grand'goule* stalked the city's inhabitants from the underground recesses of their homes. Not even the pious nuns of Holy Cross escaped this menace, risking their lives each time they ventured into the convent's subterranean storerooms. Radegund, the founder of Holy Cross, decided to confront the beast. She courageously descended into the darkness and, with the sign of the cross and the utterance of a prayer, expelled the *Grand'goule*, banishing him into the river Clain before he could claim another victim.[1] This tale, widely believed by the people of Poitiers in the later Middle Ages, proved to be supremely useful for the nuns of Holy Cross when they came under threat during this period. In the 1460s, for example, the abbess Isabeau de Couhé unfurled a banner with the image of a dragon, a reference to the vanquished serpent, to demonstrate her authority to a group of local clerics who, though traditionally in the service of the abbess, nevertheless had come to consider it 'against nature' to have a woman as their superior.[2] By 1666, any doubters of the legend had to reckon with clear proof, in the form of a stuffed crocodile, displayed on a wall of the Palais des Comtes. The specimen was mentioned by the young Lord Fountainhall, who wrote in his journal that the beast had once been much larger, but had diminished in size over the centuries.[3] It seems that, as the serpent shrank, the legend of the *Grand'goule* only increased.

The story itself originated in Poitiers many centuries after Radegund's own lifetime, from obscure traditions associated with local devotion to her as a protector of the city. The first reference to the full legend appeared in Jehan Boucet's *L'Histoire et chronique de Clotaire* of 1517, but it clearly had older

---

[1] De Chergé, *Guide du voyageur à Poitiers*, pp. 147–150. For an alternative version of the legend, see Foucart, *Poitiers et ses monuments*, p. 51, n. 3.

[2] Edwards, *Superior Women*, pp. 201–202 and 218–220; Edwards, 'Man Can Be Subject to Woman'.

[3] John Lauder, *Journals*, pp. 38–39.

Radegund. E. T. Dailey, Oxford University Press. © Oxford University Press 2023.
DOI: 10.1093/oso/9780197656105.003.0001

antecedents.[4] While the *Grand'goule* might only have appeared centuries removed from Radegund's era, belief in her power to vanquish the Devil and his agents can be traced back to early medieval times. This belief can be seen, for example, in an account of Radegund's life composed in the first years of the seventh century by Baudonivia, a nun from Holy Cross. In this *Life of Radegund*, the titular saint had acquired her power to vanquish evil by drawing close to God—a nearness that Baudonivia described in startlingly intimate language:

> With all her love she gave herself to her heavenly spouse, so that she might embrace God with a pure heart and feel Christ dwell within her. But the Enemy of Humanity, ever envious of the righteous, never ceased to persecute her, for she rejected his desires while in this world.[5]

Thus, when the denizens of Poitiers invoked Radegund as their protector, they sought the intercession of the quintessential Bride of Christ. Radegund's reputation—established in the work of Baudonivia, emphasized in times of crisis by the nuns of Holy Cross, and expressed in the legend of the *Grand'goule*—endured throughout the medieval and early modern periods. Though never entirely beyond danger, Holy Cross survived for centuries, until the 1790s, when the Revolution brought destruction upon the institution through a type of vandalism undeterred by crosses or prayers, by legends or superstitions, by ancient beliefs or by the weight of more than 1200 years of history.[6]

Long before she founded her convent in Poitiers, Radegund expected to live out her days as a queen. She was born into the royal house of the Kingdom of Thuringia, in what is today central Germany. The precise year of her birth, as with so many events in her life, cannot be determined with certainty, but it fell in either the late 510s or, more likely, the early 520s.[7] While she was still very young, Radegund lost both of her parents. Yet this tragedy was soon eclipsed by the downfall of her dynasty, and the slaughter

---

[4] Edwards, *Superior Women*, pp. 192–193 and 218–222. A panel of thirteenth-century stained glass that adorns Radegund's funerary church in Poitiers might possibly reference the legend. Lillich, *The Armor of Light.*

[5] Baudonivia, *Life of Radegund*, 5–6.

[6] Joblin, 'L'Attitude des protestants face aux reliques', p. 133, with examples drawn from Réau, *Histoire du vandalisme*, vol. 1, pp. 65–106.

[7] Fauquier, 'La Chronologie radegondienne', pp. 334–335, presents the possibilities and their implications. Radegund died in 587. Given the torments suffered by her body in her later years (discussed in Chapter 6), it is easier to imagine that she died in her early sixties than later.

of most members of her family, following an invasion by the Franks in 531. King Chlothar I took Radegund as his captive and later made her his bride. For several years, the young Radegund reigned as queen alongside the very man who had butchered many of her relatives, until Chlothar went one step further and caused her surviving brother to be killed. Following this unforgivable crime, Radegund took religious vows and, after living for a few years in a villa, she founded her grand convent in Poitiers during the 550s. There she remained, in pious devotion and ascetic self-denial, until her death in 587 (outliving Chlothar by more than a quarter century). In what might be considered her greatest single achievement, she obtained from the imperial court in Constantinople what were thought to be fragments of the 'True Cross', the wood used to crucify Jesus on the hill of Golgotha in Jerusalem. Facing down opposition from her local bishop, Radegund managed to have the relic placed within her convent, which subsequently acquired the name of 'Holy Cross'.

While there may never have been a *Grand'goule* stalking the nuns in the convent's cellars, there was certainly no shortage of enemies who threatened Radegund and her congregation. A letter she wrote to several bishops, referred to throughout this book as *Dominis sanctis* from its opening words, survives (translated here in Appendix 1), in which she sought their protection and support for Holy Cross after her death. Radegund feared that the local bishop or a royal official might harass her congregation or steal away the convent's possessions and endowments. Such fears were not unreasonable, but the greatest threat to Holy Cross actually came from the nuns themselves. Within two years of Radegund's death, a fifth of the congregation rejected their new leadership and launched an uprising that eventually led to the sacking of the convent and the desecration of its sacred confines. The affair shocked the people of Poitiers and terrified the congregation that remained in Holy Cross. Although monastic life subsequently returned to the convent, through the intervention of an ecclesiastical council and the royal court, it did so in a modified form that lacked the unique character Radegund had once conferred upon it. The reconstituted monastery instead followed what later became the standard model of female monasticism, an approach devoid of the radical potential that had previously characterized the institution.[8] Radegund's legacy endured, however, in works of hagiography (a complex

---

[8] On the declining diversity of the monastic experiment, see Diem, 'Gregory's Chess Board'; and Diem, 'Monks, Kings, and the Transformation of Sanctity'.

genre that might be described, albeit simplistically, as 'sacred biography') and in the behaviour of later queens and nuns who sought to imitate her example.[9]

* * *

When the young Radegund first arrived as Chlothar's captive to the realm possessed by the Franks, she found herself a stranger in a society experiencing rapid change. Over the previous generation, the Franks had expanded their power from their heartlands around the Rhine and the Scheldt to cover a vast territory that broadly corresponded to what the Romans had called transalpine Gaul (*Gallia*). As imperial rule faded from the West during the fifth century (and endured in the form of the Byzantine Empire in the East), the powerful Roman families of Gaul adapted to the presence of new groups, of whom the Franks were ultimately the most successful, which they regarded as bands of 'barbarians' (*barbari*). These 'Gallo-Romans' integrated with the new Frankish elite and acquired a share of the great offices of the realm. They also continued to fill important clerical posts, including that of bishop, the highest ecclesiastical office.[10] Georgius Florentius Gregorius, better known as Gregory of Tours, descended from one such family and acquired his episcopal post in 573. As the bishop of Tours, he held the special title of 'metropolitan', which gave him oversight of several dioceses—notably, not the Diocese of Poitiers, though for reasons that will become clear he intervened there nonetheless to support Radegund and her nuns, just as his predecessor had done. Radegund was Gregory's older contemporary, as well as his acquaintance and supporter, and he wrote about her in his *Ten Books of Histories* (known simply as the *Histories*) and in two of his miracle collections.[11] Gregory treated Radegund with the respect due a holy and royal woman, but he did not always share her views, especially on female religious life, and there are hints within his works that he sometimes found her autonomy and agency unsettling.[12]

As the Franks grew from their origins as a successful warband into a ruling elite, they began to adopt Christianity and to participate in the administration of the Church. Their conversion followed that of their great king, Clovis (the father of Chlothar I), who entered the baptismal font on Christmas

<hr/>

[9] Papa, 'Radegonda e Batilde'.
[10] Heinzelmann, *Bischofsherrschaft in Gallien*.
[11] On the title of the *Histories*, see Goffart, 'From *Historiae* to *Historia Francorum*'.
[12] Casias, 'Rebel Nuns and the Bishop Historian'.

Day in 508.[13] Clovis expanded the Frankish realm from a fairly modest domain centred on Tournai to a powerful kingdom poised to conqueror all of Gaul. His ruling dynasty, the Merovingians, took its name from his ancestor, Merovech, an obscure figure characterized by one medieval chronicler as, just possibly, the offspring of a sea monster.[14] Although this claim has the ring of an ancient myth, it most likely represents a satirical critique of the ruling family itself, a reminder that Merovingian kings—Chlothar included—were never able to take the loyalty of their Frankish noblemen for granted.[15] Of greater importance to the Merovingians themselves were stories that stitched together the Frankish and Roman pasts.[16] One example presented the kings of the Franks as descended from Priam, the legendary ruler of Troy who, like his compatriot Aeneas, fled the ancient city as it fell to the Greeks.[17] (Such Trojan ancestry was claimed even by Louis XIV, who reigned as King of France from 1643 to 1715.[18]) This example demonstrates how the Franks comfortably mixed the lineage of their barbarian kings with figures drawn from Virgil's *Aeneid* and Homer's *Iliad*. Such a culture created opportunities for ambitious men of letters like Venantius Fortunatus. Born near the Italian city of Treviso in the 530s and educated in the Byzantine stronghold of Ravenna, Fortunatus made his career in Gaul, where he found an eager audience among the elite of the Merovingian world. Although he composed poems in honour of many leading figures, he settled in Poitiers around the year 568 and spent two decades of his life in Radegund's service. The poetry he wrote for Radegund, or for others in furtherance of her interests, forms a key source of information about her life and the organization of her convent. After she died, Fortunatus wrote his *Life of Radegund*, a prose hagiography rich in detail (uniquely so for her early years) that also informed Baudonivia's later work.

These three authors—Gregory of Tours, Venantius Fortunatus, and Baudonivia—provide almost all the evidence available to the historian about Radegund, and any study of her life is necessarily also a study of these three

---

[13] A year of 496 for the baptism, which continues to appear occasionally in scholarship, can be definitively rejected in favour of the later date identified in Wood, 'Gregory of Tours and Clovis'. See Shanzer, 'Dating the Baptism of Clovis'.

[14] Fredegar, *Chronicles*, 3.9. Murray, '*Post vocantur Merohingii*', pp. 135–137, discussed the origin of the name 'Merovingian' and its association with the figure of 'Merovech'.

[15] Wood, 'Deconstructing the Merovingian Family', pp. 149–153.

[16] Reimitz, *History, Frankish Identity, and the Framing of Western Ethnicity*, pp. 170–174.

[17] *Liber historiae Francorum*, 1 and 5. See Wood, 'Defining the Franks', pp. 50–53; and Barlow, 'Gregory of Tours and the Myth of the Trojan Origins'.

[18] Meyer, 'Mythologies monarchiques d'Ancien Regime', p. 295.

authors. Judged by the standards of most early medieval subjects, Radegund must be considered relatively well documented. Nonetheless, a certain silence prevails in the sources. Not the conspicuous silence of quietude, not a total absence of discussion, but the reticent silence of hushed voices, of matters left unsaid amidst an otherwise active conversation. Each author wrote in pursuit of their own agenda, and according to the expectations of their audiences. For this reason, the act of conducting a historical investigation into Radegund's life is often an exercise in reading between the lines, in informed speculation, and in cautious conjecture—never more so than in attempting to discern Radegund's own thoughts and feelings. She left only one extant work by her own hand, her letter *Dominis sanctis*, a precious source, yet one both brief in length and limited in scope. This letter combined the humility expected from a pious ascetic with the language of the royal chancery, which resulted in a powerfully authoritative document.[19]

A few poems written by Fortunatus at Radegund's behest, and in her name, have sometimes been wrongly attributed to her (as discussed in Chapter 6). But even though they do not represent her voice, they may nonetheless express her opinions among Fortunatus's words. Radegund is known to have written several other works, including letters and poems, that have also been lost. Their disappearance requires little explanation, given the vicissitudes of textual preservation across fifteen centuries. *Dominis sanctis* survived largely because Gregory included a copy in his *Histories*, along with other documents such as a letter, referred to here as *Dominae beatissimae*, that Radegund received from several bishops. Occasional references in the sources indicate that Radegund also received other correspondence that has since vanished, with an important exception: a letter written by Caesaria the Younger, the second abbess of St John's convent in Arles, a religious house that inspired Radegund's own monastic project in Poitiers in important ways. But her reply, if there ever was one, has also disappeared. The silence confronted in the source material is, therefore, also the silence of loss, of words forgotten to time, the existence of which must be kept in mind even if the specific details cannot be known.

While time might be mostly to blame for the loss of so many important texts, the Merovingians also contributed to the destruction of documents, and much else, as a consequence of their civil wars. As discussed in Chapter 4, it is unfair to describe these internal conflicts as regular occurrences. Peace

[19] Smith, '*Radegundis peccatrix*: Authorizations of Virginity', p. 323.

usually prevailed, and when war broke out, it remained limited to specific regions.[20] But even so, military campaigns brought misery to those caught in their path. These civil wars resulted from ambitious, avaricious princes who fought with their coheirs over their share the kingdom.[21] Both Clovis and Chlothar eliminated rivals and consolidated their rule over the whole of the realm, only for their domains to be divided among their sons, not all of whom shared the same mother.[22] This approach to succession, more an ad hoc practice than an established system, deserves credit for its ability to manage rivalries and maintain order, but it was nonetheless unable to avert every crisis.[23] Radegund lived through some of the worst moments, though her tireless efforts at diplomacy prevented many more. She navigated this world of competing kingdoms, both as a queen while married to Chlothar, and as a stepmother to his children while cloistered in Poitiers. Her success in protecting Holy Cross from turmoil, and in preserving her own life and that of her nuns, must not be overlooked. During the second half of the sixth century, several queens met an unnatural end: Chalda was burned alive, Galswinth was murdered, and Audovera was sentenced to a 'cruel death', not to mention the ghastly demise of Brunhild (slightly later, in 613), who was tortured for several days, paraded around on a camel, and tied to the tail of a crazed horse, which tore her body apart as it bolted.[24]

The leaders of female religious houses faced perilous threats. The abbess of a convent in Tours, for example, found herself challenged by her first cousin, Berthegund, in 589. Arriving with a band of mercenaries, Berthegund stripped the convent of all its possession, seized its estates, and then returned to her home in Poitiers.[25] St John's convent in Arles was forced to relocate within the city's walls after its original site, along the road leading to Marseilles, proved to be too exposed when an army reappropriated its timbers, most likely for siegeworks, in 507.[26] In the early seventh century, the fourth abbess of St John's, Rusticula, was forced to leave the sacred confines

[20] Halsall, 'The Preface to Book V'.

[21] Ewig, Die fränkischen Teilungen und Teilreiche.

[22] Widdowson, 'Merovingian Partitions'.

[23] Wood, 'Deconstructing the Merovingian Family'; and Wood, 'Royal Succession and Legitimation in the Roman West'.

[24] Gregory of Tours, Histories, 4.20 (Chalda), 4.28 (Galswinth), and 5.39 (Audovera); Fredegar, Chronicles, 4.42 (Brunhild).

[25] Gregory of Tours, Histories, 10.12. The relationship between this incident and the roughly contemporaneous uprising in Holy Cross (discussed throughout Chapter 7) has often been the subject of speculation. See, for example, Bikeeva, 'Serente diabulo: The Revolt of the Nuns'.

[26] Cyprian, Life of Caesarius, 28.

of her convent against her will, when a royal official demanded that she answer accusations of *lèse-majesté* in the presence of the king.[27] Such incidents might have been even more frequent if there had not been so few female religious houses in Gaul during Radegund's lifetime. Although many women lived under religious vows, committed to a chaste and pious life, few of these 'virgins of Christ' organized their activities in a communal and institutional form. As discussed in Chapter 3, such communal (or 'coenobitic') monasticism remained predominantly a male pursuit in sixth-century Gaul. The precise number of female religious houses is difficult to determine, but it is clear that Radegund was a pioneer in this regard, especially outside the southern regions of Gaul that were more directly connected to the Mediterranean world.[28] The era of formalized religious life for women, cloistered within a monastery and governed by an abbess according to an established 'rule' (or set of formal regulations) had only just begun.[29] It was a process that Radegund both hastened and shaped, even though Holy Cross remained a unique institution.

* * *

This book is published with the intent of marking the 1500th anniversary of Radegund's birth, insofar as is possible, given the uncertain chronology of her life. It has been written for an audience wider than what might usually be expected for an academic work about the early medieval West. The intended audience includes not only scholars but also students and interested laypersons. In pursuing this goal of inclusivity, I have not compromised the scholarly merit of the work, which engages with prevalent theories and puts forward new interpretations to advance the field of scholarship. But I have endeavoured to present the reader with comprehensible material and entertaining prose. I have thought this marriage of scholarly and leisurely reading possible only because of the fascinating and important nature of the subject: that is, Radegund herself. But not every aspect of the Merovingian world has been so accommodating. The custom of the ruling dynasty to reuse name elements, or whole names, throughout their expansive family tree has proved challenging. I have sought simplicity and consistency where possible, and provided a genealogy to assist the reader (Appendix 2). But it is impossible to avoid such conundrums as the fact that Childebert I was the uncle

---

[27] Florentius, *Life of Rusticula*, 9–11.
[28] Hartmann, '*Reginae sumus*: Merowingische Königstöchter', p. 9.
[29] Diem, 'Inventing the Holy Rule'.

of Charibert, who was himself the uncle of Childebert II; that Bertha was the sister of Berthefled; or that Clovis had many close relations whose names began with the sequence of letters *chlo*: a wife (Chlothild), a daughter (also called Chlothild), and two sons (Chlodomer and Chlothar), not to mention those examples among his many grandchildren.

I have preferred clarity in my use of terminology, such as when I refer to Radegund's convent throughout as 'Holy Cross', even though the institution was originally dedicated to the Virgin Mary. The names of the great offices of the Merovingian realm have been translated whenever possible, but those with no clear equivalent, or with an English alternative that risks confusion, remain untranslated. Thus *dux*, a high-ranking official with military and administrative responsibilities, remains untranslated rather than rendered as 'duke', its English linguistic descendant. Likewise *comes* (pronounced in two syllables, with each vowel enunciated), a royally appointed official usually posted to a particular city, has not been translated as 'count', which might erroneously convey the sense of a hereditary title held by a landed nobleman, particular to later times. I have referred, from convention, to the holy dead with the title 'St' only in contexts related to religious devotion, and only when the saint in question died before the sixth century, rather than apply it to Radegund's contemporaries. Thus I speak of 'St Martin' (d. 397) and 'St Hilary' (d. 367), but only of 'Nicetius' (d. c. 566) and 'Monegund' (d. 570), even though these latter two figures also came to be regarded as saints.

I have kept the notes relatively slim, though not exactly minimal. I cite the necessary secondary sources, but leave aside many studies of interest. The nature of the book excludes the possibility of historiographically complete notes. With regard to primary sources, I usually refer to the texts by their English names, rather than their original Latin or Greek titles. Baudonivia wrote, for example, a *Life of Radegund* rather than a *Vita sanctae Radegundis*, while Gregory wrote a *Glory of the Martyrs* rather than a *Gloria martyrum*. But for some sources, whether out of convention or mere suitability, I have kept the Latin titles. The *Liber historiae Francorum*, a well-known anonymous work of 727, for example, retains a specificity in its original form that is lost if rendered as the *Book of the History of the Franks*, which might describe any number of medieval texts. I have also provided Latin titles for two letters (*Dominis sanctis* and *Dominae beatissimae*) that were preserved in Gregory's *Histories*, so that their identity as independent documents remains clear. When quoting from these sources, all translations are my own, though I am deeply indebted to previous translations, which appear in the Bibliography alongside the Latin edition. My contribution has been sufficient for the mistakes to belong to me, but inconsequential enough for the credit to belong to my predecessors. Biblical passages are rendered in italics typeface and translated from the (Stuttgart) Vulgate, though other *vetus Latina* versions circulated in Radegund's lifetime.

It is my sincere hope that I have provided the reader with the clarity and insight deserving of so remarkable a subject. I can do no better than to close my Introduction by quoting the opening remarks of Baudonivia, in the preface to her *Life of Radegund*, on the difficulties she faced in fulfilling the same task fourteen centuries ago:

> It is no less impossible to undertake the work you have assigned to me than it would be to touch heaven with my fingers, that I should presume to write something about the life of our holy lady, Radegund.

1

And the Lots Were Cast

I put my trust in you, O Lord,
I said, 'You are my God'.
My lots are in your hands.
Deliver me from the hands of my enemies,
and from those who persecute me.
Reveal your face to your servant;
save me in your mercy.

Psalm 30:15–17

Radegund became part of the spoils. She had fallen from princess to plunder. Two Frankish kings, Chlothar and Theuderic, captured her during their merciless war against the Thuringians. According to Venantius Fortunatus, the victorious half-brothers fought over who had the privilege of claiming the girl, likely not yet ten years old, as part of their share. They decided to cast lots for her. 'Unless they had struck upon a resolution to the disagreement', Fortunatus wrote, 'the kings would have unsheathed their swords.'[1] He neglected to detail the precise procedure; perhaps the proverbial short straw, or, more imaginatively, stones drawn from a jar until the unique stone appeared. Through this story, Fortunatus expressed the precariousness of Radegund's condition during this terrifying time. Elsewhere, he wrote that she had become a *femina rapta*—an 'abducted woman', violently carried away. The word *rapta* served as the origin for the English word 'rape', and the many senses of the modern term, from wanton pillaging to sexual violence, are also implied by its Latin progenitor, though only through layers of ambiguity. Beyond its literary purpose, however, Fortunatus's story likely also reflects a genuine moment when lots were cast for the young captive. The practice, as a means to divide loot, had immemorial origins and ubiquitous use in the early

---

[1] Fortunatus, *Life of Radegund*, 2.

Radegund. E. T. Dailey, Oxford University Press. © Oxford University Press 2023.
DOI: 10.1093/oso/9780197656105.003.0002

medieval period, including in Merovingian Gaul, where it appears in legal texts as a means of resolving disputes.[2] Fortunatus's claim is, therefore, entirely plausible.

The young Radegund found herself reduced to the same condition as the valuables she once wore as adornments, the very objects that marked her high-born status. Her jewellery perhaps resembled some of the precious items recovered by archaeologists from Thuringia that date to the period: gilt and bejewelled necklaces, silver rings and bronze buckles, beads of glass and insets of almandine.[3] Fortunatus imagined that the young Radegund had lived in a 'palace' comparable to the royal halls of Troy, and although he clearly sought to invoke the epic character of Ovid's *Heroides* in this passage, the princess probably did reside in a grand residence prior to the Frankish invasion.[4] Thuringia was not an impoverished kingdom, poorly documented though it may be. Indeed, it seems to have been the largest and most powerful kingdom beyond the old northern borders of what was once the Roman Empire in the West.[5] Its ruling family was closely connected to the courts of the Ostrogoths and Lombards, not to mention the imperial court in Constantinople.[6] Before their downfall, the kings of the Thuringians had extended their influence well beyond their heartlands, which are traditionally thought to have centred on the fertile basin that spread out beneath the Harz Mountains all the way to the Saale and the forests beyond the Hörsel, an area rich in arable land and waterways.[7] Excavations have produced evidence for a flourishing economic and cultural centre on the Unstrut river, where the ruling family was presumably based.[8] If a place of birth and upbringing for Radegund is to be guessed, it is here.[9]

Even before she had fallen into the possession of Chlothar and Theuderic, Radegund had already suffered through the tragic death of those closest to her. Her father, Berthachar, perished when she was only a few years old.[10]

---

[2] Wood, 'Pagan Religion and Superstitions', pp. 265–266.
[3] For surviving examples of the treasures available in Thuringia, including the types of objects mentioned here, see Eidam and Noll, *Radegunde*, pp. 133–157.
[4] Fortunatus, *Poems*, appendix 1, lines 5–6 (*palatium*). On the Ovidian allusions, see Fielding, *Transformations of Ovid*, pp. 187–193.
[5] Trenkmann, *Thüringen im Merowingerreich*.
[6] Pohl, '*Germania*, Herrschaftssitze östlich des Rheins', pp. 312–313.
[7] Gregory of Tours also mentioned Thuringians around the Rhine, in passages that have proved difficult to interpret. See Grahn-Hoek, 'Gab es vor 531 ein linksniederrheinisches Thüringerreich?'.
[8] Schmidt, 'Das Königreich der Thüringer'. Against this identification, and the traditional view of the Thuringian kingdom in general, see Neumeister, 'The Ancient Thuringians'.
[9] Steuer, 'Die Herrschaftssitze der Thüringer', p. 204.
[10] Gregory of Tours, *Histories*, 3.4.

Nothing is known of her mother, not even her name, and she may well have also died during Radegund's earliest years. Gregory of Tours described Radegund as an 'orphan', and although this ambiguous term might indicate either the death of both parents or that of the father alone, the absence of information about her mother suggests the former sense. It is certainly conspicuous that no source identified her among those who died at the hands of the Franks. As for the cause of her early passing, in the absence of evidence childbirth might be hypothesized, perhaps during the birth of Radegund's brother, though this is only a guess. When Berthachar died, Radegund entered the care of her paternal uncle, Herminafrid. Gregory thought that Herminafrid had been responsible for Berthachar's death, but this claim is difficult to reconcile with Fortunatus's description of Radegund as a devoted niece to Herminafrid, which he included in a poem that he composed at her behest.[11] It is not easy to understand why Fortunatus might have written this line if Radegund herself had felt otherwise. But if Gregory was mistaken, and Herminafrid was indeed the adoring uncle of Fortunatus's poetry, then it must be assumed that his death, in the aftermath of the Frankish conquest of Thuringia, troubled Radegund deeply.[12]

The reason the Franks attacked Thuringia in 531 is difficult to discern. Presumably the invasion was linked in some way to the decline in Ostrogothic influence that followed the death of Theodoric the Great in 526, the preeminent ruler in Italy, which upset the balance of power in the region.[13] The Thuringians had feared Frankish aggression before, when Odoacer, the first barbarian ruler of Italy, died in 493.[14] But Gregory of Tours provided a more dramatic motive, that of revenge, when he placed a speech into the mouth of Theuderic, who asked his warriors to recall how the Thuringians had once broken a treaty by murdering hostages that the Franks had exchanged in good faith:

> They hanged our young men from trees by the tendons of their thighs. They caused two hundred of our young women to die through cruel tortures, tying their arms to the necks of horses which, goaded by sharp prods, dashed apart and tore them to pieces. Others they stretched along the ruts

[11] Fortunatus, *Poems*, 8, line 23 (see also Fortunatus, *Life of Radegund*, 2). Wood, 'The Frontiers of Western Europe', p. 235.
[12] Gregory of Tours, *Histories*, 3.8.
[13] Schmidt, 'Die Thüringer', p. 504.
[14] Procopius, *History of the Wars*, 5.12.21.

in the road, fixed to the ground with stakes, then drove laden waggons over them until their bones were broken and they could serve as food for dogs and birds.[15]

If this story, which clearly represented the perspective of the victors, offers anything historically useful, it is to indicate that the kingdoms of the Franks and the Thuringians had long been tightly entwined.[16] Other fragmentary evidence further suggests that these two peoples were close, dynastically, politically, and probably also culturally.[17] The Frankish conquest of Thuringia, therefore, resulted from proximity, not distance, with violence resolving tensions that had grown between two sides that knew each other well.

Theuderic mentioned another motivation to his Frankish warriors, not only 'the murder of your kinspeople', but also 'the wrong done to me'. Gregory explained this remark with a story about Thuringian dynastic politics, through which the ruling family had brought disaster and misfortune upon itself.[18] The trouble started with the meddling of Herminafrid's wife, Amalaberga. Annoyed with a power-sharing arrangement between Herminafrid and his surviving brother, Baderic, after the death of Radegund's father, Amalaberga decided to shame her husband into seizing control of the whole kingdom. For one of his meals she set only half the table, and when Herminafrid asked why, she explained: 'A man who allows himself to be robbed of half his kingdom deserves to find half his table bare.' Inspired by this affront, Herminafrid secretly invited Theuderic to join him in a campaign against his brother, promising to share the spoils. Once Baderic had been defeated and killed, however, Herminafrid betrayed his Frankish ally and kept the whole kingdom for himself. This treachery inspired Theuderic to rally his half-brother Chlothar, to stir the anger of his Frankish warriors, and to invade Thuringia in revenge. Whatever the origins of this fanciful story, Gregory had his own reasons for including it, since he disapproved of women who involved themselves in political affairs.[19]

---

[15] Gregory of Tours, *Histories*, 3.7.

[16] Wood, *The Merovingian Kingdoms*, pp. 35–38.

[17] Gregory of Tours, *Histories*, 2.12, and Fredegar, *Chronicles*, 3.11–12, present a story in which Childeric I, the grandfather of Chlothar and Theuderic, took refuge with the Thuringians and acquired a wife in the process. On this episode, see Wood, 'The Frontiers of Western Europe', pp. 232–233.

[18] Schmidt, 'Die Thüringer', p. 504, n. 155.

[19] Dailey, *Queens, Consorts, Concubines*, pp. 16–45.

Radegund, in contrast, may have had an entirely different view of Amalaberga, who might even have helped to raise her during her time in Herminafrid's care. She was no meddlesome woman, overreaching her station and corrupting her husband's good judgement. Amalaberga was, in fact, a royal woman of the highest pedigree. She belonged to the Ostrogothic dynasty, the niece of Theodoric the Great and the sister of King Theodahad (d. 536). Cassiodorus, who served the Ostrogothic kings in Ravenna, described Amalaberga as well educated and as a source of wise advice.[20] She had every reason to offer her husband counsel, which she surely delivered in a manner more sophisticated than a half-set table and a sharply barbed nag. Although Radegund's feelings towards Amalaberga passed unremarked in the sources, it is at least possible to demonstrate that she regarded her children fondly. Fortunatus addressed his poem *On the Destruction of Thuringia* to Amalaberga's son, Amalfred, who had escaped the Frankish attack with his mother and found refuge in Italy, later enjoying a career in the service of the Byzantine emperor.[21] The poem also expressed deep affection for Amalaberga's daughters.[22] These children were Radegund's only surviving kin, with the notable exception of her brother (who was later murdered, a decisive moment in Radegund's life discussed in Chapter 2). It is tempting to imagine Amalaberga acting as an early mentor to the young princess, equipping her with an example, however dimly remembered, of a royal woman in her prime.

After the Frankish conquest of Thuringia, Radegund never saw her homeland or her family again. Her few relatives who escaped either lived far from Gaul or were otherwise prevented from seeing her, even after she became queen.[23] Writing at Radegund's behest many years later (as discussed in Chapter 6), Fortunatus portrayed the experience as one of profound dislocation that instilled in her an enduring sense of loss, which he expressed by placing words of lamentation into her mouth:

> If I were to speak of doomed struggles and wars lost, what first might bring me, a captive woman, to tears? What am I left to weep over? This nation beset by death, or my dear family, brought down by every misfortune?[24]

---

[20] Cassiodorus, *Variae*, 4.1.

[21] Procopius, *History of the Wars*, 8.25.11–12.

[22] Fortunatus, *Poems*, appendix 1, lines 159–160. These daughters included Rodelinda, who married the Lombard king Audoin.

[23] Scheibelreiter, 'Der Untergang des Thüringerreiches'.

[24] Fortunatus, *Poems*, appendix 3, lines 3–5.

Fortunatus also had Radegund express the heavy guilt and enduring distress she felt as someone who had survived the slaughter of her family:

> I, a barbarian woman, cannot do justice to these lamentations, to every single sorrow. I cannot swim this lake of tears. Each person has his own tears to shed, but I alone have them all. The grief of an entire people is the burden of my very self. Fortune has relieved those men struck down by the enemy, so that I, one woman, survive to weep for them all.[25]

Although fortune had spared the young Radegund from death, it nonetheless inflicted upon her a sorrow that the dead never knew: the guilt of the survivor.

These passages and others in Fortunatus's poetic works promise to provide insights into Radegund's feelings about the conquest of her homeland, but they must be used cautiously. Fortunatus wrote within a long tradition of male authors describing the emotions of women in terms of overwhelming grief, self-pity, and abject lamentation.[26] These passages also appeared in poems written as part of a diplomatic exchange with the imperial court in Constantinople (detailed in Chapter 4), and the intended audience undoubtedly influenced their contents as well.[27] Nevertheless, Fortunatus wrote these poems very much in the service of Radegund herself, who, it must be assumed, read and approved the material. Composed under what might be considered to be Radegund's authorization, Fortunatus's words, despite their literary hyperbole, were not entirely artificial. Used cautiously, these passages provide insights into Radegund's arrested adolescence, especially when they expressed a condition commonly felt as a result of traumatic experiences. Of her homeland and her family, Radegund had only what she remembered, but those memories were few and blighted by the bloodshed she had witnessed. They haunted her in a manner that she believed might arouse sympathy from other members of the ruling elite, if read in their presence at court. They reminded her of what she had lost, of what she might lose again; and they reminded others of what they too might lose, if their fortunes also turned.

* * *

---

[25] Fortunatus, *Poems*, appendix 1, lines 31–36.
[26] Nelson, 'Women and the Word'; Fielding, *Transformation of Ovid*, pp. 193–198.
[27] On gender and diplomatic letters, see Hillner, 'Empresses, Queens, and Letters', pp. 367–368.

Fortunatus suggested that it was Radegund's lot in life to suffer and endure a series of misfortunes. He used the word *sors*, literally 'lots', in the metaphorical sense of 'fate' in this context: 'envious fate', 'unfavourable fate', 'hostile fate', and 'unholy fate'.[28] Yet both poems ended with an invocation of God, as the omnibenevolent and omnipotent determiner of one's destiny. 'May the Lord now bestow upon you, the blessed ones, abundant prosperity in the present and glory in the future.'[29] Fortunatus threaded the Christian God into a long-standing literary and artistic tradition, with its roots in the Classical period, that portrayed Fortune—*Fortuna*—as a fickle goddess. In her many depictions, Fortune wore a mural crown, held a wheel, steered a rudder, and rested her leg on a sphere, all symbols that represented how she capriciously directed the lives of mortals for her own amusement, as if she were playing a game of chance.[30] 'Indeed, Fortune rules in all matters; she makes famous or obscure every affair according her impulsive feelings rather than hard truth,' wrote the Roman historian Sallust in a passage later quoted by the bishop and theologian Augustine of Hippo (d. 430) as part of his extended critique of polytheistic beliefs in his profoundly influential *City of God*.[31]

Augustine mocked the idea that Fortune herself might be subject to fortune, an implication that, he argued, led to logical absurdities. A tension clearly existed between the Classical and Christian traditions, one that intrigued Fortunatus (perhaps for reasons of nomenclature, in addition to any other), and probably also Radegund as well. The seemingly senseless vicissitudes of life, symbolized by fickle Fortune and her famous wheel, needed to be interpreted in a framework that subjected all events, ultimately, to the will of God. Fortunatus detected this tension in Radegund's own life, in which the holy woman came to devote herself entirely to God after suffering a series of seemingly senseless tragedies. As her client for many years, and her hagiographer after her death, Fortunatus clearly believed that Radegund, whatever her lot in life, was due a glorious afterlife. In his *Life of Radegund*, he asserted that tragic events might acquire a new meaning precisely because God had the power to redeem temporal suffering with eternal reward. 'Often, a misfortune leads to salvation, inasmuch as it provides another opportunity for the serendipity of the Divinity,' Fortunatus wrote, just before he referenced the tragic death of Radegund's brother.[32] It is worth considering

[28] Fortunatus, *Poems*, appendix 1, *sors invida*, *sors infausta*, *sors inimica*, and *sors nefanda*.
[29] Fortunatus, *Poems*, appendix 3.
[30] Coralini, 'Immagini di Tyche/Fortuna'.
[31] Sallust, *The Conspiracy of Catiline*, 8; Augustine, *The City of God*, 7.3.
[32] Fortunatus, *Life of Radegund*, 12.

the possibility that Radegund herself had come to adopt a similar view over the course of her life, and that she and Fortunatus had influenced each other in this regard.

The idea that Fortune ultimately served a greater power had recently found its definitive expression in Boethius's work *On the Consolation of Philosophy*.[33] As he awaited his own execution near Pavia in 524, the Roman aristocrat reflected on the meaning of seemingly absurd turns of fate, not least of which his own. Boethius placed fortune within a greater framework established by the One God, conceptualized as the expression of Being, Goodness, and Truth. 'It is the Highest Good that rules all things powerfully and arranges them sweetly', he wrote, in an important passage within the *Consolation* that echoed the biblical Book of Wisdom (8:1).[34] The scriptural verse in question contemplated the wisdom that a righteous man required in order to understand the ways of God, as well as the limitations of the human intellect—a gap that Augustine had famously tried to bridge by invoking the figure of Christ as the unity of the human and the divine.[35] The *Consolation* quickly found an audience among the Roman elite in Italy, and a commentary was produced at the monastery of Vivarium, in Calabria.[36] The abundance and the chronology of the surviving manuscripts suggests that the commentary circulated widely from an early date. It takes no great act of imagination to think that Fortunatus might have encountered Boethius's *Consolation* during his education in Ravenna (about 300 km east of Pavia), before he left for Gaul in the 560s. It is also worth contemplating the extent to which Radegund might have found such ideas useful in providing an interpretative framework for her own difficult experiences.

Radegund spent decades of her life in monastic seclusion, reflecting on the events of her life and searching for their meaning in the Scriptures, which possessed numerous references to lots and the question of fate. *The lots are cast into the basin, but they are controlled by the Lord* (Proverbs 16:33). According to Baudonivia, Radegund often rhetorically asked her nuns, after hearing a reading from the scriptures: 'If you do not understand what is read, then will you not search, unceasingly, the mirror of your souls?'[37]

---

[33] For Boethius as the definitive expression of this idea, see Frakes, *The Fate of Fortune*.

[34] Boethius, *On the Consolation of Philosophy*, 3.12. On this passage as key to understanding the *Consolation*, see Marenbon, *Boethius*, pp. 155–156.

[35] Augustine, *Confessions*, 18(24)–21(27). The dual numerals here represent the chapter numbers in early printed editions and the paragraph numbers used in the early edition produced by the Benedictines of St Maur in 1679.

[36] Troncarelli, *Tradizioni perdute*.

[37] Baudonivia, *Life of Radegund*, 9.

Radegund, unlike Boethius, did not record her own reflections for posterity, but a few passages in her letter *Dominis sanctis*, most likely written shortly before her death (as discussed in Appendix 1), provide a basis for further speculation. She described the unpredictable and transient nature of temporal existence. 'The cycles and circumstances of the human condition are uncertain', she asserted, before warning that 'the world hastens to its end'. Radegund mentioned how she had been 'loosened from worldly ties by divine providence and unmerited mercy', in a reference to her decision to end her marriage to Chlothar and take religious vows, which occurred as a result of her husband's cruelties. This claim sounded rather like Fortunatus's assertion that salvation might result from misfortune. When Radegund complained about those who 'wish to serve their own interests rather than the divine will', she identified a motivation that had inspired the perpetrators of her life's many tragedies. In a manner not altogether unlike Augustine, who turned away from his promising secular career and became a bishop and theologian, Radegund 'willingly turned to the mandate of religion and the command of Christ' when she retreated to monastic seclusion. She wanted to help others do the same. When she explained why she had founded her convent in Poitiers, she added: 'I considered how to advance other women so that—the Lord willing—my own desires might prove beneficial for others'.

Radegund may well have concluded that seemingly absurd turns of fate acquired new meaning when viewed from the perspective of divine providence, with the hand of God secretly and mysteriously guiding the believer through suffering towards salvation. In her letter *Dominis sanctis*, Radegund asserted that the sum of her experiences, many of which had involved hardship and suffering, nevertheless caused her to live as 'a devoted woman led by the zeal of God'. Baudonivia recalled an instruction that Radegund had issued to her nuns, which emphasized the eternal significance of the events that unfolded during the brief temporal life of the believer:

> Gather, gather the wheat of the Lord (cf. Matthew 3:12). For truly I say to you that there will not be long for the harvest. Consider what I say and gather it, because undoubtedly one day you will be seeking more time. Truly, truly, you will be begging for such days as these, and you will wish that you had them again.[38]

---

[38] Baudonivia, *Life of Radegund*, 19.

Radegund had come to regard this life as little more than a proving ground for the next, so that those who believed might see their faith tested by fickle fortune and found true by almighty God. She had lost the Kingdom of Thuringia; she later rejected the Kingdom of the Franks; in the end, she sought only the Kingdom of Heaven. But Radegund had acquired this wisdom in later years, after experiencing the painful uncertainty and impermanence of everything this world had to offer. She wished to help other young, high-born women follow her path because, it must be assumed, she saw her younger self in them.

* * *

The lots placed the young Radegund into Chlothar's hands. He sent her to his royal villa of Athies in Vermandois (in the Picardy region), between Amiens and Saint Quentin.[39] There she remained—guarded, watched, and raised by staff whom Chlothar selected—until he decided whether or not he wished to take her as his bride. Marriage represented a political tool that Chlothar needed to deploy to his own advantage, and at the right time. Radegund awaited her fate for a few years, passing her adolescence in Athies. In his *Life of Radegund*, Fortunatus presented this period as one of captivity, and he compared Radegund's time in Chlothar's villa to the enslavement of the Israelites in Egypt (recounted in the Book of Exodus).[40] An exaggeration, perhaps, which Fortunatus grasped so that he might include a powerful, biblical metaphor in what was a work of hagiography. But it was a metaphor based on a degree of truth. Hostages taken in war shared much in common with enslaved people, uprooted from their homeland and deprived of their kin.[41] While not unfree in a legal sense, Radegund certainly lived under a form of captivity. Fortunatus wrote that she was placed in the care of *custodes*, a term that might mean 'guardians' or 'guards'; most likely, they acted as both. She collected scraps from the table and shared them with other children. She also washed their heads. Such servile behaviour suggests that, regardless of her birth status, Radegund enjoyed little privilege in Athies. Indeed, Fortunatus characterized her treatment by those within the villa as a 'persecution'. Nor was she the only woman to find herself both a war captive and a prospective bride. In one of his sermons, Caesarius of Arles (d. 542) had rhetorically

---

[39] This Athies confusingly shares a name with two other places, Athies-sous-Laon and Athies in the Pas-de-Calais.

[40] Fortunatus, *Life of Radegund*, 2.

[41] The classic theorization is found in Patterson, *Slavery and Social Death*.

asked his congregation how it was that a brave warrior returned from victory with 'a young girl as his booty'.[42] For moralizing bishops like Caesarius, this practice had no justification. For martial men like Chlothar, it required none.

Radegund received an education in Athies, though precisely what this involved cannot be discerned in any detail. Fortunatus wrote that her instruction was 'suitable to her sex'. She may have learned weaving, a skill she certainly possessed later in life.[43] Textile production was frequently conducted on rural estates by teams of women, often of low social standing, including slaves.[44] But Fortunatus seems to have had higher learning in mind. He added that Radegund learned 'letters', *litterae*, which probably included an exposure to Latin literature, rather than mere literacy, even though the word itself allows for no certainty. The adult Radegund appreciated the written word, though it is not possible to determine how much of that appreciation traced back to her education in Athies. Gregory of Tours mentioned how she read aloud from a book while in her monastic cell, and Fortunatus referenced her composition of long and short poems on wax tablets.[45] Fortunatus also mentioned numerous texts (or their authors, or subjects), in his works dedicated to Radegund and her community of nuns, in a manner that assumed they already knew the details, which implies that these works were available in the library of Holy Cross.[46]

Radegund was apparently already a Christian when she came to Athies; Christianity must have been her religion from birth. Fortunatus certainly gave no indication in his *Life of Radegund* that she had been raised a pagan in Thuringia or converted to Christianity upon her arrival in Gaul. Nor did he have any reason to withhold details about such a conversion, as he could have used this moment to signal the spiritual progress of his saintly protagonist, in keeping with an established motif in hagiographic works.[47] Instead, Fortunatus simply noted, without further remark, that the young

---

[42] Caesarius, *Sermons*, 43.8. In these sermons, Caesarius presented his audience with material drawn from earlier sources, in particular the sermons of Augustine of Hippo; see Brown, *The Rise of Western Christendom*, pp. 150–153.

[43] Gregory of Tours, *Glory of the Confessors*, 104, mentioned the spindles on which Radegund wove in her convent, as well as the book from which she read.

[44] Harper, *Slavery in the Late Roman World*, pp. 128–135.

[45] Fortunatus, *Poems*, appendix 31, lines 1–8. The use of wax tables suggests that this may have formed part of an educational exercise.

[46] See, for example, Fortunatus, *Poems*, 8.1, lines 41–60. Riché, *Education and Culture in the Barbarian West*, pp. 292–293.

[47] Wood, 'Religion in Pre-Carolingian Thuringia'. The lone reference to household gods in Fortunatus's poem *On the Destruction of Thuringia* is best understood within the classicizing style of the work itself, which compares Thuringia to Troy (p. 318).

Radegund performed fledgling acts of Christian worship while she was in Athies. He may have included this information to foreshadow Radegund's later achievements, but he was certainly in a position to know the authentic details of her years in the villa. Together with a boy named Samuel, Radegund processed into the oratory in Athies while they were carrying a wooden cross that they had made themselves, singing psalms, and offering their pious devotions with a mature solemnity atypical for their age.[48] Radegund's early religious practices combine with other evidence to suggest that the Thuringian ruling family had adopted Catholic Christianity at an early date, perhaps even before the Frankish king Clovis had received baptism in 508.[49] They most likely did so under the influence of the Byzantine court in Constantinople, although no surviving source recorded any details that might definitively confirm this suspicion.

* * *

Each year that Radegund aged, she drew that much closer to her wedding. Although it is difficult to determine precisely when Chlothar decided to take Radegund as his bride, their marriage probably occurred sometime between 535 and 540.[50] This date range places Radegund, broadly speaking, within her teenage years. Social custom, from the ancient days of the Roman Empire and through the whole of the Merovingian period, upheld twelve as the minimal age for a girl to marry.[51] Most brides were slightly older, but not by too many years; they were usually married between the ages of fifteen and twenty.[52] Fortunatus showed no embarrassment in his epitaph in honour of Vilithuta, for example, that his subject had been married at thirteen.[53] She required an epitaph because she had died in childbirth two years after the marriage. Vilithuta's background was not so different from Radegund's: born to a wealthy, 'barbarian' (i.e. non-Roman) family in Paris, orphaned in her early years, and, at the earliest opportunity, married by her grandmother to a nobleman who lived in Poitiers, where she had no family to support her. Fortunatus wrote that Vilithuta enjoyed a happy, albeit brief,

---

[48] Fortunatus, *Life of Radegund*, 2.
[49] Wood, 'The Frontiers of Western Europe', p. 234. See also Schimpff, 'Pagan? Arianisch? Katholisch?', pp. 149–152.
[50] Fauquier, 'La Chronologie radegondienne', pp. 319–321.
[51] Wemple, *Women in Frankish Society*, pp. 15–25 and 28–43.
[52] Hopkins, 'The Age of Roman Girls at Marriage'.
[53] Fortunatus, *Poems*, 4.26.

marriage. But this claim must be considered alongside the fact that he had been commissioned to write the epitaph by the girl's husband.

In her union with Chlothar, Radegund faced marriage to a man in his late thirties, who had been married before, and whose tangle of sexual relationships was so knotted that it will require much dedicated space to sort through in what follows below. She must have regarded the idea with dread, no matter what her governors told her.[54] Chlothar had inflicted death and misery upon her family and her homeland. Nor had he any intention of changing his behaviour—or to spare even his own family from his cruelties. While Radegund still lived in Athies, Chlothar committed one of his most notorious crimes: the murder of his own nephews, who were just a few years younger than his bride to be. According to Gregory of Tours, Chlothar and his older brother Childebert conspired out of fear that the boys might inherit a share of the kingdom.[55] They captured their nephews and presented an ultimatum to their own mother, Chlothild, who had taken these grandchildren of hers into her care after they had been orphaned. 'What is your preference?', asked the messenger sent to Chlothild by Chlothar and Childebert. 'Shall they live with their hair cut short, or shall they die?' Merovingian princes wore their hair long and freely down their backs, which symbolized their dynastic right to rule.[56] Chlothild replied: 'If they are not to be raised to the throne, then I would rather see them slain than shorn.' Childebert began to lose his nerve when one of the boys grabbed his legs and begged for his life. 'Cast him aside, or you will surely die in his place', Chlothar replied, and Childebert duly complied, prising the seven-year-old away from his legs. Chlothar stabbed him with a dagger, and then served the same cruel death to the boy's ten-year-old brother, before he also ordered the execution of their attendants and tutors.[57]

Radegund's prospects of escaping marriage to Chlothar were bleak. She lacked a powerful advocate to persuade the king, perhaps through generous gifts, to agree to her release. She was not as fortunate as Rusticula, for example, who had initially suffered a similar fate. Abducted at the age of five

[54] On the questions of agency and intention in similar contexts, see Balberg and Muehlberger, 'The Will of Others'.

[55] Gregory of Tours, *Histories*, 3.18.

[56] Diesenberger, 'Hair, Sacrality and Symbolic Capital'; Wood, 'Hair and Beards in the Early Medieval West', p. 109; and Cameron, 'How Did the Merovingian Kings Wear their Hair?'.

[57] A third boy, the young prince Chlodovald, escaped the massacre, only to abandon political life altogether. Cutting his own royal locks, he lived out his days in devotion to God. According to the *Life of Cloud*, 12, he entered a monastery outside Paris. Although he lived until about 560, Chlodovald is not known to have met Radegund.

by an aristocrat and kept within his home, Rusticula was watched over by the man's mother until she became old enough to marry.[58] Her fate changed when the abbess Liliola asked King Guntram to intervene, so that Rusticula might instead be entrusted to her convent in Arles. Saved from the marriage, the presumably grateful Rusticula later refused the attempts by her mother and her kin to see her returned to her aristocratic family in Vaucluse. She opted instead to remain within the convent, where she eventually became abbess herself.[59] But Radegund had no Liliola to secure her release. No mother or kin to seek her return. And her abductor was the king himself. She had only one option: to flee.

Escape she did, though the details of her flight remain obscured by their appearance in a confusing sentence written by Fortunatus in his *Life of Radegund*:

> When Chlothar wished to accept her in marriage at [his estate in] Vitry, and after preparations had been made, Radegund slipped away with a few people in the night, through Beralcha to Athies.[60]

This passage confuses as much as it informs. Why had Radegund fled back to Athies, her place of confinement? A later scribe, equally befuddled, produced the variant reading '*from* Athies'.[61] Unfortunately, the site of 'Beralcha', presumably a place name, remains unidentified—perhaps Biaches on the Somme, near Péronne, or Baralle, southeast of Arras.[62] The word has alternatively been interpreted as a personal name (meaning 'through the help of someone named Beralcha') and even as a variant of the word for a river barge, *barca*, originally applied to the flatbottomed ships of the Nile.[63]

Fortunatus provided little clarification in his next sentence, in which he stumbled through a moment of hagiographic bathos:

> Afterwards, when Chlothar had arranged with her that she should be elevated to a queen in Soissons, Radegund avoided regal extravagance, so that

[58] Florentius, *Life of Rusticula*, 3. Riché, 'La vita s. Rusticulae', p. 371.
[59] Florentius, *Life of Rusticula*, 5. For the view that Rusticula was not rescued by Liliola so much as captured a second time, see Orlinski, 'Lost in Translation', pp. 41–51.
[60] Fortunatus, *Life of Radegund*, 2.
[61] The MSS give several alternative readings, including *ad Atteias* and *ab Attegias*.
[62] The idea that Chlothar's men captured Radegund at this location was suggested by Fauquier, 'La Chronologie radegondienne', p. 320.
[63] Rouche, 'Le Célibat consacré de sainte Radegonde'.

she might increase, not in the world, but in the eyes of the one to whom she was devoted [i.e. Christ], and she remained unchanged by worldly glory.

In his hurry to emphasize Radegund's other-worldliness, Fortunatus provided no explanation for why, or how, she had apparently failed in her escape, nor did he detail what happened to her accomplices. Neither did he believe that his audience might be confused. He thought, it seems, that the answer appeared in his text. The place to look for a resolution to this conundrum, therefore, must be in the single identifiable result achieved by Radegund's flight, as described by Fortunatus: the relocation from Vitry-en-Artois, a royal villa about 70 km north of Athies, to Soissons, the principal city of Chlothar's kingdom and home to his royal court.

Secluded and secure, Vitry was large enough to accommodate the king and his entourage, yet removed from urban life and its political complexities. A half-century later, Chilperic (one of Chlothar's sons) hid his newborn boy at Vitry, lest this precious heir suffer from the same witchcraft that had killed his brothers.[64] For Radegund, the villa must have appeared to be a gilded cage. Soissons, in contrast, offered a public venue, a marriage in the full light of day. The city also symbolized the splendour of the kingdom itself, and conferred this prestige upon Radegund as the publicly acknowledged bride of the king.[65] Chlothar's father had wrested Soissons from the late Roman ruler Syagrius, and the distinguished character of the city had endured through the years in which it served as a power centre, not only for Chlothar, but also for his sons, one of whom even constructed a circus there to host popular entertainments, in a clear attempt to evoke the grandeur of the Roman past.[66] A wedding in Soissons meant public recognition and prestige.

Although no account of the wedding survives, Fortunatus described a similar nuptial assembly in a poem written for the marriage of Brunhild to Chlothar's son Sigibert at his royal court in Metz in 566:

All things delight when, through celestial largesse, the royal court is magnified by a marriage in majesty. A great many luminaries gather in ordered ranks that serve to embroider the king, blessed by fortune in this

---

[64] Gregory of Tours, *Histories*, 6.41. In 575, an overconfident Sigibert stopped at Vitry while on campaign, and his army declared his imminent triumph by raising him on a shield. But two assassins had concealed themselves among his troops, and they stabbed him with poison daggers (4.51). More than one king considered Vitry safe; not all were right.

[65] Gerberding, *The Rise of the Carolingians*, pp. 150–159.

[66] Gregory of Tours, *Histories*, 2.27 (Syagrius), 5.17 (Chilperic I's circus).

worldly life. So many high lords rise together, meeting at the one who is their lofty summit. Behold, Mars (war) has his generals. Behold, Pax (peace) has her generosity. At the arrival of all, the palace comes to life in festivity. A people see their wishes fulfilled by the marriage of their king.[67]

Radegund's marriage to Chlothar presumably involved similar festivities in the palace in Soissons. A public ceremony mattered greatly to Radegund because it unambiguously signified two important qualities. Firstly, her status as queen, since the Merovingians lacked a specific ritual for anointing queens beyond the nuptial ceremonies themselves. Secondly, her status as wife, since many Merovingian kings kept concubines at their side (Chlothar was no exception). Neither of those qualities could be taken for granted if Radegund's marriage occurred in Vitry, with the union unwitnessed by the great of the realm and unknown to the public.

Fortunatus alluded to this distinction when, in a very different context (Radegund's later separation from her husband, discussed in Chapter 3), he wrote that the nobility of Chlothar's kingdom insisted that she could not simply be cast from the king's side as if she had no value. Fortunatus's exact phrase, placed into the mouths of these noblemen, was that they considered Radegund to be *regina non publicana sed publica*, wordplay that expressed her status as a publicly recognized queen, rather than a publicly available woman, i.e. a prostitute (deployed here as a derogatory analogue for a concubine).[68] This context explains Fortunatus's statement that, after Radegund fled the wedding at Vitry, she arranged (*dirigere*, 'set the matter straight') to be elevated to a queen in Soissons. At this moment, regardless of Fortunatus's hagiographic platitudes, Radegund showed great concern for her worldly status. Presumably she negotiated this beneficial outcome after her return to Athies, escaping not from the very notion of marriage itself, but from a relationship with Chlothar in Vitry that would be neither widely known nor clearly defined. Radegund may have lacked the power to avoid a union with the king, but she had the ability to cause enough of a stir to leverage a different venue, one that offered her greater recognition in a kingdom where she had no natural allies or supporters.

* * *

---

[67] Fortunatus, *Poems*, 6.1, lines 15–22.
[68] Fortunatus, *Life of Radegund*, 12.

Over the course of a reign that spanned five decades (511–561), Chlothar had many women at his side, some wives and others concubines, both before and after Radegund. His accumulation of sexual partners led Gregory of Tours to present him as a dissolute man driven by an exceedingly lustful disposition.[69] Most historians have concurred. But it is clear that more stood behind Chlothar's motives than his libido alone, however impulsive he may have been. What the king lacked in moral conviction he made up for in political calculation. He first married Guntheuca, Chlodomer's widow, after the latter died on campaign against the Burgundians in 524.[70] Many years later, in his final attempt at marriage in the mid-550s, Chlothar arranged to wed Wuldetrada, the widow of his great-nephew, but he encountered resistance from several bishops for his choice of bride.[71] On both occasions, by marrying the widow of a close kinsman, Chlothar aimed to consolidate his power over a part of the Merovingian realm previously beyond his control, even if that meant crossing the boundary of what many, especially among the clergy, considered to be incest. These were sins of greed as much as lust. Chlothar's other identifiable partners, however, were former slaves with no wealth or connections to offer. Here Gregory's criticism held more firmly, although a union with a low-born woman offered its own type of political benefits. The imbalance of power in these relationships afforded Chlothar the luxury to produce potential heirs and to manage the results later, either by marrying the servile woman and elevating her status, together with that of her offspring, or by dismissing her and her sons without consequence.

These women likely regarded Radegund as a threat, especially if they had ambitions to see their sons seated on a throne. Such hopes had a basis in Merovingian custom, since on a few occasions a son born to a royal father and a servile mother did manage to inherit a share of the realm alongside his legitimate half-brothers. For example, Chlodomer, Childebert I, and Chlothar, the sons of Clovis from his high-born wife Chlothild, shared the kingdom with their half-brother Theuderic, the son of a concubine. Yet this arrangement was likely a necessary compromise, rather than an expression of an ideal political system, as Theuderic was already an adult when his father died, while Chlothild's sons (Chlothar included) were still minors. More often, an attempt to include an illegitimate son in the inheritance of

[69] Gregory of Tours, *Histories*, 4.3.
[70] Gregory of Tours, *Histories*, 3.6.
[71] Gregory of Tours, *Histories*, 4.9.

the kingdom was met with opposition, often voiced by a cleric.[72] Sagittarius of Gap asserted that King Guntram's children were unable to inherit on the grounds that their mother had originally been a slave.[73] The holy man Columbanus rebuked Theuderic II for his 'adulterous relations with his concubines', asking: 'Why does he not satisfy himself with the comforts of a lawful wife so that his royal offspring might be born to an honourable queen, rather than be seen to emerge from whorehouses?'[74] And when Theuderic II asked Desiderius of Vienne whether or not he should marry his concubine, the bishop told him: 'it is better to take a wife and make your sons legitimate'.[75] For the enslaved women who gave birth to Chlothar's sons, the unsettled question of legitimacy meant that they had reason to hope, but certainly could not take for granted, that their sons might share in the inheritance of the realm. Radegund needed all the resources available to her as Chlothar's official queen to secure her position at court against her rivals and their interests.

Gregory of Tours provided an example of how a potential heir might be excluded when he described Chlothar's rejection of one woman, who did not enjoy the status of queen, and her son, a boy named Gundovald:

> Gundovald was born in Gaul, raised with great care, educated in letters, and, as is the custom of the kings here, wore his hair long down his back. He was taken to King Childebert by his mother, who said: 'Look, this is your nephew, the son of King Chlothar. Since he is detested by his father, you take him, for he is your flesh and blood.' Childebert received him and kept him by his side, as he had no sons of his own. When Chlothar heard of this, he sent messengers to his brother, saying: 'Give the boy up and send him to me.' Childebert straightaway sent the youth to his brother, who took one look at him and ordered his hair to be shorn, saying: 'This is no son of mine.'[76]

The year of Gundovald's birth is uncertain, but it most likely belongs to the early or mid-540s, while Chlothar was married to Radegund, or perhaps

---

[72] Dailey, *Queens, Consorts, Concubines*, pp. 96–99 and 110–111.
[73] Gregory of Tours, *Histories*, 5.20. Gregory had no desire to concur with this opinion in writing, quickly adding that Sagittarius was not aware that 'regardless of the birth status of their mothers, those who have been sired by kings are called the sons of kings'.
[74] Jonas, *Life of Columbanus*, 1.18.
[75] *Life of Desiderius of Vienne*, 6.
[76] Gregory of Tours, *Histories*, 6.24.

shortly thereafter.[77] In the early 580s, after a long exile spent mostly in Constantinople, Gundovald returned to Gaul and launched a war in an ultimately unsuccessful effort to claim his share of the kingdom.[78] He publicly urged anyone with reservations about his paternity to ask Radegund, who was then ensconced in her convent in Poitiers and advanced in years, on the grounds that she knew the truth of the matter.[79] Such an assertion suggests that Gundovald felt confident about his claim, and that he expected Radegund to know the details of Chlothar's sexual relationships with other women.[80]

Gregory identified some of the women who had children from Chlothar before he married Radegund. Or, in some instances, perhaps not long *after* the wedding, which probably took place between 535 and 540. The king's son Chramn, for example, was born to a concubine perhaps around 537.[81] Another concubine, Ingund, had three sons who were older than Radegund and who had already reached adulthood before she married Chlothar.[82] But Ingund also had two other sons born very close to the wedding itself, the youngest in 535 or 536.[83] Between these younger two boys, Ingund's sister Aregund also gave birth to a son from Chlothar.[84] Gregory of Tours wrote that the king had eventually married these two sisters and former slaves, but there are reasons to doubt the claim, especially since it appeared in the context of a story that inspires little confidence about the historicity of its details. He wrote that Ingund, after she married Chlothar, used her influence to ask the king to find a suitable partner for her sister. Chlothar went to the villa where Aregund lived in servitude, but he audaciously arranged to marry her himself. He then returned to Ingund and told her the good news:

---

[77] Ewig, 'Die Namengebung bei den ältesten Frankenkönigen', pp. 62–63. Gundovald had apparently spent time painting the walls and vaults of oratories prior to Chlothar's death in 561 (Gregory of Tours, *Histories*, 7.36), so he cannot have been born too late into the 540s. Unless the reference to painting instead represents nothing more than a slight upon Gundovald's character, for which possibility see Johnsson, 'Locks of Difference', p. 67.

[78] Gregory of Tours, *Histories*, 7.14. See Wood, 'The Secret Histories of Gregory of Tours', pp. 263–266.

[79] Gregory of Tours, *Histories*, 7.36. Or, Gundovald said, they could ask Ingitrude, a nun in Tours and relative of the royal house.

[80] Goffart, 'The Frankish Pretender Gundovald', p. 5.

[81] Ewig, 'Die Namengebung bei den ältesten Frankenkönigen', p. 62.

[82] Gregory of Tours, *Histories*, 3.21.

[83] Gregory of Tours, *Histories*, 4.3. Ingund also had at least one daughter, Chlodoswintha.

[84] Ewig, 'Die Namengebung bei den ältesten Frankenkönigen', pp. 55–56.

I have done the favour that you, my sweetness, asked of me. You wanted a man both wealthy and wise for me to join to your sister, and I have found no one more worthy than myself.[85]

Gregory offered this amusing tale to support his view of Chlothar as enthralled to his own lust, and he emphasized that the king's behaviour created instability in the realm by elevating meddlesome women to high status and increasing the likelihood of civil wars between their sons over the matter of inheritance.

If truth is to be found in Gregory's claim that Ingund and Aregund were regarded as queens, it is probably retrospectively. When Chlothar died in 561, he was survived only by the sons born to these two sisters (Gundovald excepted). His kingdom was divided between them. Gregory of Tours began to write only after these sons had taken up dominion over their share of the realm. By the time Gregory rested his pen, it had likely become customary, and perhaps politically prudent, to consider the mothers of these kings to be queens in their own right, at least as a matter of legacy, and to imagine that their relationship with Chlothar had been a marriage. That outcome occurred for two reasons. Firstly, Ingund and Aregund successfully arranged for their sons to be incorporated into Chlothar's rule at the expense of his sons from other women, who (like Gundovald) were rejected by their father. Secondly, none of Chlothar's high-born wives, Radegund included, produced a legitimate heir.

Unsurprisingly, no source recorded Radegund's feelings about her infertility. Baudonivia, Gregory, and Fortunatus all knew Radegund after her separation from Chlothar, when she lived as a woman under religious vows, pledged to a life of sexual abstinence in devotion to God. Only Fortunatus discussed her marital life in any detail, and he did so only to support his dubious claim that she had always wished to live as a nun rather than a wife (as discussed in Chapter 2). Yet it cannot be imagined that those governors appointed by Chlothar to guide the young Radegund through her adolescence in Athies had encouraged her to adopt a life of avowed chastity. Such an idea can only have come to her later. The young Radegund never enjoyed the privilege to freely choose her own goals or ambitions. In her role as queen, her value was deeply associated with her fertility. She must have felt pressure to produce a son, especially as her rivals secured important roles for their own

---

[85] Gregory of Tours, *Histories*, 4.3.

sons within the kingdom.[86] Perhaps she also found the idea of having a child comforting, even if, it must be assumed, she detested the father. For a woman who, in her earliest years, had her home and her kin taken from her, and who knew only loss, a child might have offered the opportunity for her to see her family continue, and to have someone all her own to love. Such ideas must remain speculative, but it can be said with more confidence that, whatever her personal feelings on motherhood during this period of her life, Radegund faced an enduring precariousness, even after her wedding, at the hands of her rivals and their sons, and that her condition might improve if she gave birth to an heir, as was surely expected of her.

* * *

Once she had embraced the religious life, if not before, Radegund recited the psalms regularly. The cry of Psalm 30, *my lots are in your hands; deliver me from the hands of my enemies*, must have brought memories to her mind of the moment when lots were cast for her, when fortune placed her in the hands of Chlothar and sent her to Gaul. The Scriptures mentioned lots on several occasions, many of them in the context of war and the division of spoils. Perhaps the best-known example of the practice occurred in Acts 1:20–26, when the eleven remaining apostles cast lots to select Matthias as the replacement for Judas Iscariot. But for Radegund, the most meaningful of such biblical passages may just have been those in which lots were cast to select the animals offered as a sacrifice for the forgiveness of sin in the Temple of Jerusalem. In the books of the New Testament, these sacrifices were associated with Jesus's crucifixion, interpreted as a sacrifice for the salvation of humanity that rendered the Temple unnecessary. In the Gospels, Roman soldiers had even cast lots to determine who might keep Christ's cloak, since it served no use if divided up (John 19:23–24, a passage that quoted Psalm 21:19 on the casting of lots). As detailed in Chapter 6, an older, biblically literate Radegund took a passionate interest in the Crucifixion, beyond that of even the most devout among her contemporaries. She dispatched envoys to Constantinople, where she obtained fragments of the Cross from the imperial court, and placed them in her convent, which served as a new temple. Perhaps Radegund had come to see her own experience of suffering and loss as a form of sacrifice, which she offered for the redemption of her soul, that allowed her to partake in the redemptive suffering of Christ on the Cross.

---

[86] Nelson, 'Queens as Jezebels', p. 38.

If so, such theological insights remained for the future. When Radegund married Chlothar in Soissons, the founding of a monastery was furthest from her mind. Fortunatus's presentation of Radegund—not only in her destiny, but also in some sort of metaphysical sense—as a nun by vocation even from her earliest days is obviously little more than a hagiographic topos. The goal of the young Radegund was surely to achieve a measure of security in life and to capitalize on the opportunity to increase her standing in the kingdom once it came. What other option did she have but to embrace Gaul as her new home and to make a success of the life allotted to her? Alongside any developing sense of divine purpose, which ought not be disregarded, Radegund also acquired a renewed sense of her birthright—her entitlement to the status of queen, and to whatever benefits she might secure in a worldly life that she had not yet come to reject. *Blessed be the Lord, for he has exalted me with his mercy in a walled city*, continues Psalm 30, in a verse that might just as fittingly apply to Radegund the queen, reigning from Soissons, as to the later nun, secluded behind the walls of her convent in Poitiers. Now that Radegund had become Chlothar's wife, she aimed to put the miseries of her childhood behind her, to whatever extent that might be possible, and to establish herself as a royal woman who enjoyed God's favour as she reigned from Soissons.

2

A Temple Consumed by Fire

Radegund received an invitation from the noblewoman Ansifrida to a *prandium*, a sort of brunch, though more a grand banquet than a pleasant elevenses. Even for such a quotidian event as a meal, Radegund travelled in splendour, with an entourage in train. Now a queen, she had become the esteemed guest of the illustrious women of the realm, welcomed to the houses and villas of the elite. Much had changed, in quick order, since her time in Athies. Radegund possessed significant resources and commanded great respect. She also had enemies, even though she had the means to confront them. While still on her way to the *prandium*, Radegund stopped to challenge a cohort of Franks. In a scene portrayed in Baudonivia's *Life of Radegund*, they maintained a pagan sanctuary (described as a *fanum*, a 'shrine' or 'temple') about a mile off the road, an edifice that the queen ordered to be destroyed:

> She commanded her servants to set fire to the temple, which the Franks revered, because she considered it an outrage to honour the deceptions of the devil and insult the God of Heaven. Hearing this, the entire crowd of Franks tried to protect their shrine with swords and cudgels, and by every diabolical incantation. The holy queen remained unmoved, steadfast with Christ in her heart. The horse, on which she had long sat, did not stir until the flames fully consumed the shrine. By her prayers, the people established peace with one another, and, on account of this deed, they all admired the virtue and conviction of the queen and blessed the Lord.[1]

In this story, Radegund confronted and stood down the same sort of Frankish warriors who had eagerly spearheaded the invasion of Thuringia, and she did so full of confidence and conviction. She had crossed a frontier, from captive to queen.

[1] Baudonivia, *Life of Radegund*, 2.

Radegund. E. T. Dailey, Oxford University Press. © Oxford University Press 2023.
DOI: 10.1093/oso/9780197656105.003.0003

This story is most valuable for what it reveals about Baudonivia's portrayal of Radegund, and the manner in which she was remembered by the nuns of Holy Cross. Its details are doubtful, since there is little evidence to support the idea of a thriving Frankish paganism, or the existence of temples substantial enough to be destroyed in a dramatic conflagration, during Radegund's lifetime (even though pagan practices had not yet wholly disappeared among the Franks).[2] For Baudonivia, however, the story possessed a greater thematic significance. Radegund had come to set fire not merely to a shrine, but also to an entire social order, one in which an old guard of warrior elite caused havoc across the land as they pursued their personal ambitions, ignorant of any fear of God. Now, those days were over. The Frankish warriors sheathed their swords and submitted to their 'holy queen', and ultimately to Christ. Venantius Fortunatus had portrayed Radegund as a woman uncomfortable with her queenship, eager to renounce the trappings of worldly power. Although Baudonivia had read Fortunatus's *Life of Radegund*, and although she too believed that Radegund had transcended the troubles of the world, she and the nuns of Holy Cross clearly thought that Radegund had never stopped being their queen.[3]

While the story of the burning temple served as a metaphor for Radegund's sacred presence in the kingdom, and for her righteous authority, Baudonivia also insisted on its veracity. 'I bear witness to what I have seen and I speak of what I have heard', she asserted, rather conspicuously. Nevertheless, she willingly sacrificed plausibility for dramatic effect, gradually building a tension in her account between the righteous queen and her heathen opponents, which she then resolved, abruptly and almost inexplicably. As the shrine turned to ash and ember, Radegund prayed, peace was made, and the pagans blessed the Lord. The staccato structure of this sequence conveyed a sense of the miraculous, with divine intervention silently bridging the gaps between events that otherwise failed to connect through cause and effect. Through this literary technique, Baudonivia elevated the passage to match other stories of saints destroying pagan shrines, a common hagiographic topos.[4] She and her community of nuns in Holy Cross clearly wished to remember a bold, valiant, and even audacious queen who ranked among the righteous

---

[2] Hen, 'Paganism and Superstitions', pp. 232–234. See also Effros, 'Monuments and Memory'.

[3] Baudonivia, *Life of Radegund*, preface, on her acknowledged debt to Fortunatus.

[4] A hagiographic topos that appears, interestingly enough, in the versification of the *Life of Martin* by Fortunatus (§1), and the earlier prose version by Sulpicius Severus (§13).

vanquishers of the Devil and his ignorant acolytes. They also wished to remember a queen unashamed of her worldly power, even though she was also unbeholden to it.

If Baudonivia's adherence to hagiographic convention provides reasons for suspicion, her story nonetheless contained incidental details that are themselves believable—and useful for understanding Radegund's life as a queen. The name Ansifrida, irrelevant to the story's theatricality, surely referred to a genuine individual, a woman of high status who managed a large and important household, and who was honoured by Radegund's presence. Baudonivia described Radegund as travelling with a *comitatus*, a personal entourage befitting a queen (or, in fact, a king). She also celebrated Radegund's 'worldly pomp', in a clear contrast to Fortunatus, who wrote that Radegund avoided the 'royal pomp' available to her as a queen.[5] Elsewhere in her *Life of Radegund*, Baudonivia even compared Radegund to Helena, the mother of the Roman emperor Constantine I, a woman who, according to legend, had discovered the Cross of the Crucifixion on her journey to Jerusalem in the early fourth century (as discussed in Chapter 5).[6] Baudonivia's claim that Radegund faced opposition from an old guard of Frankish warriors may also accurately reflect the circumstances in which she lived, as preserved in the collective memory of the nuns in Holy Cross, even if the queen never personally stared down a mob of recalcitrant pagans as their shrine burned in an inferno.

* * *

Fortunatus might not have included this story about the burning temple in his *Life of Radegund*, but he provided details elsewhere in his works that align with Baudonivia's portrayal of Radegund as an influential and affluent queen. He revealed the great wealth she enjoyed, ironically, when he described everything that she renounced in her pursuit of ascetic piety, unintentionally confirming Baudonivia's presentation of Radegund as a resplendent queen. Fortunatus wrote that she travelled in a glittering coach, her hand weighed down by jewellery inset with emeralds. She slept in a bed with gilded posts. She possessed, among the many luxurious garments in her wardrobe, an especially beautiful shawl, of the finest line-fibre linen, adorned with gold

---

[5] Baudonivia, *Life of Radegund*, 2 (*pompa saecularis*); Fortunatus, *Life of* Radegund, 2 (*pompa regalis*).

[6] Baudonivia, *Life of Radegund*, 16.

and gems.[7] She had other clothes dyed in purple, the colour of emperors and kings, decorated with gems and jewels, and accompanied with a heavy golden belt.[8] Fortunatus mentioned other adornments, too: chains, necklaces, hairnets, and brooches all made of gold.[9] His description recalls the contents of a Merovingian sarcophagus, dating perhaps to the 630s, discovered in 1959 under the Basilica of Saint-Denis (now located in a northern suburb of Paris): precious gold jewellery such as pins, earrings, brooches, and a ring engraved with a woman's name; a large glass vase; a linen tunic embroidered in gold; a wool dress with a long belt; and leather shoes.[10] Baudonivia wrote of exquisite gold adornments covered in gems and pearls.[11] Caesaria the Younger, an abbess of Arles who wrote to Radegund, also mentioned pearl necklaces and earrings.[12] So impressive were these valuables that they have been cited in scholarship as proof that Radegund had access to the royal treasury.[13] And surely she did (nor was she the only queen to have this privilege).[14] Indeed, she came close to confirming this herself in her letter *Dominis sanctis*, when she wrote that she had received wealth directly from Chlothar, which she later donated to her monastery in perpetuity.

Other queens received wealth from a range of sources, including tax revenues, and it might be assumed that Radegund enjoyed similar benefits.[15] Gregory of Tours wrote that Fredegund (the wife of Chlothar's son Chilperic I), for example, had to explain to the Frankish warriors of her kingdom where she had obtained the great wealth that she gave to her daughter upon her marriage. Fredegund assured them that she had not taken it from the royal fisc; it had come instead from the assets she had accumulated herself, the gifts she had received from leading men, and the tax revenues she had collected in her own right.[16] As a former slave, Fredegund had not brought any wealth into her marriage, nor had she received any from her family. Yet she was

---

[7] Fortunatus, *Life of Radegund*, 9. See Müller, *Die Kleidung nach Quellen*, pp. 263–264.

[8] Fortunatus, *Life of Radegund*, 13.

[9] Similar items have been recovered from Merovingian burial sites. On their social significance, see Halsall, 'Female Status and Power'.

[10] This sarcophagus is known by the name *Arnegundis*, which appears on the ring. Attempts to associate this burial with the sixth-century figure named 'Aregund' (the sister of Ingund) have proved unconvincing due to the dating of the tomb offered by Périn, 'À propos de la datation et de l'interprétation de la tombe n° 49'.

[11] Baudonivia, *Life of Radegund*, 4.

[12] Caesaria the Younger, *Letter to Richild and Radegund*, 3.

[13] Wood, *The Merovingian Kingdoms*, p. 137.

[14] Stafford, *Queens, Concubines and Dowagers*, pp. 134–139; Stafford, 'Queens and Treasure in the Early Middle Ages'.

[15] Dailey, *Queens, Consorts, Concubines*, p. 110.

[16] Gregory of Tours, *Histories*, 6.45.

still able to load her daughter's wedding caravan with so much gold, silver, and other treasure that her husband worried he might have nothing left.[17] Presumably, Fredegund needed to reassure the elite of the realm that this particular treasure had come solely from revenue under her direct control because she had access to the treasury and might have drawn from it instead. Another queen, Galswinth, had received revenues from five cities upon her marriage, and after her death these eventually fell to her sister, Brunhild, as a matter of inheritance.[18] Radegund's financial resources were likely of a similar nature. Indeed, Fortunatus probably referred to such an arrangement when he described Radegund travelling around to collect 'tribute'.[19]

Such revenues, together with her possessions and property, made Radegund a powerful figure in Chlothar's kingdom. As Fortunatus asserted in one of his poems, she 'ruled the hights of the royal court'.[20] Yet to accumulate and display such wealth as a queen also meant to acquire enemies. It is noteworthy that Fredegund was compelled to explain the source of her wealth to 'the Franks', the same group of powerful warriors who confronted Radegund in Baudonivia's story of the pagan sanctuary. These elite men and their families had formed a kind of military aristocracy after the Merovingians had expanded their rule across Gaul in the early sixth century. They occupied the upper ranks of society alongside older aristocratic families that traced their ancestry back to the days of the bygone Roman Empire. They had broadly adopted Christianity (Baudonivia's story notwithstanding), though perhaps often more out of loyalty to their king than out of zeal for the religion. The Franks clearly felt that, in a certain sense, the treasure of the realm belonged to them in common, with the king holding his personal share and acting as a kind of custodian over the rest. Radegund may have been a princess by birth, but, like the lowborn Fredegund, she had brought no wealth into her marriage and had no family resources to draw upon. Her access to resources depended entirely on her status as Chlothar's queen, whether such wealth came straight from the royal treasury or through other routes like tax revenues or personal gifts. The Franks had every reason to grumble about this foreign captive turned sanctimonious queen, who paraded through the kingdom with a sizable entourage on her way to luncheons as the guest of honour.

[17] The treasure fell into the hands of Gundovald. See Gregory of Tours, *Histories*, 7.9–10.
[18] Gregory of Tours, *Histories*, 9.20.
[19] Fortunatus, *Life of Radegund*, 3 (*tributum*).
[20] Fortunatus, *Poems*, 8.1.

Radegund needed to gather the bulk of her support from elsewhere within the kingdom. Her many donations to the Church indicate where she found it: among the clerical elite, in which the old aristocratic families of Gaul enjoyed abundant representation. Not that the secular and clerical elites neatly split into two distinct factions, nor that these loudly echoed a 'barbarian' and 'Roman' social divide.[21] Nothing was ever so straightforward in Merovingian Gaul.[22] Elite families had long intermingled, shifting their identities and obtaining the great offices of the realm regardless of such traditional distinctions.[23] Radegund navigated a complex terrain in which the loyalties of any single individual could not be taken for granted on the basis of their presumed pedigree.[24] Nonetheless, she found ecclesiastical benefaction and visible piety the surest path to securing a base of support. Fortunatus wrote that, after collecting her 'tribute', Radegund immediately gave away the first portion as 'tithes' (*decimae*), before accepting any of the money herself.[25] She then visited monasteries, handed out more treasure, and dispatched gifts to those institutions that she was unable to reach in person. 'Even a hermit could not hide himself from her munificence,' Fortunatus wrote. Although generous almsgiving appears ubiquitously in hagiographic literature, what Fortunatus described here is different: Radegund travelled in a circuit and redistributed wealth into the hands of ecclesiastical institutions, in addition to the poor and needy, on an unprecedented scale.

Radegund also went further than most in her efforts to associate herself with holy places, where the clergy oversaw access to the divine. She put candles, fashioned with her own hands, into oratories, physically connecting her to sites of divine power.[26] She also restitched her clothes into cloth to cover the altars of churches and shrines.[27] Fabric that once rested upon Radegund's body now stretched out over the very place where, in the form of the Eucharist, the divine sacrifice that Jesus made on the Cross was reproduced by a priest and offered to the faithful. Radegund also honoured ecclesiastical figures. Fortunatus wrote that, when one of the 'servants of God' visited her, Radegund and her attendants met the holy ascetic outside, washed his feet with warm water, and offered him a refreshing drink.[28] This

[21] Pohl, 'Christian and Barbarian Identities'.
[22] Halsall, 'Transformations of Romanness'; Mathisen, 'Roman Identity in Late Antiquity'.
[23] Salzman, *The Making of a Christian Aristocracy*.
[24] Buchberger, *Shifting Ethnic Identities in Spain and Gaul*, pp. 107–178.
[25] Fortunatus, *Life of Radegund*, 3.
[26] On the significance of the practice, see Fouracre, 'Lights, Power, and the Moral Economy'.
[27] Fortunatus, *Life of Radegund*, 7 and 9.
[28] Fortunatus, *Life of Radegund*, 8.

gesture carried great weight with the clergy. In one of his sermons, Caesarius of Arles had rebuked nobles who refused to allow people to wash the feet of clerics out of pride.[29] He also encouraged his congregation to give money to monks and clerics when they asked. Radegund anticipated such requests, rewarding bishops with gifts when they visited her before they had even asked, and she kept these visiting bishops in her company to discuss the 'principles of salvation' for long periods.

Radegund also presented herself as a holy queen to the wider population. In Athies, which she continued to visit once she had become queen, Radegund built a house to provide beds for needy women. She washed them in warm baths and mixed medicines to revive those weak from fever.[30] She also acquired a reputation as a source of mercy and clemency in the kingdom, influencing Chlothar to be lenient towards those he had sentenced to execution.[31] When some criminals escaped imprisonment in Péronne, they fled to Radegund's nearby villa, perhaps, because they were aware of her reputation, in the hope the she might offer protection.[32] Through such behaviour, Radegund imitated the actions of certain high-profile bishops: organizing care for the poor, maintaining holy sites, and negotiating the release of prisoners. The parallels are so conspicuous, in fact, that it has been suggested they resulted from Fortunatus modelling his depiction of Radegund on the protagonists of 'episcopal biographies'.[33] While the possibility of such literary inspiration must be taken seriously, it is likely that the modelling began with Radegund herself, rather than with her hagiographer. Fortunatus even asserted as much when he wrote that Radegund made her own bread in conscious imitation of Germanus, a fifth-century bishop of Auxerre (though this example concerns her religious life after she separated from Chlothar, detailed in Chapters 5 and 6).[34] She had apparently learned more than the principles of salvation from her conversations with bishops. She had acquired an example of pious behaviour that reinforced her status and her authority through charitable service, generous benefaction, and political intervention.

[29] Caesarius, *Sermons*, 202.1.
[30] Fortunatus, *Life of Radegund*, 4. The institution has been considered the first of its kind in its focus on helping poor women. See Horden, 'Public Health', p. 309.
[31] Fortunatus, *Life of Radegund*, 10.
[32] Fortunatus, *Life of Radegund*, 11. In Fortunatus's account, the criminals had assumed, wrongly, that Radegund's prayers had set them free, and they sought to show their gratitude.
[33] Kitchen, *Saints' Lives and the Rhetoric of Gender*, p. 123.
[34] Fortunatus, *Life of Radegund*, 16. Compare with Constantius, *Life of Germanus*, 3.

* * *

Fortunatus provided a glimpse into Radegund's marital relationship with Chlothar in a passage unprecedented in the hagiographic genre:

> When she lay with the king at night, she sought permission to rise and relieve herself. Departing from the bedchamber, she tossed a hair shirt in front of the privy and lay prostrate upon it in prayer for a long time. As she lay still, the cold ran through her until only her spirit remained warm. Unconcerned for her tormented body, her flesh prematurely dead, she kept her mind focused on paradise. She considered her burdens light, lest she lose her value in the eyes of Christ. When she returned to the bedchamber, she found it almost impossible to warm herself, either by the fireplace or in the bed.[35]

Fortunatus portrayed Radegund as a penitent woman. The cold and narrow privy foreshadowed her monastic cell in Holy Cross, where she secluded herself during Lent and tormented her body (as discussed in Chapter 6). Without specifically mentioning sexual intercourse, the passage certainly alluded to what Fortunatus and many among his audience considered an act of bodily pollution, with the filth of the privy a metaphor for the indignity of sex. In a poem that praised virginity, Fortunatus, himself a chaste man, described chastity as

> the original state, shining without stain, revered throughout the world. The good that belongs to nature is not to be violated. Precious, it preserves the value of the body unhurt and retains forever the riches unknown to the thief.[36]

Fortunatus presented Radegund's marital bed as another source of suffering, which acquired a redemptive purpose in the context of her asceticism.

Although it is, of course, impossible to discern how Radegund interpreted this experience herself, it seems unlikely that she agreed with the view expressed by Fortunatus, at least during this stage of her life, or that she ascribed the same theological significance to her sexual life in order to make sense of it (however unpleasant it may have been for her, given the

[35] Fortunatus, *Life of Radegund*, 5.
[36] Fortunatus, *Poems*, 8.3, lines 322–325.

conditions). Admittedly, Fortunatus knew Radegund well. His correspond-ence with her suggests a closeness that might even have led him to believe he understood her most intimate experiences. But even if Radegund had felt comfortable enough to discuss this aspect of her life with a male asso-ciate, and there is absolutely no reason to believe that she did, she could offer Fortunatus only a perspective altered by hindsight. Baudonivia, who might have provided a female perspective on the matter, passed over this material without comment, except to point her readers to Fortunatus's earlier work and to state that Radegund's marital life was already a matter of record.[37] Baudonivia brushed aside Radegund's time as a wife by stating that God had simply allowed her to experience the marital condition so that she might serve as a model for pious laywomen. This interpretation conferred a spir-itual purpose upon Radegund's secular life while subsuming it within her greater identity as a nun and saint. Baudonivia, herself avowed to the celibate life, clearly found the subject uncomfortable.

What these views hold in common is a denial of the possibility that, at this moment in her life, Radegund wished for a child (regardless of how she felt about the means). Some of her possible motivations have already been identified in Chapter 1. Ample biblical examples existed to provide Radegund with a model of a married woman who prayed for, and ultimately received, offspring of her own. Perhaps her prayers echoed those of Hannah, who asked for a son so incessantly that she was considered either drunk or mad (1 Samuel 1:1–20). There is certainly no basis to imagine, as has been suggested, that her nocturnal journeys to the cold privy were simply 'a con-traceptive tactic' because they cooled Chlothar's passions.[38] Admittedly, any attempt to guess Radegund's thoughts and desires at this moment requires an act of the imagination, but the value of such an exercise is to emphasize the dynamic character of her beliefs. The newly married Radegund cannot have been the predestined, yet momentarily frustrated, nun of hagiography. Instead, her desires and her self-conception developed in response to events. She eventually learned that she was no Hannah, because her prayers went unanswered. But only from this later perspective did a monastic calling truly make sense. Radegund's longing for the religious life represents the final product, not the guiding purpose, of her early years, when a growing awareness of her own infertility (itself perhaps caused by trauma and abuse)

[37] Baudonivia, *Life of Radegund*, 1.
[38] Rouche, 'Le Célibat consacré de sainte Radegonde' (*une tactique anticonceptionnelle*).

inclined her to the message of holy men and women who spoke to her about the superiority of an ascetic life.

* * *

Radegund avoided royal banquets by 'making excuses to the king' to spend more time in devotion to God.[39] She departed from such festivities, singing the psalms as she left, and she ensured that the poor, who were waiting outside the doors of the great hall, were provided with food. When Chlothar took his meals in private, Radegund avoided joining him at the table and said that 'she had her hands full with the affairs of God', an explanation that angered the king. 'He had quarrels with his wife,' Fortunatus wrote, 'such that he subsequently compensated her with gifts in return for the wrong done through his tongue.'[40] This gesture might suggest a hint of remorse. But Fortunatus mentioned the gifts, not to offer a partial rehabilitation of Chlothar's legacy, but to demonstrate the king's concern for his public image, in contrast to Radegund's desire for approval in the eyes of God above all else. The comparison may seem rather forced, given the very public displays of charitable almsgiving and ecclesiastical benefaction that Radegund regularly performed. But there is little reason to doubt Fortunatus's suggestion that Radegund and Chlothar clashed over her private devotions, or that she took advantage of moments when Chlothar left the royal residence to spend long periods in prayer. Neither is it difficult to believe that the king was concerned with his own reputation, rather than Radegund's feelings. Fortunatus concluded his critique of Chlothar by declaring that Radegund's good deeds 'incited him to his roughest behaviour, but she softened his anger to some extent, and what remained she endured discreetly, as a stern scolding delivered by her husband.'[41]

Fortunatus mentioned that Radegund used a hair shirt, which frequently appeared in his *Life of Radegund* (and in Baudonivia's work as well). A coarse and uncomfortable garment, the hair shirt was worn as an ascetic practice by those who embraced self-denial as a form of piety. Though mostly worn under other clothing, hair shirts had multiple uses. The letters of Jerome (d. 420) reveal that his supporter Paula had chosen to sleep between the folds of a hair shirt laid out on the floor, rather than under the warm covers of her bed.[42] Jerome's letters proved highly influential with the aspiring ascetics

[39] Fortunatus, *Life of Radegund*, 4.
[40] Fortunatus, *Life of Radegund*, 7.
[41] Fortunatus, *Life of Radegund*, 6.
[42] Jerome, *Letters*, 108.15.

of sixth-century Gaul. Fortunatus, in a poem written on Radegund's behalf, praised Paula for her self-denial, which suggests that Radegund was familiar with these letters (though at what point she became so remains unclear).[43] Radegund also used her hair shirt as a prayer mat, in addition to wearing it under her clothes.[44] According to Fortunatus, she had asked a woman named Pia, who lived under religious vows, to provide her with a hair shirt covered discreetly by linen, which she wore under her royal robes during Lent.[45] When Radegund became a nun, she continued to wear her hair shirt, and the object even survived her death to become a relic in Holy Cross, valued by her community for its miraculous power.[46] These references cannot all concern the very same hair shirt (Pia took her gift back after Lent, and Radegund sourced several hair shirts throughout her life), but, as a point of literary continuity at least, the hair shirt associated Radegund's asceticism, and her later life as a nun, with her earlier time as queen.[47] Fortunatus was thus able to assert that people openly said Chlothar had 'married himself to a nun rather than a queen', a defining remark in his *Life of Radegund*.

Radegund was not, however, the first queen to conceal a hair shirt under her regal attire. An inscription, now lost but once displayed in Lyon, praised Caretena (d. 506), the wife of the Burgundian king Gundobad, for wearing coarse vestments under her purple robes.[48] It also described how she assisted the poor, hid her fasting behind a radiant face, urged the king to release prisoners, and gave 'her royal limbs to a secret cross', which likely referenced private acts of asceticism and perhaps even self-mortification.[49] It further declared that Caretena had 'sought the wonderous work of Solomon', an implicit comparison to the biblical Queen of Sheba (who travelled to Jerusalem with her regal entourage to ask questions of the great king of Israel), and that she had built a 'temple', a statement that contained scriptural allusions but also referred specifically to her construction of the Church of St Michael at Lyons.[50] The language of the epitaph, though not entirely clear on this point, may even suggest that Caretena had taken religious vows after her reign as

---

[43] Fortunatus, *Poems*, 8.1, line 41.

[44] Kneepkens, 'Supra sanctae Radegundis cilicium', p. 173.

[45] Fortunatus, *Life of Radegund*, 6.

[46] Fortunatus, *Life of Radegund*, 22 and 34; Baudonivia, *Life of Radegund*, 15.

[47] Another example occurs in Baudonivia, *Life of Radegund*, 4.

[48] For Caretena as the wife of Gundobad, see Shanzer and Wood, *Avitus of Vienne*, p. 209, n. 2.

[49] *Epitaph of Caretena*, lines 6–10 and 21–22. The epitaph vanished in the wars of the seventeenth century. See Coville, *Recherches sur l'histoire de Lyon*, p. 209.

[50] Dolbeau, 'La Vie en prose de saint Marcel de Die'.

queen.[51] It states that she undertook her ascetic practices *post diadema* (literally, 'after the crown'), which might express the sense of 'after she ceased to be a queen', or alternatively 'after she became queen'. Either way, the epitaph contains remarkable parallels with Radegund (further illustrated in Chapter 6), though with one important exception: Caretena had children, including Sigismund, who became king after the death of his father in 516.

Radegund, of course, cannot have met Caretena, who died before she was born, and it is extremely unlikely that she had any direct knowledge of the inscription in distant Lyon. But she may have encountered a similar expression of royal piety in the person of Chlothild, her mother-in-law, who, like Caretena, belonged to the Burgundian royal house.[52] Although Chlothild's family tree is confused in the sources, it seems likely that her father was Chilperic of Lyon, who had himself married a woman of great piety and ascetic virtue.[53] Sidonius Apollinaris, an aristocrat from Lyon and eventual bishop of Clermont, noted that this unnamed woman admired the asceticism practised by Bishop Patiens of Lyon, and (in another intriguing parallel to Chlothar and Radegund) quipped that she preferred fasts while her husband preferred feasts.[54] Chlothild's sister, Chrona, took religious vows.[55] And Chlothild herself spent most of her long widowhood, from 511 to 545, in pious devotion in Tours, where she acquired a reputation for her good works.[56] She was later remembered as the founder of convents in Les Andelys and Chelles.[57] Her final years overlap with Radegund's marriage to Chlothar, which raises the possibility that she may have influenced her daughter-in-law.[58] Unfortunately, the sources record no meeting between the two: it is not known if Chlothild journeyed to Soissons for Radegund's wedding, if Radegund travelled to Tours thereafter, or if the two ever found themselves in Paris at the same time (a city that Chlothild is known to have visited). Yet it remains an intriguing possibility that Chlothild passed on to Radegund

---

[51]   Kampers, 'Caretena', p. 19.

[52]   Though married into the royal family, Caretena may not herself have been a Burgundian. See Wood, 'Assimilation von Romanen und Burgundern'.

[53]   Dailey, *Queens, Consorts, Concubines*, pp. 40–41. The reconstruction of the Burgundian royal family deployed here differs from that often found in scholarship, most recently Mathisen, 'Sidonius' People'.

[54]   Sidonius Apollinaris, *Letters*, 5.7.7 and 6.12.3.

[55]   Gregory of Tours, *Histories*, 2.28.

[56]   Gregory of Tours, *Histories*, 3.18.

[57]   *Life of Chlothild*, 11; *Life of Balthild*, 18. Papa, 'Radegonda e Batilde'.

[58]   A possibility discussed in Delaruelle, 'Sainte Radegonde'.

certain ideas about ascetic piety and queenly power, which she had acquired during her upbringing at the Burgundian royal court.

* * *

Radegund endured her marriage to Chlothar until a single tragic event compelled her to attempt, at considerable risk, to permanently separate from her husband: the murder of her brother. This crime clearly affected Radegund deeply, but any attempt to understand, let alone narrate, its occurrence is frustrated by the lack of detail in the surviving sources.[59] Neither Baudonivia nor Radegund herself, in her letter *Dominis sanctis*, mentioned the murder directly, even though they referenced what is essentially the same moment (i.e. when Radegund decided to live under religious vows) and identified the unseen hand of God at work in a counterintuitive, mysterious way. In his *Life of Radegund*, Fortunatus expressed a similar sentiment in direct reference to this incident: 'Her innocent brother was killed so that she might live with greater devotion.'[60] This rationalization may well have resulted from Radegund's own reflections on the experience in her later years, which filtered through to Fortunatus and the nuns of Holy Cross. In a single sentence in his *Histories*, Gregory of Tours identified Radegund's husband as the culprit: 'Chlothar caused her brother to be slain by evil men.'[61] But Gregory failed to explain the king's motive, or to provide any further details. Given the impossibility of coherently linking together a sequence of events that might explain the murder, an analysis of this incident must instead parse a few vague details provided by Fortunatus in his poem, *On the Destruction of Thuringia*, written in Radegund's voice and addressed to her cousin Amalfred.[62]

In a passage of about thirty lines, Fortunatus provided enigmatic details about the death of Radegund's brother that, although they fall short of a coherent explanation, nevertheless deserve more attention than they often receive. The very name of Radegund's brother, for example, has always been considered lost to history, yet it may well appear in this very passage. The possibility depends on the interpretation of the word *germanus*, which can mean 'brother', but which can also represent a personal name, as seen in the

---

[59] Kroll and Bachrach, *The Mystic Mind*, pp. 132–133, speculates about how the murder may have altered Radegund's psychological wellbeing.

[60] Fortunatus, *Life of Radegund*, 12.

[61] Gregory of Tours, *Histories*, 3.7.

[62] Fortunatus, *Poems*, appendix 1, lines 124–154.

earlier example of 'Germanus of Auxerre'. (Latin did not use capital letters to distinguish proper names from other words; the distinction must instead be discerned from context alone.) Fortunatus opened his passage on the murder by having Radegund rhetorically ask Amalfred why he had not made more of an effort to communicate with her *de nece germani*, which might be translated as 'about the murder of Germanus', or alternatively as 'about the murder of [my] brother'.[63] Four subsequent references to this sibling use another word, *frater*, which also meant 'brother', in a sequence interrupted by a second use of the word *germanus*, when Fortunatus had Radegund call out to her deceased brother (by name?) amid her regret that she had been prevented from attending his funeral:[64]

> Germanus, believe me. I stand before you, accused and accursed, as I bid you farewell. Of your death I alone had responsibility, yet I gave you no tomb.[65]

The word *germanus* appeared here in the vocative case, used to address or invoke a person, which may well suggest a personal name, even if the alternative meaning, 'Brother, believe me', cannot be excluded.

The passage indicated that Radegund blamed herself for her brother's death, or at least for her failure to oversee his funeral rites. This insight aligns with the other details Fortunatus provided to present a fuller, if ultimately incomplete, picture. Radegund's brother died as a result of violence, an 'unnatural killing'. He was 'innocent'. He faced an 'unjust plot'. And he was taken from the world through *fides opposita*, imprecise language that brings the question of his loyalty into the discussion, either because 'his loyalty stood in the way' (of escaping, perhaps), or because 'his loyalty had been put forward' (as matter of doubt).[66] Fortunatus added that Germanus—if he may be called that—died while he was still 'youthful', with his beard still 'delicate', like the 'down of plants'.[67] Although none of these details truly explain what happened, they do offer clues. The reference to Germanus's first beard, for

---

[63] Fortunatus, *Poems*, appendix 1, line 124.

[64] Fortunatus, *Poems*, appendix 1, lines 141 (*frater*), 143 (*frater*), 145 (*germanus*), 148 (*frater*), and 151 (*frater*).

[65] Fortunatus, *Poems*, appendix 1, lines 145–146.

[66] Fortunatus, *Poems*, appendix 1, lines 147–152. The translated words are *nex*, *insons*, and *insidiae iniquae*. On the potential meanings of *fides opposita*, see Roberts, *Venantius Fortunatus*, p. 890, note for line 126 (listed in the Bibliography under Fortunatus, *Poems*).

[67] Fortunatus, *Poems*, appendix 1, line 133: *iuvenis*, *tener*, and *lanugo*.

example, indicates that he had reached adulthood and, it might be assumed, become politically dangerous. This detail also provides evidence against the idea that Germanus's death was related to two uprisings in Thuringia in the mid-550s.[68] He could not have been an adolescent at this time, since he had been born more than two decades earlier, before the destruction of the Thuringian royal house in 531.

Although the vocabulary used by Fortunatus suggests a political context for the death of Radegund's brother, one in which the loyalties of a maturing prince held importance, any explanation must also consider why Chlothar had kept the boy alive for so many years. After all, he killed every other significant member of the Thuringian royal family upon whom he was able to lay his hands. None of the sources, it must be noted, actually provided a location for Radegund's brother, and it remains possible that he survived elsewhere (perhaps in Italy, where Amalaberga and Amalfred fled, as discussed in Chapter 1) until Chlothar eventually managed to arrange his murder. It seems more likely, however, especially in light of the details provided by Fortunatus, that he was kept as a hostage by Chlothar, perhaps at his court or in a royal villa, and that his fate was entwinned with that of his sister. If Radegund failed to prove her usefulness as a wife and queen, then Chlothar had one less reason to keep her brother alive. She may therefore have suffered another, more enduring form of captivity, in which the menace to her brother's life limited her options and controlled her behaviour. This hypothesis suggests a further reason Chlothar decided to kill her brother: he had lost interest in his childless marriage. Because he no longer valued Radegund as a wife, he had less cause to keep her brother alive. But once her brother had died, tragic though this may have been, Radegund had an opportunity, one in which, with the benefit of hindsight, it was possible to discern the hand of God at work: an opportunity to leave her husband and risk the consequences, in the knowledge that now she gambled with her life alone.

---

[68] Fredegar, *Chronicles*, 3.50–51 and 4.15; Gregory of Tours, *Histories*, 4.10; Marius of Avenches, *Chronicle*, anno 556. Another reference to a campaign against the Thuringians appears in Fortunatus, *Poems*, 6.1a, in which a young Sigibert participated before he became king. For an attempt to link the revolts to the murder, see Pietri, *La Ville de Tours*, p. 229.

3

What Can Man Do unto Me?

Radegund left Chlothar and came directly to Médard, the bishop of Noyon. She intended to 'exchange her clothes', to discard the resplendent robes she wore in the royal palace for the simple attire of a pious ascetic. She asked the bishop to 'consecrate her to the Lord', thereby confirming her new status as a woman under religious vows.[1] But Médard hesitated, unprepared to provide what was, essentially, his ecclesiastical sanction for the separation of the queen from her husband. 'He forestalled the queen', wrote Venantius Fortunatus, 'to avoid clothing her in the garb of a nun.' Baudonivia confirmed that Radegund's monastic vows required her to 'separate from her earthly king', though she provided no additional details to Fortunatus's account.[2] Radegund's request was certainly unusual. Although it was possible for marriages to be dissolved in Merovingian Gaul, there was no straightforward means by which a woman might unilaterally initiate or achieve a divorce, least of all if she were married to a king.[3] A woman might *ask* her royal husband to allow her to return to her family, perhaps offering to leave her wealth behind, but examples are rare.[4] She was more likely to simply hope that her husband might increasingly ignore her. Instead, a queen usually wished for her rivals to suffer such a repudiation, which was a fate that more often befell concubines than wives. But Radegund initiated the separation herself. The sources are remarkably consistent on this point: Fortunatus, Gregory of Tours, and Baudonivia all described Radegund as the active party.[5] In her letter *Dominis sanctis*, Radegund herself, after crediting divine providence for her withdrawal from the secular life, added: 'I willingly turned to the mandate of religion and the command of Christ.' The exchange of a marital life for a monastic one was not something done to Radegund; it

---

[1] Fortunatus, *Life of Radegund*, 12.

[2] Baudonivia, *Life of Radegund*, 3.

[3] Wemple, *Women in Frankish Society*, pp. 42–43.

[4] Galswinth at least thought this might be a possibility, though she was mistaken, according to Gregory of Tours, *Histories*, 4.28.

[5] Gregory of Tours, *Histories*, 3.7; Baudonivia, *Life of Radegund*, 3. Radegund was also described as the active party in the late seventh-century *Life of Bathild*, 18.

Radegund. E. T. Dailey, Oxford University Press. © Oxford University Press 2023.
DOI: 10.1093/oso/9780197656105.003.0004

was something she achieved. Perhaps for the first time, she pursued a goal that was all her own, despite considerable risk.

Médard certainly feared the consequences of sanctioning her choice. Although bishops enjoyed both power and prestige within the Merovingian kingdoms, they did not live beyond the wrath of the king.[6] Removal, exile, and even murder happened to a surprising number of bishops during this era, for varying degrees of political insubordination.[7] Not unreasonably, Médard momentarily withheld his episcopal approval. Radegund had apparently not chosen Médard for his courage. Indeed, she may have approached him merely because of his proximity. Noyon lay between Athies and Soissons; Athies had no bishop to offer, and Soissons's episcopal throne was inconveniently empty at the time (if a story in the twelfth-century *Life of Bandaridus* has any truth to it, at least).[8] Not that Médard was unknown to Radegund. Indeed, she had very likely met him at Chlothar's royal court. Or possibly earlier, perhaps even during her captivity in Athies. Médard hailed from Vermand, a mere 13 km east of Athies, where he first served as bishop during the early 530s, before moving his episcopal seat to Noyon. It is not difficult to imagine Médard attending the royal villa in Athies, in the fulfilment of his clerical duties, while the young Radegund lived there in captivity. Perhaps he even provided her with some basic instruction in the Christian faith. If so, Radegund might have found his hesitancy to consecrate her particularly disappointing.

Médard's relationship with Chlothar is even more difficult to determine, but he seems to have been loyal by instinct. The king inspired fear in most bishops, and made an example out of those who failed to show him obeisance. According to Gregory of Tours, Chlothar exiled Nicetius, bishop of Trier, who had bravely, and 'frequently', excommunicated the king for his 'unjust deeds'.[9] The other bishops, presumably Médard included, supported the banishment because they were all 'sycophants toward the king', in Gregory's words. Nicetius returned from exile only after the king's death.[10] In another example, when Germanus of Paris went to visit Chlothar unannounced, the king left him waiting outside the palace until he eventually gave up and returned home.[11] Fortunatus had no desire to tarnish Médard's legacy, and

---

[6] Halfond, *Bishops and the Politics of Patronage*, pp. 29–40.

[7] Fouracre, 'Why Were So Many Bishops Killed'.

[8] *Life of Bandaridus*, 5.

[9] Gregory of Tours, *Life of the Fathers*, 17.2–3.

[10] *Life of Goar*, 7–11.

[11] Fortunatus, *Life of Germanus of Paris*, 23. Fortunatus claimed that Chlothar fell ill as a result, only to receive a cure from Germanus when he licked the saint's cloak in repentance.

he even wrote a poem dedicated to the bishop, in which he presented the site of his burial as a place of miracles.[12] His rather unflattering depiction of Médard in the Life of Radegund, therefore, probably portrayed the bishop's response to Radegund authentically. A Life of Medard, probably also written by Fortunatus, included a story of doubtful historicity in which Médard demanded that Chlothar surrender the plunder he had taken on a campaign around the Oise and Somme.[13] This passage, which appeared in what is essentially a list of Médard's miracles, more or less admitted that opposing Chlothar required supernatural strength.

When Fortunatus tried to explain why Médard hesitated to fulfil Radegund's request, he cited a scriptural passage in justification: Art thou bound unto a wife? Seek not to be loosed (I Corinthians 7:27).[14] The argument is not entirely apt, since this passage refers to a separation initiated by the husband.[15] But more importantly, Médard's own concerns were clearly less about this biblical injunction, and more about the fact that Radegund was bound unto a king. Médard came under intense pressure to refuse her request. According to Fortunatus, armed men confronted him in his church and demanded that he respect Radegund's marital status:

> The noblemen harassed the blessed man. They forcefully carried him from the altar and through the basilica, so that he might not veil the wife of the king—so that a bishop might not be seen to even dare to take away a king's wife, who was a public figure, not some public woman.

As discussed in Chapter 1, Radegund had secured a marriage to Chlothar in his royal centre of Soissons, which conferred public recognition upon her as a queen, and which distinguished her from the king's concubines (alluded to in this passage by the derogatory term publicana, 'public woman', i.e. a prostitute). If Médard consecrated Radegund, and thereby separated her from her husband, he risked placing his own authority above that of the king.

---

[12] Fortunatus, Poems, 2.16.

[13] Fortunatus, Life of Médard, 7. On the question of authorship, see Heinzelmann, 'L'hagiographie mérovingienne', pp. 62–63.

[14] Fortunatus, Life of Radegund, 12.

[15] See the discussion in Smit, 'Man or Human?'. I Corinthians 7:27, in fact, refers specifically to whether or not a man should pursue a marriage in the first place, in view of the impending Eschaton. Verses 10–11, in contrast, refer to marital separation, but not in a manner that is entirely favourable to Radegund's own behaviour.

Médard had very little principle to stand on. Married women were not permitted to take religious vows, especially without their husband's consent. Not in theory, at least; enough examples exist to demonstrate that, in practice, it did happen on occasion, though these anecdotes do not concern the wives of kings. When Gunthedrud received a cure of her blindness at St Martin's shrine in Tours, for example, she decided not to return to her married life in Vermandois. 'Quickly forgetting her husband and children, she changed her clothing and, by the inspiration of the Lord, passed into the Church's religious life', wrote Gregory of Tours.[16] When Monegund, a wealthy woman from Chartres, experienced the tragic death of her children, she entered a hermitage on her estates and 'had nothing more to do with her husband'.[17] Whether or not her husband initially agreed to the separation (Gregory is unclear about this point), he later refused to accept the arrangement. Once Monegund had become a nun in Tours, he decided to forcibly retrieve her, in circumstances discussed below. Although Gregory recorded these pious stories with approval, he seems to have behaved differently when he found himself confronted by a woman who wished to abandon her husband for a convent in Tours. Gregory opposed her actions and told her to return to her husband's side, lest she suffer eternal damnation.[18] Whatever stories might have circulated about women abandoning their marriages to answer God's call to the religious life, the clerical establishment was unlikely to support such a choice in the face of opposition from a powerful husband.

Radegund forced Médard's hesitant hand. No longer content to wait, she changed into 'monastic attire', in Fortunatus's description, and proceeded to the altar herself.

> She said to the blessed Médard: 'If you hold back from consecrating me, fearing man more than God, then from your hand, O shepherd, he will demand the soul of his sheep.' Shaken by the impact of her argument, he laid his hands upon her and consecrated her as a deaconess.[19]

Radegund appealed to Médard's sense of honour as a bishop, alluding to two important biblical themes: the injunction to fear the power of Almighty God, and the metaphor of God's people as a sheepfold. *You are my Lord; I will*

---

[16] Gregory of Tours, *The Virtues of St Martin*, 2.9.
[17] Gregory of Tours, *Life of the Fathers*, 19.1.
[18] Gregory of Tours, *Histories*, 9.33.
[19] Fortunatus, *Life of Radegund*, 12.

not fear what man does to me (Psalm 117:6). *For He is our God and we are the people of his pasture, and the flock of his hand* (Psalm 94:7). Radegund succeeded because she presented her request, not merely as her own desire, but as the will of God. That she might do so plausibly indicates just how much prestige she had acquired, especially among the clergy. Her enemies might disagree, of course, but they still needed to reckon with the passionate support she received from those who accepted her as their holy queen. Radegund had invested tremendous resources in achieving this reputation; now she received the dividends. Her proximity to divine power served as her defining characteristic for the rest of her life, determining both the influence she enjoyed and its limits. Médard ultimately decided not to defy her wishes, because he feared that he might jeopardize his own standing in the eyes of God, and thereby in the eyes of his congregation and his clergy. *Am I seeking to satisfy mortal men or God? Am I seeking to please mere mortals? If I were thus to please men, I would not be a servant of Christ* (Galatians 1:10).

Fortunatus's use of the word 'deaconess' (*diacona*) in this passage has proved difficult to interpret. There is no reason to accept, however, the theory that Médard actually rejected Radegund's request to be consecrated as a nun and made her a deaconess *instead*, as a compromise based on a custom of the early Church that allowed a woman to become a deaconess while still remaining married.[20] In fact this ancient practice focused on male agency, permitting a married man to be consecrated as a deacon, together with his wife, as long as she agreed to practice sexual abstinence. There is, of course, no basis to imagine that Chlothar had entered the diaconate to facilitate Radegund's plans. Neither can Fortunatus be thought to have used the term *diacona* in a manner that undermined the very story he wished to tell, in which Médard's consecration represented an unequivocal victory for Radegund, after which she exchanged her regal clothing and lifestyle for that of a nun (*monacha*), a 'slave of the Lord' (*ancilla Domini*).[21] 'From this time onward', he wrote, 'she was veiled, having been consecrated by the blessed Médard.'[22] For Fortunatus, the term *diacona* likely functioned, not as a mutually exclusive alternative to 'nun', but as an overlapping, complementary title.[23] Merovingian church councils had formally rejected the ancient 'order of deaconesses', which as a result unmoored *diacona* from its technical

---

[20] As suggested by Rouche, 'Le Célibat consacré de sainte Radegonde'.
[21] Fortunatus, *Life of Radegund*, 13–14.
[22] Fortunatus, *Life of Radegund*, 15.
[23] See Aigrain, *Sainte Radegonde*, pp. 60–61.

meaning, unintentionally releasing it to function as an undefined honor-
ific title for pious women in common parlance.[24] Fortunatus may even have
thought the term particularly appropriate for Radegund, as she was an atypical sort of nun, neither an unmarried virgin nor a rededicated widow.

The word 'nun' translates *monacha*, *monialis*, and *nonna*, Latin terms that
must be understood according to a broader meaning, in the context of sixth-
century Gaul, than the more precise meaning particular to later periods.[25]
Radegund lived during an early era of female asceticism, distinguished
by its diversity and creativity.[26] The appearance of convents with enclosed
grounds, headed by an abbess, and regulated by codified strictures had only
just begun, and the paucity of such institutions left many women to fulfil
their religious vows on their own estates.[27] Consecrated to God, pledged
in perpetual virginity, and attired in simple yet distinctive garb, these nuns
followed a more ancient, less formal approach to asceticism.[28] Both Gregory
of Tours and Fortunatus mentioned examples of this practice.[29] In the fifth
century, Bassula had chosen to live with her son-in-law, Sulpicius Severus,
and his close friends in his villa of Primuliacum as a community under religious vows.[30] Farther afield, Macrina had lived as an avowed virgin within
her family home in the Black Sea region of Asia Minor, and when her
brother tragically died in 357, she convinced her mother to convert her entire household to the monastic life.[31] Radegund may be best remembered
for founding the convent of Holy Cross, a formal religious house for women
that represented an important contribution to the professionalization of female ascetic practice in central and northern Gaul, but when she first left
Chlothar's side, she fulfilled her religious vows for several years in a much
less formal setting.[32] In the villa of Saix, in the region of Vienne (10 km south
of the eponymous river's confluence with the Loire), Radegund lived as a

---

[24] The Second Council of Orléans (533), canon 17; and the Third Council of Orléans (538), canon 27(24). Binder, 'The Evolution of the Female Diaconate'.
[25] Helvétius, 'L'Organisation des monastères féminins'.
[26] See Dey, 'Bringing Chaos out of Order'.
[27] See Diem, 'Merovingian Monasticism'.
[28] See Elm, *Virgins of God*, pp. 84–89; and Cooper, *The Virgin and the Bride*, pp. 68–91.
[29] Fortunatus, *Poems*, 6.4, lines 8–9, 13–14, and 17–18 (Berchild); Gregory of Tours, *Glory of the Confessors*, 33 (Georgia); and Gregory of Tours, *Life of the Fathers*, 19 (Monegund).
[30] Percival, 'Villas and Monasteries in Late Roman Gaul'; Alciati, 'And the Villa Became a Monastery'. A parallel example in Radegund's time is found with Pelagia and her son Aredius; see Gregory of Tours, *Glory of the Confessors*, 102; and Gregory of Tours, *Histories*, 10.29.
[31] Rousseau, 'The Pious Household and the Virgin Chorus'.
[32] Bailey, *The Religious Worlds of the Laity*, pp. 36–37.

woman avowed to God and committed to pious service and personal devotion, yet also as a royal woman in retreat on a country estate.[33]

In Saix, Radegund had female 'attendants' and 'loyal followers'.[34] She dispatched a priest named Magnus to obtain the relics of saints, and in particular those of St Andrew, which she placed on an altar in the villa.[35] She hosted bishops and sent them away laden with gifts.[36] She distributed bread to the needy, made out of flour that she ground herself.[37] She washed the poor with her own hands (the whole bodies of women, but only the heads of men), and applied oil to their sores.[38] Women who arrived in dirty rags departed in new clothes. The poor came hungry and left fed. Radegund served them herself. She cleaned their hands and mouths, and cut their bread and meat; the blind she fed with a spoon. Radegund also acquired a reputation for wonderworking within the local population.[39] The infirm brought her leaves to bless, which they used to cure their illnesses, while others were healed after they sent candles to be burned in her presence throughout the night.[40] When a group of lepers arrived and announced their condition, as a warning to anyone who might approach them in ignorance, Radegund rushed to greet them and arranged a feast.[41] She wrapped her arms around leprous women and kissed their faces, to the great alarm of one of her attendants, who asked: 'Most holy lady, who will kiss you, now that you have embraced these lepers?' Radegund replied: 'Truly, if you will not kiss me, it is no concern of mine.'

* * *

By arranging the murder of Radegund's brother, Chlothar revealed that he no longer valued his marriage. Radegund may even have feared that her life had become equally expendable. Chlothar surely expected her to react, though he may well have been surprised by her boldness in straightaway pursuing ecclesiastical support for her decision to take religious vows. If he no longer had much regard for his marriage (as discussed in Chapter 2), however, then the question of his honour was another matter entirely. In quickly securing

[33] Baudonivia, *Life of Radegund*, 3.
[34] Baudonivia, *Life of Radegund*, 3 (*fideles*). Fortunatus, *Life of Radegund*, 19 (*ministrae*).
[35] Baudonivia, *Life of Radegund*, 13.
[36] Fortunatus, *Life of Radegund*, 18.
[37] Fortunatus, *Life of Radegund*, 16.
[38] Fortunatus, *Life of Radegund*, 17.
[39] Fortunatus, *Life of Radegund*, 28.
[40] Fortunatus, *Life of Radegund*, 20.
[41] Fortunatus, *Life of Radegund*, 19. See Peyroux, 'The Leper's Kiss'.

consecration at Médard's hands, Radegund presented Chlothar with a fait accompli; to oppose the separation now represented a show of weakness, an acknowledgement that he had been outmanoeuvred by his wife. Chlothar may have found it easier to accept these new arrangements than to admit he had not intended them. It is noteworthy, therefore, that Fortunatus presented Chlothar's noblemen, rather than the king himself, as the principal opponents of Radegund's consecration. Chlothar's reluctance to oppose the separation, at least initially, finds a parallel in a story that Gregory of Tours related about the husband of Monegund.[42] The unnamed man offered no apparent resistance when Monegund left to become a hermit on their estates, and then to become a nun in Tours, even though he later changed his mind, gathered a band of men, and forcibly returned Monegund to his estates.[43] His motivation, at least according to Gregory, was not principally romantic: he decided to act only after Monegund gained wide recognition as a holy woman, ashamed that she had grown in stature independent of him.

Chlothar apparently experienced a similar change of heart. Baudonivia recorded two distinct attempts by the king to restore Radegund to his side, with the first set during her time in Saix.[44] Of the two, the second attempt, set in Poitiers (and discussed below), is the more believable, but the first attempt deserves consideration too, at least as a representation of the fear that Radegund likely felt, if not as a genuine account of the king's intentions. Baudonivia presented Radegund as perpetually menaced by the thought that Chlothar might return her to her married life. She wrote that, while living in Saix, Radegund heard a rumour that Chlothar regretted allowing 'such a great and distinguished queen to depart from his side'.

When she heard this, the most blessed woman became panicked with extreme terror, and gave herself over to the abundant tortures of her roughest hair shirt, affixed upon her soft flesh. To this she added the weight of tortuous fasts and nightlong vigils, pouring herself out in prayer.

Radegund asked a hermit named John, who lived in a cell attached to a church in Chinon (about 20 km east of Saix), if he might gain an insight into the truth of the rumour from the Holy Spirit.[45] She presented John with a

[42] Jones, *Social Mobility in Late Antique Gaul*, p. 151.
[43] Gregory of Tours, *Life of the Fathers*, 19.1–2.
[44] Baudonivia, *Life of Radegund*, 4.
[45] Gregory of Tours, *Glory of the Confessors*, 23.

generous gift, an immensely valuable ornament cast in gold and set with gems and pearls. After accepting the donation, John felt a divine message come to him: 'Although this is indeed the king's wish, God will not permit its fulfilment; the king will be punished by the judgement of God before he takes her back as his wife.'[46] Relieved, Radegund began to plan the foundation of a convent in Poitiers.

Baudonivia certainly indulged in melodramatic excess, especially when she claimed that Chlothar felt 'no deep desire to carry on living unless he retrieved Radegund'. Her account gave rise to a later medieval legend, the 'Miracle of the Oats', in which Radegund learned of Chlothar's approach and immediately fled into a field of oats. Recognizing the vulnerability of the saint, the oats quickly grew so high that Radegund was concealed from view. Chlothar arrived and questioned the local ploughman, who said that no one had ventured into the field since it had been sown. The king realized that he had no hope of finding his former wife and abandoned his pursuit.[47] This story is, of course, without any factual basis, and there is also little reason to believe Baudonivia's original claim that Chlothar intended to retrieve Radegund at this time. Yet the idea that such a rumour might circulate, independent of Chlothar's actual intentions, seems plausible, as does the possibility that an anxious Radegund sought solace from a holy man. Even more interesting is Baudonivia's claim that Radegund wore a hair shirt and engaged in severe fasting in order to offer spiritual resistance to the king's purported efforts. Baudonivia wrote in full knowledge of the memories preserved in Holy Cross, and her revelation about the link between Radegund's deep fears and her extreme asceticism is not only believable, but also insightful.

Equally intriguing is Baudonivia's statement that Radegund felt unflinching determination to defy any attempt by Chlothar to retrieve her:

> If the king sought her return, then she wished to end her own life first, rather than to be united a second time to her earthly king, because she was already bound and joined to her heavenly king.

Radegund's threat to kill herself is truly remarkable, especially in light of the stigma associated with suicide, and in particular the view, expressed within

---

[46] Baudonivia, *Life of Radegund*, 4.
[47] The legend had taken shape at least by the thirteenth century, when it was depicted on stained glass within the Church of St Radegund in Poitiers. See Edwards, *Superior Women*, p. 193.

the Patristic tradition, that to kill oneself represented an affront to God.[48] Indeed, the passage is without precedent in the hagiographic genre.[49] The letters of Jerome, however, mentioned a circumstance in which it might be acceptable to take one's own life: when a woman chose to die rather than see her chastity violated.[50] Ambrose of Milan provided a detailed justification of such righteous suicide in a work addressed to his sister, Marcellina.[51] Heroic examples of like-minded women, portrayed as martyrs, were provided by Eusebius of Caesaria in his *Ecclesiastical History*.[52] As discussed in Chapter 5, the letters of Jerome and Rufinus of Aquileia's Latin rendition of the *Ecclesiastical History* were likely available to Radegund in Holy Cross. She may therefore have seen herself in a similar position to the noble matrons and devout virgins who had chosen death over dishonour at the hands of the villain of Eusebius's account, the great persecutor of Christians, Maximinus Daza. Indeed, her embrace of extreme ascetic practices might even represent an attempt to reproduce the sort of tortures that these holy martyrs suffered at the hands of Maximinus's agents. Radegund had no choice but to undergo such torments. In her mind, she could never accept a return to Chlothar's side because, through her religious vows, she had instead become a bride of Christ.

* * *

After several years in Saix, Radegund founded a convent in Poitiers, where she spent the remaining three decades of her life. Perhaps surprisingly, Chlothar approved the project and financed its construction.[53] Radegund herself confirmed that she had received Chlothar's support, as well as the support of his sons once they had become kings, in her letter *Dominis sanctis*:

> A monastery for girls was constituted and established in the city of Poitiers at the order and expense of the most excellent lord, King Chlothar. After its foundation, I endowed the monastery with however much wealth I had received from the generosity of the king.

---

[48] Murray, *Suicide in the Middle Ages*, vol. 2, pp. 98–121.

[49] Kroll and Bachrach, *The Mystic Mind*, p. 132.

[50] Jerome, *Letters*, 22 (to Eustochius).

[51] Ambrose, *Concerning Virgins*, 3.7. This view was not without its dissenters, most notably Augustine, *The City of God*, 1.17.

[52] Eusebius, *Ecclesiastical History*, 8.12 and 8.14.

[53] The document that purports to be the foundational charter of Holy Cross is in fact a forgery. Poitiers, Médiathèque François-Mitterrand (bibliothèque municipale), MS 130, 75^r–76^v.

In her *Life of Radegund*, Baudonivia concurred:

> Inspired and assisted by God, and through the arrangement of the excellent
> king, Chlothar, Radegund constructed for herself a monastery in Poitiers.[54]

She added that construction finished 'swiftly', which suggests that Radegund benefited from the sort of continuous flow of funds that was possible only through the support of the king.[55]

Chlothar's motivations can only be guessed, but several possibilities merit consideration. If he worried about how his separation from Radegund might have been regarded within the elite circles of his kingdom, then supporting her foundation of Holy Cross certainly gave the impression that he had always agreed with her departure. The convent represented an official version of the story, one written in stone, in which its foundation was as much his idea as it was hers. The convent also offered Chlothar an opportunity to atone, in a publicly recognized way, for his many misdeeds. For each buttress that he financed, he reinforced not only her convent but also his reputation. The closest parallel is perhaps to be found in seventh-century Britain. The Northumbrian ruler Oswiu murdered his cousin and fellow king, Oswine, in a crime that met with 'universal disgust', according to Bede, the monk and scholar who produced an account of the incident in his *Ecclesiastical History of the English People*.[56] Oswiu then built a monastery over the site of the murder, where, in a show of repentance, prayers were offered for him and his victim alike.

Chlothar had used conspicuous acts of generosity to restore confidence in his rule before. When he met with unexpected resistance to his efforts to claim a third of the ecclesiastical revenues of Tours, for example, he publicly recompensed the people of the city with a tax exemption.[57] Chlothar also offered gifts to the local bishop, Injuriosus, in the expectation that the bishop would invoke the power of St Martin on his behalf in return. When the Basilica of St Martin in Tours burned down several years later, in the aftermath of his war with his rebellious son Chramn, Chlothar ordered the building restored to its prior splendour.[58] None of these grand gestures,

---

[54] Baudonivia, *Life of Radegund*, 5.
[55] Labande-Mailfert, 'Les Debuts de Sainte-Croix', p. 35, estimates that construction began in 552 and finished by 557.
[56] Bede, *Ecclesiastical History*, 3.14.
[57] Gregory of Tours, *Histories*, 4.2.
[58] Gregory of Tours, *Histories*, 4.20.

however, compared to the display of penitent benefaction that Chlothar performed on a pilgrimage to Tours in the final year of his life (as detailed below). These deeds are known because, as the bishop of Tours, Gregory took particular interest in them. The king likely performed similar acts elsewhere in his kingdom that escaped mention within the historical record. The financing of Holy Cross falls within this pattern of using royal benefaction as a means to influence public perception and to secure support from the clergy and the wider population. Chlothar may not have been a man of moral rectitude, but he understood the value of associating himself with centres of spiritual power. By supporting the construction of Holy Cross, Chlothar became a partaker in Radegund's reputation for sanctity. He repaired his own image without needing to offer a single prayer himself.

By providing funding for Holy Cross, Chlothar also strengthened his authority in Poitiers itself, a city that had long held strategic significance for the Franks. His father, Clovis, had acquired Poitiers when he defeated the Visigoths at the Battle of Vouillé in 507.[59] Situated on a plateau above the Clain and Boivre rivers, the early medieval city emerged from the ancient Roman settlement of *Pictavium*, which had featured a typical grid layout, the east-west *decumanus* intersecting the north-south *cardo*, and a centrally located forum.[60] From the late third century, thick walls enclosed Poitiers and reached up to ten metres in height.[61] Radegund built her convent within these walls, in the old Roman districts of the city, near the cathedral and the baptistry of St John. Limited archaeological excavations in 2005 indicated that this location, though once a thriving neighbourhood, had been largely abandoned by the end of the fifth century and replaced with a necropolis. The rows of tombs contained burial assemblages characteristic of the period, including fragments of weapons and a belt buckle.[62] Because burials within an urban district were still unusual for the time (due to an ancient Roman custom that opposed the practice), this necropolis might be thought to include Frankish warriors, newcomers established in this quarter of Poitiers perhaps in the aftermath of Clovis's victory. Four decades later, this intramural district may still have been at the disposal of the king, now Chlothar

[59] Mathisen, 'Vouillé, Voulon, and the Location of the Campus Vogladensis'.
[60] Maurin, *Topographie chrétienne des cités de la Gaule*, vol. 10, pp. 73–76.
[61] Hiernard, 'La Topographie historique de Poitiers'.
[62] The rescue archaeology was conducted by the Institut national de recherches archéologiques préventives (INRAP) during the construction of a residential building in 2005. The excavations were restricted to the ancillary parts of the monastic complex.

rather than Clovis, when it served as the basis for Radegund's monastic complex.

When planning her monastic foundation, Radegund took inspiration from the Convent of St John in Arles, established by Caesaria the Elder.[63] This religious house had also been constructed within the city's walls, even though this arrangement had not been Caesaria's original plan. Monasticism represented an attempt to escape from the world and its temptations, and to live in holy seclusion in the wilderness, an ambition that poorly fit an urban setting.[64] Instead, Caesaria had initially intended to construct her convent in the ancient Alyscamps, a large Roman necropolis that spanned both sides of the road leading to Marseilles, which housed several impressive mausolea and sarcophagi, including the tomb of St Genesius. But during the winter of 507, the same army that won Poitiers for Clovis also besieged Arles, dismantling the monastery, which was still under construction, and reusing the beams (probably for siegeworks). After this setback, Caesaria decided to build her convent within the city walls. She found another way to separate her nuns from the world: an uncompromising form of enclosure that restricted access to the institution and prevented the nuns from leaving, except under limited circumstances. When Radegund established her convent in Poitiers, she imitated Caesaria's plan B, both the intramural location and the uncompromising rule (as discussed further in Chapter 5).[65]

Aside from the Convent of St John in Arles, Radegund had relatively few established female religious houses to draw upon as precedent, especially of a size suitable to serve as a model for her own ambitious plans in Poitiers.[66] Holy Cross eventually housed two hundred nuns, the same number as St John's and considerably more than any other such institution of which she might have known.[67] Precisely how many female religious houses existed in Gaul at this time is difficult to determine, but only a few appear in the sources, usually in oblique references. It is clear, however, that southern Gaul featured more female religious houses, and that they were often closely associated

---

[63] Rudge, 'Dedicated Women and Dedicated Spaces'.

[64] See Dailey, 'Introducing Monastic Space'.

[65] Compare the layout in Arles and Poitiers presented in Vieillard-Troiekouroff, *Les Monuments religieux de la Gaule*. The excavations in Poitiers, discussed in Eygun, 'Circonscription de Poitiers', and Labande-Mailfert, 'Poitiers: Abbaye Sainte-Croix', can be compared to those in Arles reported in Heijmans, *L'Enclos Saint-Césaire à Arles*.

[66] Weidemann, 'Urkunde und Vita der hl. Bilhildis', pp. 77–83 (*Anhang*).

[67] On the number of nuns in Holy Cross, see Gregory of Tours, *Histories*, 9.39, and Fortunatus, *Poems*, 8.4. For Arles, see Messianus and Stephanus, *Life of Caesarius*, 47.

with major monasteries for men.[68] Caesaria herself had received her early monastic training in St Saviour's convent in Marseilles, which was affiliated to the male religious house founded by John Cassian.[69] Caesaria had also established her convent in Arles with the assistance of her brother, Caesarius, who served as the bishop of the city, and who authored her convent's rule. In another example, the Convent of La Balme in the Jura had been founded by the sister of Romanus and Lupicinus, two influential figures who established several male religious houses in the region.[70] La Balme had adopted a strict approach to enclosure and seclusion, probably even before St John's convent, under the inspiration of religious literature that featured the pioneering ascetics of late Roman Egypt, the Desert Fathers, and in particular Pachomius and his monastery in Tabenna (in the Thebaid of Upper Egypt).[71] Jerome had translated the *Praecepta* of Pachomius into Latin in 404.[72] Since Radegund apparently had access to other works of Jerome, she may have read the *Praecepta* as well, and drawn upon the same source that had guided practices in La Balme, an additional and easily overlooked source of inspiration for Radegund, alongside the example of St John's in Arles.

The quotidian responsibilities of managing Holy Cross and its two hundred nuns, who were of high status and of varying ages (but often young), must have been extensive.[73] Radegund assigned these duties to a close confidante, Agnes, whom she appointed as abbess. According to Baudonivia,

> Radegund submitted herself to the abbess, chosen and confirmed, and handed over all her power, keeping none of the rights particular to her station, so that she might hasten, unencumbered, after the footsteps of Christ, and amass for herself as much in heaven as she alienated in this world.[74]

Baudonivia may have characterized Radegund's decision to invest Agnes with the authority to govern Holy Cross as an act of profound humility, but

---

[68] Hartmann, '*Reginae sumus*: Merowingische Königstöchter', p. 9.

[69] Dailey, 'Confinement and Exclusion', pp. 305–310.

[70] As detailed in the *Life of the Jura Fathers*.

[71] For a consideration of Pachomius that also looks forward to Radegund, see Cooper, 'The Household and the Desert'.

[72] Rousseau, *Pachomius*, pp. 48–53. The *Praecepta* reflect a broader Pachomian tradition rather than the sole work of Pachomius himself.

[73] The diverse ages of the nuns in Holy Cross can be inferred from the various stories offered by Fortunatus, Baudonivia, and Gregory of Tours. Most of the nuns who appear on a list of people who died in Faremoutiers, within two decades of the monastery's foundation by Burgundofara in 620, were young. Jonas, *Life of Columbanus*, 2.11–22.

[74] Baudonivia, *Life of Radegund*, 5.

it also seems to have been entirely in keeping with her regal demeanour. The ardours of daily administration neither merited the attention nor befit the grandeur of a queen. It must be assumed, after all, that Radegund had not burdened herself with the quotidian operations of the royal palace, either, when she had been married to Chlothar. Radegund knew that Agnes, her close personal confidante, was not inclined to act in a manner out of step with her own wishes, even when their relationship experienced moments of tension that inevitably occur between two people working closely together for so many years.[75] In her letter to the bishops, *Dominis sanctis*, Radegund indicated that Agnes was younger than she and had spent considerable time under her care and patronage:

> I appointed as abbess my sister and *domina*, Agnes, whom I had loved and raised from a young age in the place of a daughter. I submitted myself in regular obedience to her authority, next to that of God.

Although the language Radegund used spoke of her humble submission to Agnes, characterized as a transfer of authority, the nature of their relationship suggested only a transfer of responsibility. There is certainly no reason to accept the suggestion that Radegund honoured Agnes as her abbess out of 'recognition of the superiority of her virgin state.'[76] Radegund appointed Agnes precisely because the honour belonged to her, as a holy queen, to pursue her spiritual goals unencumbered.

* * *

When an aging Chlothar entered the fiftieth year of his reign, he journeyed to the Basilica of St Martin in Tours and offered himself as a penitent before the saint's relics:

> When he came to Tours, Chlothar went to the tomb of Bishop Martin and reflected upon all of the deeds that he might have thoughtlessly committed. He prayed, in great lament, that the blessed confessor request the mercy of the Lord for his mistakes, and by his intercession wash away those deeds which he had foolishly committed.[77]

---

[75] Roberts, *The Humblest Sparrow*, pp. 303–305, detected evidence of occasional tension between Radegund and Agnes in Fortunatus, *Poems*, appendix 13, lines 9–14.

[76] The suggestion appears in McNamara and Halborg, *Sainted Women of the Dark Ages*, p. 89, n. 89.

[77] Gregory of Tours, *Histories*, 4.21.

Gregory of Tours presented this journey as a pilgrimage, conducted by the king in the aftermath of perhaps the most sorrowful episode of his reign: the failed rebellion of his eldest son, Chramn. Tours may have seemed a fitting destination, since the Basilica of St Martin had been badly damaged in a fire set by one of Chramn's supporters.[78] The revolt itself, however, had started in Poitiers, around the middle of the 550s, where the rebellious prince established his own royal court, in defiance of his father's rule.[79] Although Chramn's behaviour in Poitiers received little attention in this source, his presence cannot have been pleasant for Radegund and her nuns. While in Clermont, Chramn had abducted young women from prominent local families and given them over to his own supporters (merely one of his many misdeeds).[80] Radegund and her newly founded convent, perhaps still partially under construction, cannot have escaped these events unscathed, even though the details went unrecorded.[81]

Chlothar's regret, however, had little to do with any trouble that Chramn's rebellion might have caused Radegund. Instead, the king sought to atone for his decision to execute his son—or, at least, this is the impression given by Gregory of Tours. The king had ordered Chramn, together with his wife and their daughters, to be shut within the humble cottage of an impoverished family.[82] Once the prince had been strangled and tied to a bed, Chlothar set fire to the hovel, so that the body of his eldest son was consumed by the blaze, while his daughter-in-law and granddaughters burned alive.[83] Gregory found intrafamilial conflict particularly distasteful, especially when it led to civil war, and he infused his account with a deep sense of gravitas. The downfall of Chramn recalled the death of the Roman emperor Flavius Valens, at the hands of the Goths, who set fire to the hut in which the wounded emperor lay following his ignominious defeat at the Battle of Adrianople in 378.[84] Gregory further claimed that, at the very moment when Chlothar defeated Chramn on a plain in Brittany, swarms of locust were fighting their own

---

[78] Gregory of Tours, *Histories*, 4.20.

[79] Gregory of Tours, *Histories*, 4.16.

[80] Gregory of Tours, *Histories*, 4.13; Gregory of Tours, *Glory of the Martyrs*, 65.

[81] As his rebellion progressed, Chramn pursued the *dux* Austrapius, one of Radegund's key supporters, who was saved only by the miraculous intervention of St Martin; see Gregory of Tours, *Histories*, 4.18.

[82] See also *Liber historiae Francorum*, 28, which provides the name 'Chalda' for Chramn's wife.

[83] Gregory of Tours, *Histories*, 4.20.

[84] These details appear in one account of the demise of Valens, though others existed. Ammianus Marcellinus, *Res Gestae*, 31.13.14–16. On the thematic similarities between the *Histories* and the *Res Gestae*, which suggest that Gregory may have known the work of Ammianus, see Pizarro, 'Gregory of Tours and the Literary Imagination', pp. 367–373.

battle on the plain of Romagnat near Clermont. Gregory also cited the biblical story of the war between King David and his son Absalom, who perished at the hands of David's commander, Joab. *In great sorrow the king ascended the high gatehouse and wept, declaring as he went: 'O my son Absalom, my son Absalom, were it granted to me, I would die in your place; my son Absalom, my son Absalom.'* (II Samuel 18:33).

After the death of Chramn, Chlothar took his youngest son, Sigibert, and set off on his pilgrimage to St Martin's shrine. Through this grand show of repentance, Chlothar made a statement about his own absolution from sin, just as his brutal execution of Chramn had made a statement about the fate of rebellious princes. Chlothar made other ostentatious efforts to repair his reputation around this time. He had already begun to construct a church in Soissons over the tomb of the recently departed Médard, where he intended to be buried himself.[85] He may have wished to appropriate burgeoning popular devotion to the late bishop, since Gregory of Tours reported that a chapel made from small branches had been erected over Médard's tomb already. When Chlothar had the branches removed (to enable the new construction), people took slivers of the wood and used them to cure their ailments.[86] Meanwhile in Poitiers, Radegund wondered if she might be part of the king's plans to secure his legacy. According to Baudonivia, Radegund heard from messengers what she feared most:

> As though for the sake of devotion, the excellent king, with his most excellent son, Sigibert, had come to Tours, whence he might more easily travel on to Poitiers in order to reclaim his queen.[87]

Although it is difficult to determine the authenticity of Baudonivia's claim, it certainly fits the political context described by Gregory of Tours. By restoring Radegund to his side, Chlothar might have hoped to confer upon himself an aura of redemption. Perhaps he also hoped to improve his standing with the Thuringians, whose restlessness, along with that of the rebellious Saxons, had forced him to send an army into his eastern domains in 555 and 556 (the very opening Chramn used to launch his rebellion).[88]

---

[85] Gregory of Tours, *Histories*, 4.19.

[86] Gregory of Tours, *Glory of the Confessors*, 93. The slivers of wood were particularly effective against toothaches, an ailment of interest for Gregory.

[87] Baudonivia, *Life of Radegund*, 6.

[88] Gregory of Tours, *Histories*, 4.14 and 4.16.

Radegund asked for help from Germanus, bishop of Paris, who was accompanying Chlothar on his pilgrimage, and to her relief he came to her aid. Throwing himself at the feet of the king, before the tomb of St Martin, Germanus pleaded with Chlothar not to travel to Poitiers.[89] According to Baudonivia, the king realized the request had come from Radegund herself, and he felt sadness in his heart that she so feared the thought of returning to his side. Chlothar then renounced the 'evil advisers' who had counselled him to retrieve his queen. Baudonivia compared the demise of these advisers to the infamous death of Arius, a heretical priest of the fourth century:

> Divine vengeance came immediately upon the evil advisers. As with Arius, who turned against the Catholic faith and shat his very entrails into the privy, so it happened to those who acted against the blessed queen.

By referencing Arius, the archetypal heretic of the ancient Church, Baudonivia drew a parallel between these men and Radegund's other enemies, such as the heathen Franks who had once opposed the queen when she sought to destroy their pagan sanctuary (discussed in Chapter 2).[90] Baudonivia thus suggested a continuity between those who had opposed Radegund when she was married to Chlothar, and those who later wished to see her restored to the king's side. This perspective depended upon Baudonivia's assertion that the opposition Radegund faced in life ultimately came from a single source, 'the Enemy of Humanity', i.e. the Devil.[91]

Germanus travelled to Holy Cross in Poitiers, where, 'in an oratory dedicated to the name of Our Lady Mary, he prostrated himself at the feet of the holy queen and begged forgiveness for the king'.[92] Radegund granted the request and forgave Chlothar's sins—'benevolently', Baudonivia concluded. The king's reputation had been secured, but on Radegund's terms. Chlothar himself headed north, away from Poitiers and towards the old heartlands of his kingdom, where he spent what proved to be his final days hunting in the forests of Cuise-la-Motte. There is little evidence in Gregory's *Histories*

[89] Baudonivia, *Life of Radegund*, 7.
[90] Baudonivia, *Life of Radegund*, 2. Arius's particular manner of death, first described by Athanasius and repeated in Eusebius, *Ecclesiastical History*, 10.4, was cited three times alone in the *Histories* of Gregory of Tours: 3.0 (prologue), 5.43, and 9.15. It was also mentioned by Fortunatus, *Poems*, 2.15, line 12.
[91] Baudonivia, *Life of Radegund*, 16 (*inimicus humani generis*).
[92] Germanus consecrated Agnes as abbess of Holy Cross, perhaps at this time. See Gregory of Tours, *Histories*, 9.42 and Baudonivia, *Life of Radegund*, 7. A different trip to Poitiers was also recounted in Fortunatus, *Life of Germanus of Paris*, 45.

to support Baudonivia's claim that, at this late moment in his life, 'the king feared the judgement of God', or that he realized 'his queen had been fulfilling the will of God' even during their marriage.[93] When Chlothar fell ill, he was taken to his royal residence in Compiègne, where he breathed his last, one year to the day after he ordered the execution of Chramn and his family.[94] Gregory placed a few final words into the king's mouth, an ironic testimony to both his seemingly limitless power in this life, and the utter insignificance of this power in the presence of Almighty God. 'Ah, can you imagine what sort of Heavenly King it is, who kills so great a king as me?', uttered the dying Chlothar.

The king's body was taken by his four surviving sons—Charibert, Guntram, Chilperic, and Sigibert—to Soissons and, in an ostentatious ceremony, placed in the still unfinished church that housed the tomb of Bishop Médard.[95] The church was later finished by Sigibert, who eventually took his resting place alongside that of his father, and honoured with a celebratory poem by Fortunatus upon its completion. The tomb of Médard became a site of miracles, with the holy bishop curing sick pilgrims, sheltering desperate refugees, and punishing wicked thieves.[96] No such miracles were reported for Chlothar's tomb, though his reputation must have benefited in some way from his proximity to the great intercessor Médard. There is no record of Radegund ever visiting her late husband's grave, or of her attending his funeral. Her residence within the cloistered environment of Holy Cross, described in Chapter 6, may have offered a convenient excuse, if any such expectations existed—and perhaps they did not. With Chlothar now dead, his four sons were poised to dominate Gaul for the remainder of Radegund's life. Meanwhile, in Poitiers, Radegund began the construction of her own funerary church, dedicated to St Mary. There she planned to be interred alongside her fellow nuns. Far away from Chlothar.

[93] Gregory of Tours, *Histories*, 4.21, recorded Chlothar's request that St Martin implore the Lord to show him mercy, but left open the question of whether this prayer had been answered.

[94] The royal residence appears specifically in Gregory of Tours, *Histories*, 6.35. Gregory drew attention to the significance of the timing. But this chronology also fits the information presented by Marius of Avenches, *Chronicle*, anni 555 and 561.

[95] Gregory of Tours, *Histories*, 4.21.

[96] Fortunatus, *Poems*, 2.16; Gregory of Tours, *Histories*, 4.51.

4

They Will Be as Bears and Wolves

When Jesus arose, baptized, from the waters of the Jordan river, he entered the desert to face temptation from the Devil. He fasted for forty days and nights, and overcame three tests, before angels arrived and attended to him. For one of his tests, the Devil took Jesus to a high mountain and showed him all the kingdoms of the world.

> 'I will give these all to you', the Devil said, 'if you will fall down and worship me.' Jesus replied: 'Begone Satan, for it is written: You shall worship the Lord your God and serve him alone.' And then the Devil left him. (Matthew 4:8–10)

This story influenced many of who, like Radegund, sought spiritual perfection through ascetic discipline, rejecting the temptations of the world. They secluded themselves in the proving ground of the desert, or a suitable alternative—alone in a hermitage, or together in a monastery—to be tested and to triumph, against the Devil and against themselves. But not all succeeded. *For the doorway is tight and the road narrow that leads to life, and they are few who find it* (Matthew 7:14). The world had ample temptations, and it tempted some more than others. Many found an offer of all the kingdoms of the earth too alluring to decline. Or even a share of just one.

Radegund watched, from the secluded confines of her monastery, as Chlothar died and his domains fell to a new generation of kings, his four (acknowledged) sons, each tempted by what he might receive. As soon as Charibert, Guntram, Chilperic, and Sigibert had buried their father in the church of St Médard, they began to fight over their share. Matters were complicated by the fact that Chilperic had a different mother from that of his half-brothers (in convoluted circumstances discussed in Chapter 1). In the opening gambit of what proved to be a series of civil wars, Chilperic seized his late father's treasury and entered the palace in Paris, before his half-brothers quickly united to oust him from the city.[1] They then divided the kingdom

---

[1] Gregory of Tours, *Histories*, 4.22.

Radegund. E. T. Dailey, Oxford University Press. © Oxford University Press 2023.
DOI: 10.1093/oso/9780197656105.003.0005

among themselves, and although they included Chilperic in the distribution, they gave him only the humblest share. For much of the remaining quarter century of Radegund's life, Chilperic strove to enlarge his portion, while his half-brothers took up arms in various configurations of rivalry and alliance with one another and with him. Poitiers repeatedly changed hands, and each time Radegund came to terms with life under the rule of a different stepson.

According to Baudonivia, Radegund tried to prevent these wars, for the sake of her city and her convent:

> She trembled whenever she heard acrimony stir among the kings, and dispatched letters of a similar nature to one king and to the others, so that they neither took up arms nor waged war with one another, but deepened their peace, lest the realm come to ruin. [...] By her intercession came peace among the kings, relief from armed conflict, and security to the realm.[2]

While it is easy enough to believe that Radegund used diplomacy to encourage her stepsons to beat their swords into ploughshares, she cannot have been quite as successful as Baudonivia claimed. Writing in the early seventh century, Baudonivia had the luxury of forgetting the conflicts that had threatened Poitiers during Radegund's time in Holy Cross. Not that Merovingian rule should be equated with the perpetual threat of civil war. On the contrary, peace prevailed across most of the realm most of the time. But the 570s and 580s experienced particularly intense internal conflict that disproportionately impacted Poitiers and Tours.[3] Gregory of Tours witnessed these conflicts and recorded their terrible details.[4] 'It saddens me to recall the multiplicity of civil wars that grievously wore down the Franks and their kingdom.' He punctuated this distinctive passage in his *Histories* with a stern rebuke:

> Because you keep not the peace, you have not the grace of God. Why does one of you take away what belongs to the other? Why does one desire what another possesses? I beg you, heed the words of the Apostle: *If you eat and consume one another, beware, lest you be consumed in turn* (I Galatians 5:15).[5]

---

[2] Baudonivia, *Life of Radegund*, 10.
[3] Wood, *The Merovingian Kingdoms*, pp. 88–101.
[4] On this theme within the *Histories*, see Halsall, 'The Preface to Book V'.
[5] Gregory of Tours, *Histories*, 5.0 (prologue).

Gregory urged warmongers to expend their energies differently, fighting against their own temptations so that they might triumph in 'the war that is waged in the heart of every man', rather than in these bloody battles.

A later legend interpreted this era as one of conflict hastening towards decline, with Chlothar's sons representing the last generation of Merovingian kings to enjoy their dynasty's talent for rule. Although a later invention, the legend took the form of an ancient prophecy, set in the days of Childeric I (d. 481).[6] On the night of his wedding, the king was instructed by his bride, Basina, to rise from his bed and look beyond the gates of the palace. On three separate occasions he witnessed a sign: first a lion, unicorn, and leopard gathered outside; then bears and wolves; followed by lesser beasts, the size of mere dogs or even smaller, tugging at one another. When dawn came, Basina offered her interpretation:

> A son will be born to us who has the mark and likeness of a lion. His sons will possess, in their strength, the mark of the leopard and unicorn, and from them will next come men who display the strength and voracity of bears and wolves. What you saw third are those who will remove the foundations of this kingdom. They will rule in the manner of dogs and lesser animals, which they will resemble in their strength. Those lesser beasts, twisting and tugging one another, are the people destroying one another without the fear of kings.[7]

The story appears in the *Chronicles* of Fredegar, who also elucidated the meaning of the prophecy and identified Clovis as the lion, Chlothar and his brothers as the leopard and unicorn, and Chlothar's sons—Charibert, Guntram, Chilperic, and Sigibert—as the ravenous bears and wolves, destined to produce a generation of dogs.

Fredegar wrote in the seventh century, seven generations after Childeric I, during an era of political instability in which the Merovingian dynasty was particularly vulnerable to criticism.[8] His views do not represent those prevalent in Radegund's lifetime, even if he was not the first to regard the sons of Chlothar as the source of many ills.[9] The legend's undeniable debt to the

---

[6] Childeric I is perhaps best known from his grave goods, discovered when his tomb was unearthed at Tournai in 1653, and lost when they were stolen and melted down for their gold content in 1831. See Effros, *Merovingian Mortuary Archaeology*, pp. 28–35.

[7] Fredegar, *Chronicles*, 3.12.

[8] Wood, 'Deconstructing the Merovingian Family', p. 151.

[9] Wallace-Hadrill, 'Fredegar and the History of France'.

biblical Book of Daniel suggests that it formed within ecclesiastical circles, and it may be that, the legend aside, these underlying scriptural prophecies had long been interpreted as a critique applicable in some way to the Merovingian dynasty.[10] Although Radegund and her congregation clearly lived before Basina's prophecy had been invented, they probably anticipated some of its sentiments, insofar as they had been pulled distressingly into the conflicts fought among these bears and wolves. Not only was Poitiers often contested, but also the nuns of Holy Cross were closely related to the elite of the realm—its powerful lords, bishops, and even kings. Chance references in the sources reveal that the convent's congregation included the daughters of two officials of the highest rank, the *viri illustres* Leo of Poitiers and Pientus of Tours; the nieces of two bishops, Gregory of Tours and Salvius of Albi; and the daughters of the kings Charibert and Chilperic.[11] These two princesses, mentioned last in the list, caused their own turmoil, within two years of Radegund's death, when they subjected the convent to a disaster worse than anything inflicted upon it by warring kings (as detailed in Chapter 7).

Such trying times were, in the view of the prophecies recorded in the Book of Daniel, a test that distinguished believers from unbelievers, a refining flame that separated out unwanted impurities from molten gold in the crucible of temporal life. *Many will be chosen and purified, tested as through fire; the wicked will continue to act wickedly—they will not understand—but the wise will understand* (Daniel 12:10). Radegund may not have been tempted by the kingdoms of the world, but she nonetheless found herself imperilled by kings and their wars. For this very reason, if for no other, she was unable to truly abandon all concern for secular politics. Poitiers fell into the hands of Chlothar's sons more or less in sequence (certain complexities aside): first Charibert, then Sigibert, Chilperic, and finally Guntram. With each changeover, Radegund faced new challenges and sought new opportunities for her monastic project. She continued to influence the affairs of the realm: she fuelled opposition to Charibert, found support from Sigibert, faced peril under Chilperic, and finished her work, before dying peacefully, under Guntram.

* * *

[10] Murray, '*Post vocantur Merohingii*', p. 150.

[11] See Baudonivia, *Life of Radegund*, 15; Fortunatus, *Life of Germanus of Paris*, 34; and Gregory of Tours, *Histories*, 7.29, 9.39, and 10.15. On the identity of 'Leo of Poitiers', see Halfond, 'Ecclesiastical Politics in the Regnum Chramni', pp. 479–482.

Charibert, the first of Chlothar's sons to rule over Poitiers, seems to have always had a poor relationship with Radegund. Perhaps the problems began when the king blocked one of Radegund's supporters from becoming the next bishop of the city and selected a cleric loyal to himself instead.[12] But the decisive moment came later, when Charibert married Marcovefa, a former slave, a sister of one of his earlier wives, and, most importantly, a woman who lived under religious vows.[13] A council of bishops met in Tours in 567, presided over by Germanus of Paris, which issued promulgations that implicitly rebuked Charibert for his choice of bride.[14] The Council of Tours had not been called for this reason, and the link between the promulgations and the marriage is itself an inference, but it is an inescapable one nonetheless.[15] The Council forbade a man from marrying the sister of his previous wife, on the grounds that this constituted a form of incest, and condemned any woman who renounced her religious vows in order to marry.[16] Anticipating resistance to this decree, the bishops included a series of quotations from authoritative texts, citing biblical material, previous conciliar promulgations, a decretal of Innocent I (bishop of Rome, 401–417), and the *Theodosian Code* (a compilation of Roman law).[17] Such illicit unions, they warned, might result in military defeat, which the biblical Hebrews had suffered after they entered into marriages that displeased God (in Ezra 10:1–44 and Nehemiah 13:23–31). Only when these wives and their sons were rejected did victory return. For a Merovingian king, whose authority derived largely from his ability to lead his Frankish warriors successfully in battle, such a proclamation directly threatened his authority as a ruler.

Radegund unquestionably opposed the marriage of women who had taken religious vows. When Chilperic tried to reclaim one of his daughters from Holy Cross and marry her to a Visigothic prince in 584, she resolutely refused. Gregory of Tours even had Radegund declare: 'It is not right that a girl dedicated to Christ should be given back to the pleasures of the world.'[18]

---

[12] Gregory of Tours, *Histories*, 4.18; Baudonivia, *Life of Radegund*, 5.

[13] Gregory of Tours, *Histories*, 4.26.

[14] Halfond, 'Charibert I', pp. 23–28.

[15] Wood, 'Incest, Law and the Bible', pp. 302–303.

[16] Second Council of Tours (567), canons 21–22.

[17] Mikat, *Die Inzestgesetzgebung*, pp. 41–127. The *acta* omitted the important phrase *adhuc illa vivente* from Leviticus 18:18 on marriage to a wife's sister.

[18] Gregory of Tours, *Histories*, 6.34. Chilperic is probably the king of *Histories*, 6.16, who allowed a man named Pappolen to reclaim his fiancée from a convent in Bazas, against the wishes of her family. Her uncle, Felix of Nantes (a bishop who, curiously enough, attended the Council of Tours), had forced her to enter the convent.

Radegund, of course, had also used this principle to justify her separation from Chlothar, and to resist his efforts at reconciliation.[19] Germanus of Paris, who presided over the Council of Tours, had helped Radegund to successfully avoid her forced return to marital life. He also consecrated Agnes as abbess, and he received praise through the pen of Venantius Fortunatus, two indications that he was one of Radegund's supporters.[20] Radegund received a letter, *Dominae beatissimae*, from several bishops, including Germanus, apparently while they were attending the Council of Tours, in which they agreed to excommunicate any nun from her convent who renounced her vows and took a husband.[21] Besides the similarities in content, the letter and the council feature very similar lists of signatories and attendees.[22] This link, together with Radegund's connection to Germanus, suggests that she was in communication with the bishops gathered in Tours in 567, and that she probably also influenced their decree against the marriage of avowed women, which had become of great political relevance following Charibert's marriage to Marcovefa.

When Charibert ignored the decrees issued by the Council of Tours, Germanus excommunicated him and his wife.[23] Remarkably so, it must be added. Little precedent existed for the use of this ecclesiastical sanction against a reigning king and queen.[24] Merovingian kings expected bishops to submit to their will, if not out of deep respect, then at least out of self-interest (or perhaps self-preservation).[25] But Germanus, now in his seventies, had both the clout and the inclination to back up his threats and to issue the excommunication. In a remarkable turn of events, Marcovefa soon died,

---

[19] The *Praeceptio Chlotharii*, which forbade a man to marry a woman under religious vows (preserved in the *Capitularia regum Francorum*, 7–8), was likely *not* a decree of Chlothar I, but instead that of Chlothar II. See Esders, *Römische Rechtstradition*, pp. 88–108.

[20] Fortunatus, *Poems*, 2.9 and 8.2. Fortunatus also wrote a *Life of Germanus of Paris*, after the death of the bishop, which detailed his many miracles, including one episode (§34) in which he brought a dying girl back to life; she later became a nun in Holy Cross.

[21] Gregory of Tours, *Histories*, 9.39.

[22] Halfond, 'Charibert I'. The letter was sent by Germanus of Paris, Euphronius of Tours, Praetextatus of Rouen, Felix of Nantes, Domitianus of Angers, Victorius of Rennes, and Domnolus of Le Mans. These bishops also signed the promulgations of the Council, except for Euphronius, whose attendance is at the Council is confirmed his signature on another document. Two other bishops, Chaletricus of Chartres and Leudobaudis of Seés, attended the Council but did not sign the letter. The bishop of Poitiers, presumably Maroveus by this time, neither attended the Council nor signed the letter.

[23] Gregory of Tours, *Histories*, 4.26. Halfond, 'Charibert I', p. 25.

[24] Germanus might be considered the first bishop to excommunicate a ruling Merovingian, but for the vague statement in Gregory of Tours, *Life of the Fathers*, 17.2, that Nicetius of Trier had excommunicated Chlothar 'frequently'.

[25] See Hen, 'The Church in Sixth-Century Gaul'; and Dumézil, 'La Royauté mérowingienne'.

followed by her unrepentant husband. It is difficult to determine precisely how soon, but the Council issued its decrees on 18 November 567, and Charibert's brothers were already dividing up his kingdom in 568. Gregory of Tours expressly connected Charibert's death to his refusal to reject Marcovefa, and he was surely not alone in this interpretation. The moment seems to have been widely regarded as replete with otherworldly significance. A comet that crossed the sky in this year was remembered as auguring the demise of the king.[26] A woman later claimed that she had earned herself a reputation as a soothsayer by predicting Charibert's death to the hour.[27] Euphronius, the bishop of Tours and an attendee of the Council, was credited with a similar insight, when he abandoned a trip to see Charibert at the last moment, with horses saddled and his entourage waiting, and said: 'The king you are forcing me to visit has died; if we depart, we will only discover that he lives no more.'[28]

For all the stories recorded about Charibert's death, no contemporary source mentioned the location of his tomb. Only the *Liber historiae Francorum*, an anonymous work of 727, identified Blaye, a fortified site about 30 km north of Bordeaux, as his place of burial.[29] Yet this identification seems to be a mistake. A later, and considerably less significant, ruler of the same name, Charibert II (d. 632), had his powerbase in Aquitaine, and a burial in Blaye makes much more sense for him.[30] But if the *Liber historiae Francorum* was able to confuse one Charibert for another, then the location of the king's grave must have already been lost by the early eighth century. Such obscurity suggests that the king had died in disgrace.[31] His brothers, even those who perished by an assassin's blade, were all interred in prominent locations. Sigibert was buried in the Basilica of St Médard in Soissons, alongside his father.[32] Chilperic came to rest in the Church of St Vincent in Paris, the city that had previously served as Charibert's power centre, which also featured the Basilica of St Geneviève and the tomb of their great ancestor, Clovis.[33]

---

[26] Gregory of Tours, *Histories*, 4.51.

[27] Gregory of Tours, *Histories*, 5.14.

[28] Gregory of Tours, *Glory of the Confessors*, 19. The clergy in Tours also regarded Charibert's death as a manifestation of divine judgement according to Gregory of Tours, *The Virtues of St Martin*, 1.29.

[29] *Liber historiae Francorum*, 31. Blaye possessed a church with the relics of St Romanus, whose cult enjoyed local popularity, according to Gregory of Tours, *Glory of the Confessors*, 45.

[30] Fredegar, *Chronicles*, 4.57 and 4.67 (on Charibert II and his powerbase).

[31] Fortunatus, *Poems*, 6.2, praised Charibert during the king's lifetime; he wrote nothing similar after the king's death.

[32] Gregory of Tours, *Histories*, 4.51.

[33] Gregory of Tours, *Histories*, 6.46. Chilperic had been initially buried in haste in Lambres, near Vitry.

Guntram had his final repose in a church within the monastic complex of St Marcel, which he had built for himself on the outskirts of Chalon-sur-Saône, the home of his royal court.[34] It must be concluded that Germanus's excommunication of Charibert, together with the unexpected death of the king and his wife soon thereafter, affected how he was memorialized. If Radegund had indeed encouraged the Council of Tours to implicitly rebuke Charibert's marriage to an avowed woman, then she likely saw her reputation grow as a result of the king's sudden demise.

Her opinion about the irrevocability of religious vows also seems to have experienced a moment of increased support, one that others quickly exploited for political advantage. Charibert had left behind an abundance of daughters and former wives, who might potentially confer a sense of legitimacy, through marriage, to any king or prince who asserted a claim over the late king's domains. Thus one of Charibert's former wives, Theudogild, tried to offer herself and her treasure to Guntram, but he rejected her marriage proposal, stole her money, and sent her to a convent in Arles, presumably that of St John.[35] Other women close to the late king found themselves dispatched into female religious houses, which made them unavailable for politically advantageous marriages. His daughter Berthefled entered a convent in Tours, where she showed 'no regard for the holy offices'.[36] She left many years later. His daughter Chlothild became a nun in Holy Cross. The troubled circumstances of her departure, more than twenty years later, are detailed in Chapter 7. His former wife, Ingoberg, spent her remaining years devoted to the 'religious life', though in what context remains unclear.[37] Only one daughter, Bertha, avoided the monastic life; she was married to a prince in Kent, across the Channel, who was not himself a Merovingian.[38] Radegund may not have intended to sweep an entire cohort of princesses into convents, but that outcome seems to have resulted nonetheless from her opposition to the marriage of avowed women and from her surprisingly successful efforts to rebuke Charibert for his marriage to Marcovefa.

* * *

[34] Fredegar, *Chronicles*, 4.14.
[35] Gregory of Tours, *Histories*, 4.26. The monastery is not named in the passage, but Arles was known for the Convent of St John. Aurelian of Arles wrote a rule for nuns, which has led to the belief that he may have founded another convent in the city.
[36] Gregory of Tours, *Histories*, 9.33.
[37] Gregory of Tours, *Histories*, 9.26 (*vita religiosa*).
[38] Gregory of Tours, *Histories*, 4.26 and 9.26; Bede, *Ecclesiastical History*, 1.25–26, 2.3, and 2.5.

The mostly likely architect of this strategy is Sigibert, the youngest of Chlothar's sons, who also acquired control of Poitiers upon Charibert's death. That he deserves credit can be inferred from the fact that he clearly held the upper hand during the division of Charibert's kingdom, receiving by far the greatest share.[39] Guntram received noticeably less, and Chilperic the least. When Guntram rejected Theudogild's offer of marriage, he probably acted in deference to his younger (but more powerful) brother. Even though Sigibert's motives were political, Radegund may have appreciated how he upheld her views on the irrevocable nature of religious vows. Neither was this policy the only area in which the interests of the queen and her stepson aligned. The two formed a constructive relationship for the duration of his reign. It surely helped that, unlike his brothers, Sigibert rejected his father's pro-clivity for what biblical idiom referred to as the desires of the flesh: he mar-ried only one woman, Brunhild, and he had no concubines (none of record, at least). Together, Sigibert and Brunhild produced a legitimate son and heir, Childebert II, in whom many in the kingdom invested their hopes.[40] Gregory of Tours praised the king for choosing a high-born bride, since Brunhild was a Visigothic princess:

> When King Sigibert saw that his brothers were taking unworthy wives and even joining themselves to slaves in worthless marriages, he sent a dele-gation to Spain with many gifts to ask for Brunhild, the daughter of King Athanagild. She was a girl refined in her ways, charming to behold, honour-able and modest in her manners, sensible in her advice, and cultured in her speech.[41]

Fortunatus, in a poem he delivered at their wedding in Metz, also praised the royal couple and imagined a future in which the kingdom flourished under the rule of their children.[42]

Shortly after the wedding, Fortunatus came to Poitiers, where he spent most of his life in Radegund's service. Sigibert and Brunhild had dispatched the poet to her, presumably as an expression of their support for Holy Cross—one of many hints that Radegund enjoyed a mutually beneficial re-lationship not only with Sigibert, but also with his queen.[43] Radegund had

[39] Esders, '"Avenger of All Perjury"', pp. 24–27.
[40] Dailey, *Queens, Consorts, Concubines*, pp. 94–96.
[41] Gregory of Tours, *Histories*, 4.27.
[42] Fortunatus, *Poems*, 6.1.
[43] Thomas, 'The "Second Jezebel"', pp. 185–191.

met Brunhild's sister, Galswinth, when she travelled through Poitiers on her way to marry Chilperic.[44] According to Fortunatus, who witnessed the encounter, Radegund treated Galswinth 'with the love of a mother', and she frequently received missives (*missi*) from the princess once she had become Chilperic's queen.[45] The marriage, however, lasted only a short while. According to Gregory of Tours, Galswinth was murdered on the orders of her husband.[46] Chilperic acted 'out of love for Fredegund', one of his concubines whom he had dismissed as a condition of his marriage. After publicly mourning Galswinth's death for 'a few days', Chilperic not only took Fredegund back, but even made her his wife, elevating the former slave to the rank of queen.[47] Gregory considered the whole affair to be an outrage, and he depicted Galswinth almost as a martyr, with miracles occurring at her tomb. Fortunatus went even further, placing Galswinth in the heavenly court next to the first martyr, St Stephen, as well as St Peter and the Virgin Mary, in his poem *On Galswinth*. Radegund presumably commissioned this poem to console Brunhild, the bereaved sister, and to show that she planned to take her side in her enduring rivalry with Fredegund.

Just as Radegund met Galswinth when she travelled to her wedding, she may well have met Brunhild in the same way a year earlier, when she came to marry Sigibert. Although the two sisters ultimately travelled to different destinations—Brunhild to Metz, Galswinth to Rouen—the first part of their journeys was likely the same: from Toledo, across the Pyrenees to Narbonne, then Poitiers, and on to Tours.[48] Brunhild was escorted by Gogo, a prominent official at Sigibert's court, and she seems to have become his patron in later years.[49] Gogo also became a friend to Fortunatus, who wrote four poems to the official, which further reveal that they exchanged gifts and letters.[50] The close relationship between these two men suggests that their respective patrons, Radegund and Brunhild, were also on good terms. The same might be said of Sigoald, another prominent official at court, who had escorted

[44] Roberts, 'Venantius Fortunatus's Elegy'.

[45] Fortunatus, *Poems*, 6.5, lines 225–228.

[46] Gregory of Tours, *Histories*, 4.28.

[47] Fredegund's origins are implied in Gregory of Tours, *Histories*, 9.34, and expressly stated in the *Liber historiae Francorum*, 31.

[48] Fortunatus, *Poems*, 6.5, lines 209–236, described the route taken by Galswinth.

[49] Gogo remained prominent in the kingdom after Sigibert's death, and he served as the *nutritor*, or 'governor', for Brunhild's son, Childebert II, according to Fortunatus, *Poems*, 7.4, lines 25–26. The claim made by Fredegar, *Chronicles*, 3.59, that Brunhild turned Sigibert against Gogo and had him killed, cannot be true because Gogo lived into the early 580s (several years longer than Sigibert himself), as noted in Gregory of Tours, *Histories*, 6.1.

[50] Fortunatus, *Poems*, 7.1–4. See Redellet, 'Tours et Poitiers'.

Fortunatus through Sigibert's kingdom when he first arrived in Gaul from his home in Italy.[51] Fortunatus wrote three poems in Sigoald's honour, which apparently hint that the official might have served as the *comes* of Poitiers after Sigibert's death.[52] These details indicate a network of clients linked to both Radegund and Brunhild, one that developed during Sigibert's reign but endured thereafter.

Gregory of Tours can be counted as part of that network.[53] Fortunatus mentioned that he received his post as bishop of Tours in 573 through the favour of Sigibert and Brunhild, and that he was consecrated in Reims, an important power centre in their kingdom, even though ecclesiastical regulations held that bishops should be consecrated in their new episcopal see after they were selected by the local population and the clergy.[54] Fortunatus implied that Sigibert and Brunhild circumvented these regulations specifically for Radegund's benefit, in a poem he addressed *To the Citizens of Tours*, written for this very occasion:[55]

The generous hand of father Aegidius [of Reims] consecrated Gregory to the Lord, to renew the people and for Radegund to love. A cheering Sigibert and Brunhild favoured this honour.[56]

Fortunatus apparently wrote this poem to convince the people of Tours to accept Gregory as their bishop, because his appointment caused some controversy.[57] Gregory delayed his arrival in Tours, and he experienced much anxiety in the meantime, perhaps because the local clergy had favoured one of their own for the post. Radegund may have preferred Gregory because he was a relative of the previous bishop of Tours, Euphronius, who had provided his services to Holy Cross when the local bishop, Maroveus, refused (in circumstances discussed shortly).[58] If so, she made a wise choice: Gregory fulfilled the same role when Maroveus made himself unavailable to preside

---

[51] Fortunatus, *Poems*, 10.16, lines 1–4.

[52] Fortunatus, *Poems*, 10.16–18. Gregory of Tours, *Histories*, 7.14. The hints are identified in Martindale, *Prosopography of the Later Roman Empire*, vol. 3B, p. 1151 (Sigvaldus 3).

[53] Gregory of Tours, *Histories*, 4.28.

[54] Such royal appointments, however, were not uncommon. See Gaudemet, *Les Élections dans l'Église*, pp. 56–62.

[55] See Van Dam, *Saints and their Miracles*, p. 63. Words of caution appear in Roberts, *The Humblest Sparrow*, pp. 110–111.

[56] Fortunatus, *Poems*, 5.3, lines 13–15.

[57] Wood, *Gregory of Tours*, pp. 10–13; and Van Dam, *Saints and their Miracles*, pp. 63–66.

[58] Gregory of Tours, *Histories*, 4.15. Gregory claimed that he was related to most of his predecessors (*Histories*, 5.49). See Mathisen, 'The Family of Georgius Florentius Gregorius'.

over Radegund's funeral (discussed in Chapter 6), and the nuns of Holy Cross remembered Gregory well, with Baudonivia describing him as a 'devout man, full of God'.[59]

Radegund's relationship with Sigibert and Brunhild enabled her to accomplish one of her principal ambitions: to acquire fragments of the Cross of the Crucifixion from the imperial court in Constantinople. The exchange occurred when Sigibert sought a political accord with the emperor, Justin II, most likely concerning their mutual interests in Italy.[60] Radegund had her own connections with the imperial court in the form of her cousin Amalfred, who had made a career for himself in the service of the Byzantine emperors, and she had already dispatched at least one embassy into eastern provinces of the Empire in search of relics (discussed further in Chapter 5).[61] Sigibert surely found these connections useful in his attempts to deepen his relationship with the rulers of Constantinople.[62] Baudonivia described how Radegund collaborated with Sigibert to acquire the fragments of the Cross as a gift from Justin II and his wife, Sophia:

> Radegund dispatched letters to King Sigibert, the most excellent lord, under whose authority our homeland had fallen. She asked that he allow her to seek the wood of the Lord's Cross from the emperor, for the protection of the entire realm and the stability of his kingdom. Sigibert most benevolently consented to the holy queen's request. [...] As a result of the holy woman's petition, the emperor sent legates with gospel books adorned with gold and gems; and the wood, upon which the salvation of the world once hung, came to the city of Poitiers, with a congregation of saints.[63]

Baudonivia understood that this imperial gift belonged to Sigibert's broader political programme, and her words, 'for the protection of the entire realm and the stability of his kingdom', echoed common formulae used in prayers for the health of the king.[64]

Baudonivia's words also recalled a belief in the protective power of the great relic, which found expression in eastern sources that recorded how the

---

[59] Baudonivia, *Life of Radegund*, 23.
[60] Esders, '"Avenger of All Perjury"', pp. 33–34.
[61] Procopius, *History of the Wars*, 8.25.11–12. As discussed in Chapter 5, Radegund probably dispatched her first embassy not long after the death of Charibert.
[62] Brennan, 'The Relic of the True Cross'.
[63] Baudonivia, *Life of Radegund*, 16.
[64] Esders, '"Avenger of All Perjury"', pp. 36–37.

Figure 4.1 A jewelled reliquary containing fragments of the True Cross, sent to Rome during the reign of Justin II (565–578), as depicted in 1779—before its more recent alterations—by the antiquarian Stefano Borgia, *De cruce Vaticana*.

first Christian emperor, Constantine I, had placed a fragment of the Cross in a statue that stood atop a porphyry column in the forum of Constantinople, to protect the city and the empire.[65] The power of the relic had also been referenced by Rufinus of Aquileia, in his Latin rendition of Eusebius's *Ecclesiastical History*, which associated the victories of Constantine I with his acquisition of the wood of the Cross and the nails of the Crucifixion.[66] Justin II and Sophia invoked that tradition when they sent other fragments of the Cross to Rome, in a majestic cruciform reliquary that still survives (though in modified form) and bears the inscription 'With the wood through which Christ overcame the enemy of man, Justin gives his strength to Rome, and his companion [Sophia] gives her grace'[67] (Figure 4.1). The gift was clearly intended to protect the city through its spiritual power. The imperial couple had surely intended the same for Poitiers, which at this time formed part of

---

[65] See Klein, 'Constantine, Helena, and the Cult of the True Cross'; and Fowden, 'Constantine's Porphyry Column'. The column survives, minus the statue, in Çemberlitaş Meydanı in Istanbul.

[66] Rufinus, *Ecclesiastical History* 10.8. Specifically his victories over the Sarmatians in 334 and Goths in 332.

[67] See Belting-Ihm, 'Das Juztinskreuz'; and Pace, Sante, and Radiciotti, *La crux vaticana*.

Sigibert's kingdom.[68] Later evidence about the landscape of Metz, Sigibert's centre of power, indicates that a church dedicated to the Holy Cross stood on a mound, referred to as 'Holy Cross Hill', next to the royal palace, in circumstances that might date back to Sigibert's reign.[69] Justin II and Sophia hoped to strengthen their political ties with the Franks, and to improve their standing in the eyes of the clergy in the Latin West, while Sigibert benefited not only from the honour associated with imperial benefaction, but also from the protective power of the relic itself.[70]

Baudonivia wrote that Radegund had acquired the fragments of the Cross not merely to glorify Sigibert's kingdom, but also 'for the honour of this place [i.e. Poitiers] and the salvation of the people in her monastery'. But not everyone in Poitiers appreciated the gift. In a dramatic moment, Maroveus, the bishop of Poitiers, refused to install the fragments of the Cross in Radegund's convent. According to Gregory of Tours,

> When the envoys returned with their quest fulfilled, the queen asked her
> bishop to deposit the relics in her monastery with all due honour and the
> chanting of psalms. But Maroveus regarded her request with contempt.
> Having mounted his horse, he departed for his villa.[71]

The full details of this remarkable conflict are discussed in Chapter 5, but the salient point here concerns Radegund's response: in the face of such defiance from her local bishop, she wrote to Sigibert to ask that he dispatch another bishop to perform the task. Sigibert instructed Euphronius of Tours to transfer the fragments of the Cross to Poitiers. He brought his clergy 100 km south and installed the relic in Radegund's convent with all due liturgical ceremony.[72] Radegund had apparently lost the support of her local bishop during Charibert's reign, but now, with Sigibert ruling over Poitiers, she gained the service of the bishop of Tours (first Euphronius, then Gregory) because of her positive relationship with the new king. Sigibert's reign over Poitiers, though relatively brief (568–575), proved to be Radegund's most productive period.

---

[68] Klein, 'Sacred Relics and Imperial Ceremonies'.

[69] Esders, ' "Avenger of All Perjury" ', pp. 36–37.

[70] Cameron, 'The Early Religious Policies of Justin II'.

[71] Gregory of Tours, *Histories*, 9.40.

[72] Baudonivia, *Life of Radegund*, 16, states that, in the meantime, the fragments of the Cross had been kept in a male religious house in Tours founded by 'the king', presumably Sigibert.

* * *

From the moment when Sigibert acquired control over Poitiers, his rule was challenged, and ultimately ended, by Chilperic. The conflict principally concerned land, although the untimely death of Galswinth, and the suspicion that she had been murdered, surely added a personal wound to the rivalry. Chilperic had received the least from the division of Charibert's kingdom; worse still, his territories in southern Gaul were not connected to his powerbase in Soissons. To visit these far reaches of his kingdom, he required the grace of either Guntram or Sigibert, so that he and his entourage, or at least his officials, might pass through their domains. If Chilperic captured Tours and Poitiers, however, then he linked his holdings in Picardy, Normandy, Maine, and Anjou to his possessions in the Gironde and Gascony. This political objective put Radegund and Holy Cross squarely within Chilperic's path to greater power. He launched his first effort to conqueror Poitiers soon after the division of Charibert's kingdom, when he sent his son Chlodovech with an army to the city, only to withdraw as soon as Sigibert and Guntram made a united show of force.[73] But when that alliance soured in 573, Chilperic renewed his efforts. He dispatched his son Theudebert, who defeated an opposing force near Poitiers and who, in the words of Gregory of Tours, 'made a great slaughter of the people there'.

Although Gregory provided no further information about the effects of this campaign on Poitiers, he detailed the destruction Theudebert unleashed elsewhere, in Cahors and across the Limousin:

> He set fire to churches, confiscated their plate, and killed their clergymen.
> He destroyed the monasteries of men, dishonoured those of girls, and laid
> waste to everything. In the churches there was a greater cry of sorrow than
> had occurred even during the persecution of Diocletian.[74]

Here Gregory referenced the great persecution of Christians ordered by the Roman emperor Diocletian (r. 284–305). According to Rufinus's rendition of Eusebius's *Ecclesiastical History*, Diocletian had ordered his men to destroy all the churches they found, to force the leaders of these churches to worship idols, and to burn the sacred scriptures.[75] Gregory could make no more terrifying association than this.

---

[73] Gregory of Tours, *Histories*, 4.45.
[74] Gregory of Tours, *Histories*, 4.47.
[75] Rufinus, *Ecclesiastical History*, 8.2.4.

Rufinus included a story of Christian women who faced torture and rape during Diocletian's persecution, and who chose to drown themselves rather than lose their honour.[76] Gregory may also have referenced the threat of rape, when he described how Theudebert's army mistreated convents, by using the verb *deludere*, translated above as 'dishonour'. Although the word commonly meant 'to delude' or 'to mock', this passage implies more than mere ridicule or trickery. Its grammatical structure paired the meaning of *deludere* with that of *deicere*, 'to destroy', suggesting that the threats faced by the monasteries of men and women were equally serious. Gregory probably used *deludere* in the same sense in another passage, in which he described how Fredegund brought about the downfall of her husband's former wife, Audovera, and her children. Fredegund murdered Audovera and her son, and then she turned to her daughter, Basina, who was, according to Gregory, 'dishonoured by the slaves of the queen and sent into a monastery'.[77] Most translations interpret this phrase to mean that Fredegund's slaves *tricked* Basina into the monastery, a reading that, though certainly possible, stands at odds with Fredegund's otherwise brutal approach to her rival's family (and her many other victims in the *Histories*).[78] The monastery that received Basina was, in fact, Holy Cross, and it seems less likely—in Gregory's sympathetic portrayal, at least—that Radegund would acquiesce to such trickery than that she might offer refuge to a victim of sexual violence.

Whatever the precise meaning of *deludere*, it can be assumed that the 'great slaughter' brought to Poitiers by Theudebert's army involved much distress for the population, and that this misery must have touched Radegund's congregation in some way. The nuns surely found the experience profoundly disturbing, whether or not they faced a choice between death and dishonour.[79] One story preserved in Holy Cross calls attention to itself in this context, because it articulated the fear felt by the congregation at the dangers beyond the convent's walls—even though, in Baudonivia's telling, the menace took the form of demons rather than soldiers. One night, a nun saw 'thousands of thousands of demons' standing on the walls of the convent. They appeared in

[76] Rufinus, *Ecclesiastical History*, 8.12.3–5, which differs significantly from Eusebius's original.

[77] Gregory of Tours, *Histories*, 5.39 (*in monasterio delusa a pueris reginae transmittitur*). The interpretation of *deludere* to mean 'rape' in this passage appears in Dumézil, *La Reine Brunehaut*, p. 201. I would like to thank Shelley Puhak for encouraging me to seriously consider this possibility while this manuscript was in draft. The issue has now been treated in detail by Singer, 'Gregory's Forgotten Rebel', pp. 190–192 (but without reference to Dumézil).

[78] See the translations of the *Histories* by Dalton, vol. 2, p. 212; Thorpe, pp. 304–305; and Murray, p. 110.

[79] See Vihervalli, 'Wartime Rape in Late Antiquity'; and Joye, *La Femme ravie*, pp. 241–249.

the image of goats, but their demonic nature was apparent to the nun, who became greatly distressed. At that very moment, Radegund happened to be keeping vigil, praying for the protection of her monastery. When she raised her hand to make the sign of the cross, the demons fled. 'Never to appear again', Baudonivia concluded.[80] The power of the cross, invoked by a pious gesture from Radegund's hand, protected the convent and prevented the evils of the world from encroaching upon its sacred confines.[81] The nuns of Holy Cross clearly regarded the outside world as a source of perilous danger, in large part because of their own experiences. Without any further details, it might be assumed that the congregation had also relied on Radegund, and the power of the Cross, to survive Theudebert's campaign.

After Sigibert restored his rule in Poitiers, he sought to end his conflict with Chilperic once and for all, through a decisive victory, even though this involved an act of fratricide.[82] The year, 575, was marked by a portentous comet, which Gregory compared to 'that comet once seen before the death of Chlothar'.[83] Germanus of Paris, now approaching his eightieth year, admonished Sigibert by alluding to scripture (specifically Proverbs 26:27), when he warned the king: 'He who shall dig a hole for his brother, into it shall he himself fall.' Germanus also implored Brunhild, in a letter that survives, to influence her husband to change his mind, like the biblical Esther, and to thereby save him from divine retribution.[84] Germanus wrote that a desire for more power was no justification to kill one's own brother. He cited Matthew 18:7, *woe to the man through whom temptation comes*, and referenced the sin of Judas, who had betrayed Christ for a mere thirty pieces of silver. But Sigibert ignored the warning. Chilperic's kingdom was, after all, no mere potter's field. When he reached as far as Vitry-en-Artois, the royal villa in which Chlothar had once planned to marry Radegund, Sigibert sat upon a shield, which his men then raised high while proclaiming him to be the king of his half-brother's domains. But before Sigibert's feet returned to earth, he felt the sting of an assassin's blade (wielded, at least in Gregory's opinion, by the agents of Fredegund). Sigibert died: from imminent victor to ignominious victim. Chilperic found his reprieve. The portentous comet had not blazed for him. Sigibert's son, Childebert II, now inherited his father's

---

[80] Baudonivia, *Life of Radegund*, 18.

[81] Rusticula, abbess of St John's convent in Arles, used her fragment of the Cross (discussed further in Chapter 5) to vanquish demons. *Life of Rusticula*, 13.

[82] Gregory of Tours, *Histories*, 4.49.

[83] Gregory of Tours, *Histories*, 4.50–51; Gregory of Tours, *On the Course of the Stars*, 34.

[84] *Epistulae Austrasicae*, letter 9.

kingdom, while Chilperic took advantage of the moment and captured Tours and Poitiers for himself.[85]

* * *

The death of Sigibert diminished Radegund's influence and over the remaining twelve years of her life prevented her from achieving anything remotely comparable to her acquisition of the relics of the Cross. In Poitiers, as in Tours, the advent of Chilperic's rule emboldened old enemies. Those who had opposed the appointment of Gregory as bishop, for example, took advantage of the new political circumstances and accused him of spreading a rumour that Fredegund had committed adultery.[86] At his trial in Berny-Rivière, he pleaded his innocence to Chilperic and a heavily pregnant Fredegund.[87] His enemies became so confident in his inevitable demise that they took an inventory of the cathedral treasury, a procedure normally undertaken after the death of a bishop.[88] Fortunatus, presumably at Radegund's direction, composed a panegyric in honour of the king and delivered it during the trial, in what appears to have been an attempt to support Gregory by flattering the man who decided his fate.[89] Long before, Radegund had acquired a reputation for persuading her husband, Chlothar, to show mercy to those on trial and the condemned; now she directed those same efforts to her stepson.[90] Her intervention may have proved decisive. But by the end of the trial, Gregory was allowed to acquit himself by saying Mass at three altars and swearing his innocence, a remarkable outcome for someone who had been in such jeopardy.[91]

Radegund seems to have made other efforts, in light of the new political reality in Poitiers, to curry favour with Chilperic and Fredegund. Fortunatus wrote two poems to console the royal couple following the death of two of their sons, and he composed two corresponding epitaphs for the princes.[92] His words, though not necessarily insincere, were probably more a product of expedience than remorse; as soon as Chilperic died, his blandishments

[85] Gregory of Tours, *Histories*, 5.41.

[86] Gregory of Tours, *Histories*, 5.49.

[87] See Dailey, 'Gregory of Tours and the Paternity of Chlothar II'. For the idea that Fredegund was pregnant with the child of questionable paternity at this time, see Smith, '"Carrying the Cares of State"', p. 238.

[88] Wood, *Gregory of Tours*, p. 16.

[89] Fortunatus, *Poems*, 9.1. See George, 'Poet as Politician'.

[90] Fortunatus, *Life of Radegund*, 10.

[91] Gregory of Tours, *Histories*, 5.49. See Van Dam, *Saints and their Miracles*, pp. 70–73.

[92] Fortunatus, *Poems*, 9.2–5.

ceased. Fortunatus wrote no epitaph for the king, and no consolation for his wife, when an assassin struck Chilperic dead as he dismounted his horse while hunting near Chelles in 584. Gregory produced an epitaph of sorts—a lengthy diatribe that damned Chilperic as the 'Nero and Herod of our time'.[93] He wrote that the king had laid waste to several regions in Gaul, unjustly confiscated property, allowed the episcopate to atrophy, and indulged his appetite for food and flesh. He ignored the needs of the poor, slandered priests, and invented new methods of torture for undeserving victims. Gregory even reported a vision, which Guntram apparently experienced, of Chilperic melting away in a boiling cauldron, an obvious symbol for the torments of Hell.[94] With Chilperic now cast into the abyss, Guntram became the ruler of Poitiers for the final three years of Radegund's life, though the question of who rightfully deserved control over the city remained unsettled.[95]

A few months after Radegund's death in 587 (described in Chapter 6), Guntram formally transferred the city into the possession Childebert II, the son of Sigibert and Brunhild.[96] The following year, Fortunatus met with Brunhild and Childebert II, when they undertook a lengthy boat ride from Metz to Andernach, near Koblenz.[97] In a poem celebrating the Feast of St Martin, Fortunatus depicted the recently departed Radegund as a beloved figure who now stood in the heavenly court, flanked by other saints, ready to offer her intercession in support of the new rulers of Poitiers.[98] He also forced allusions to fertility into his poem, portraying the heavenly Radegund as 'plump', even though her extreme fasts had surely left her body gaunt in life, and he referenced the burgeoning belt of St Martin, which encased his 'sacred loins'.[99] Radegund and Martin made an odd pairing for a fertility cult,[100] but Fortunatus understood the desires of his audience:[101] Brunhild had recently arranged for her daughter to marry a Spanish prince, and to thereby

[93] Gregory of Tours, *Histories*, 6.46.
[94] Gregory of Tours, *Histories*, 8.5.
[95] Gregory of Tours, *Histories*, 7.3, 7.12–14, 7.24, 7.28, 8.26, 9.7, and 9.9.
[96] Gregory of Tours, *Histories*, 9.20 (the Treaty of Andelot). Radegund died on 13 August; the treaty was agreed on 28 November.
[97] Meyer, *Der Gelegenheitsdichter*, p. 22; and Koebner, *Venantius Fortunatus*, pp. 208–209.
[98] Fortunatus, *Poems*, 10.7–9 and appendix 5–6, honour of Brunhild and Childebert II; they probably all belong to this moment.
[99] Fortunatus, *Poems*, 10.7, lines 25–28. The words translated here are *opima* and *sacri lumbi*.
[100] Radegund had visited sites associated with St Martin (Fortunatus, *Life of Radegund*, 14), and she asked Fortunatus to versify the saint's *Life*. See Roberts, 'Venantius Fortunatus's *Life of Saint Martin*'.
[101] Brunhild had once sought sanctuary in a church dedicated to St Martin, and she founded a monastic complex in Autun, where her remains were later interred, that was also dedicated to him. See Gregory of Tours, *Histories*, 5.2; and Gregory I, *Register*, 13.5.

unite through their offspring the Merovingian and Visigothic dynasties, and she also hoped for her daughter-in-law to give birth to a son.[102] Yet these ambitions ultimately proved fruitless: Brunhild lived long enough to see her dynasty collapse, and the thrones of her husband in Gaul, and her father in Spain, pass out of her family's hands. Captured by Fredegund's son in 613, Brunhild was tortured for several days, paraded around on a camel, and tied—by her hair, an arm, and a leg—to the tail of a crazed horse, which tore her body apart when it bolted.[103]

Radegund understood the violence at the heart of the Merovingian political system better than most. She watched as Brunhild and Fredegund made every effort to increase their political power and to pursue their personal vendetta. The two women acted with the same determination that had driven the sons of Chlothar to vie for their father's kingdom at each other's expense. They also paid a similar price. To command respect, to inspire fear, and to eliminate enemies necessitated the use of violence. Unlike kings, Brunhild and Fredegund were unable to wield the sword openly, because legitimate violence belonged only to men, but they had the cloak and dagger, and they had male agents willing to act on their behalf.[104] They also had their sons, whom they raised to carry their grudges and to exact revenge.[105] Gregory of Tours presented Fredegund as the principal source of the evils that befell the ruling family, but later authors remembered Brunhild as the more malevolent figure. In the words of Jonas of Bobbio (d. post 659), she was a 'second Jezebel', a reference to the great villainess of the biblical Book of Kings.[106] For this reason, Brunhild and Radegund came to be regarded as occupying the opposite extremes of Merovingian queenship.[107] Not only does this interpretation overlook the support that they provided each other in life, but it also obscures the similarities between these two women—each a foreign princess attempting to survive and succeed in a dangerous and unfamiliar world—at least in regard to the challenges they faced, if not the manner in which they tried to overcome them.

[102] Gregory of Tours, *Histories*, 8.37, 9.4, 9.16, 9.20, and 9.38; Fredegar, *Chronicles*, 4.5, 4.7, and 4.27. These hopes were expressly addressed in the concluding prayer by Fortunatus, *Poems*, 10.7, lines 59–64.

[103] Fredegar, *Chronicles*, 4.42.

[104] This interpretation differs from that of Gradowicz-Pancer, *Sans peur et sans vergogne*.

[105] For Fredegund and her son Chlothar II, see Fredegar, *Chronicles*, 4.42. For Brunhild and Childebert II, see Gregory of Tours, *Histories*, 7.14.

[106] Jonas, *Life of Columbanus*, 1.18.

[107] See the remarks of Wood, *The Merovingian Kingdoms*, p. 139.

Radegund had no descendants, no sons to champion her cause, but she had her nuns and her supporters, who helped her in life and who memorialized her in death. Once a reigning queen herself, Radegund was forced by the murder of her brother to leave her husband and to transfer her queenship to the celestial realm. *We know that we are from God, and the whole world is placed in wickedness* (I John 5:19). Radegund treated Holy Cross as an outpost of the heavenly kingdom, a sanctuary in which to endure, and perhaps even flourish, through a generation of kings who behaved as ravenous bears and wolves. She avoided the fate of Brunhild and the reputation of a Jezebel that, rightly or wrongly, awaited those women who retained prominence at court beyond the lives of their husbands. If any queen had taken up Germanus's advice, and chosen the path of the biblical Esther—who rejected an offer of half the Persian Empire, in order to save her people—it was she. Radegund chose, instead, to dedicate herself to the service of God, in the seclusion of her convent, trusting the fragments of the Cross to protect her and her congregation of nuns.

> *Have no desire for the world, nor for those things which are in the world. If anyone loves the world, then the love of the Father is not in him. For everything that is in the world—the desires of the flesh, the desires of the eyes, the vanities of life—whatever is not from the Father, is from the world. And the world and its desires pass away. But whoever does the will of God abides in eternity.* (I John 2:15–17).

5

The Lord Knows His Own

> What Helena did in an eastern land, the blessed Radegund did in
> Gaul.
>
> Baudonivia, *Life of Radegund*, 16

The Abbaye Sainte-Croix in Saint-Benoît, just outside Poitiers and 6 km from
the original site of Holy Cross, houses a small plaque, with sides measuring
less than 6 cm, as depicted in Figure 5.1, an eighteenth-century drawing
(in a condition more complete than what survives today).[1] It contains five
fragments of wood arranged in the shape of a double-barred cross, believed
to be pieces of the Cross of the Crucifixion.[2] The reliquary itself is likely an
eleventh-century replacement for the original gift that Radegund received
from Justin II and Sophia.[3] But the fragments of wood that it contains might
just possibly date to her lifetime. Indeed, they may even sit in something like
their original arrangement. A double-barred cross appears on Merovingian
coins of the period, inspired by Byzantine coinage and intended to symbolize
the True Cross.[4] Although small, these fragments were still reasonably sized:
no mere splinters. Radegund was not the first inhabitant of Gaul to seek out
relics of the Cross. Bassula, the mother-in-law of Sulpicius Severus, for example, had relied upon her personal networks to obtain a tiny sliver of the
Cross for the villa monastery of Primuliacum (mentioned in Chapter 3) in the
early fifth century.[5] At about the same time, Avitus of Vienne demonstrated
an interest in obtaining a fragment from Elias, bishop of Jerusalem.[6] But

---

[1] The drawing appears in Poitiers, Médiathèque François-Mitterrand (bibliothèque municipale),
MS 547, fol. 165.

[2] Hahn, 'Collector and Saint'. See also Schulenburg, 'Female Religious as Collectors of Relics'.

[3] See Skubiszewski, 'La Staurothèque de Poitiers'; and Buckton, 'Byzantine Enamels in the
Twentieth Century'.

[4] Grierson and Blackburn, *Medieval European Coinage*, vol. 1, p. 117.

[5] Paulinus of Nola, *Letters*, 31.2 and 32.7–8. See Frolow, *La Relique de la vraie Croix*, pp. 169–170.

[6] Avitus of Vienne, *Letters*, 20. He was probably successful in his efforts. See Shanzer and Wood,
Avitus of Vienne, p. 154.

Figure 5.1 Drawing of the reliquary of the True Cross in Poitiers from an eighteenth-century manuscript, which depicts the object in a more complete form than what survives today. This sketch is adapted from Conway, 'St Radegund's Reliquary at Poitiers'. The original drawing appears in Poitiers, Médiathèque François-Mitterrand (bibliothèque municipale), MS 547, fol. 165. The reliquary itself is kept in the Abbey Sainte-Croix in Saint-Benoît.

there is nothing to suggest that the result of such efforts survived, either materially or even simply in memory, into Radegund's lifetime, by which point it had become very difficult to obtain a fragment of the Cross from Jerusalem.[7] And in a clear departure from these earlier efforts, Radegund sought her relic from the imperial court in Constantinople.[8]

When Radegund received her prized relic, she had it placed in an oratory within the inner confines of her convent, which subsequently took the name 'Holy Cross'. These fragments of wood were venerated intently by Radegund and her nuns as the object upon which Christ had died to redeem humanity. She may have distributed small pieces of the relic to her closest associates, since two other places with links to her convent acquired shards of the True Cross around this time. Details are scarce, but one such shard apparently resided in an oratory in Tours, built in the courtyard of the Basilica of St Martin.[9] Another found its way to the Convent of St John in Arles, where it inspired a major building programme. Rusticula, the fourth abbess of the convent, and a younger contemporary of Radegund, constructed several shrines and a new church, and she dedicated this church to the Holy Cross, in honour of the piece of wood that it possessed. Yet this church, though

---

[7] Veneskey, 'Jerusalem Refracted', p. 65 and n. 9.

[8] On the significance of Constantinople in particular as the source of Radegund's gift, see Jones, 'Perceptions of Byzantium', pp. 114–116.

[9] Gregory of Tours, *Glory of the Martyrs*, 14.

presumably the result of great effort and expense, proved to be unsuitable for so glorious a relic in the eyes of God, according to the *Life of Rusticula*:

> In a revelation, Rusticula was shown a building of wondrous size, constructed in heaven, which she understood to be a command of the Lord to replicate this building on earth.[10]

Rusticula began anew, erecting a grander 'temple of shining beauty' that reproduced the church she had seen in her vision. She then transferred her fragment of the True Cross to this larger building. Elsewhere in the *Life of Rusticula*, the abbess used the relic to expel demons, who testified to its power before they abandoned their hosts, in a manner that recalled how Jesus expelled demons as they affirmed his divinity in the Gospels.[11] *And when the unclean spirits saw him, they fell down before him, and exclaimed: 'You are the Son of God'* (Mark 3:11). Though the *Life of Rusticula* provided no explanation for how the convent in Arles came to possess this relic, the source was surely Holy Cross in Poitiers.

Rusticula reconsecrated the smaller church to St Michael the Archangel. This unusual dedication calls attention to a story preserved in Radegund's convent, which featured the Archangel. According to Gregory of Tours, when the nun Disciola passed away, a man possessed by a demon went into a fit. He had come to Poitiers in the hope that the True Cross might free him from demonic influence. Now he pulled out his hair, fell to the ground, and uttered an impassioned lament, expressed in juridical language:

> Alas, alas, alas for us who have suffered so punitive a ruling. The trial has been adjourned, and this soul has been removed from our jurisdiction, before the inquiry had even begun![12]

When asked the meaning of these words, the demoniac explained that St Michael had carried Disciola's soul to heaven before the Devil had been given a chance to lay his claim upon her. This statement echoed Jude 9, a verse of scripture that referenced the Archangel's dispute with the Devil over the body of Moses, an event detailed in apocryphal literature.[13] St Michael the

---

[10] Florentius, *Life of Rusticula*, 8.
[11] Florentius, *Life of Rusticula*, 13.
[12] Gregory of Tours, *Histories*, 6.29.
[13] This dispute is thought to have been detailed in the now lost sections of the Assumption of Moses.

Archangel also featured prominently in the final victory over the Devil in Revelation 12:7–12. Just as Rusticula likely received her relic of the Cross from Radegund, she may also have taken her interest in St Michael the Archangel from the devotional practices and traditions observed in Holy Cross.

Gregory's story about Disciola recalled a passage in his *Glory of the Martyrs* that presented his version of the Assumption of Mary, in which the resurrected Jesus entrusted the soul of his mother to St Michael before her body was taken into heaven.[14] Gregory is usually considered the first author writing in Latin to give an account of the Assumption of Mary, which had previously appeared only in texts of eastern origin.[15] It is perhaps more significant, however, that his source may well have been the nuns in Poitiers. Their influence is suggested by the fact that he placed his version of the Assumption just before he described one of his visits to Radegund's convent, during which he learned about miraculous occurrences there and witnessed the wondrous power of the relic of the Cross himself.[16] In what must be more than a mere coincidence, Fortunatus also alluded to the Assumption of Mary in his description of the celestial court, when he referenced the Blessed Virgin together with Elijah and Enoch, the two biblical prophets who were taken directly into heaven. 'Elijah comes in one chariot, Enoch in the other chariot,' Fortunatus wrote, before adding, 'and by the gift of her son, the Virgin Mary comes first.'[17] Although subtle, this reference likely took for granted the audience's knowledge of the Assumption of Mary, an event similar to that experienced by Elijah and Enoch, but of greater prestige because it involved the Blessed Virgin. Taken together, these references point to Holy Cross as an incubator and disseminator of the belief in the Assumption of Mary in the West. Radegund had sent more than one mission to the East, including Jerusalem in particular, which (as discussed below) served as a source of precious relics and ecclesiastical lore. She and her congregation had every reason to take a keen interest in this story, and to share it with Gregory, Fortunatus, and the nuns in Arles.

Gregory of Tours also recounted a story about a church dedicated to Mary in Jerusalem, built according to the engineering instructions provided by the Blessed Virgin herself in a vision to the architect.[18] Although he provided

---

[14] Gregory of Tours, *Glory of the Martyrs*, 4.
[15] Dailey, 'The Horizons of Gregory of Tours', p. 22.
[16] Gregory of Tours, *Glory of the Martyrs*, 5.
[17] Fortunatus, *Poems*, 8.3, lines 135–136.
[18] Gregory of Tours, *Glory of the Martyrs*, 8.

few details, Gregory presumably referred to the building that marked Mary's (briefly occupied) tomb in the Kidron Valley. In an interesting parallel, the nuns in Arles were buried in a funerary church dedicated to the Virgin Mary.[19] Radegund also built a funerary church for her nuns and dedicated it to the Virgin Mary.[20] In her letter *Dominis sanctis*, she insisted that she be buried there:

> When God decides to take me from the light, my dear body ought to be interred in the basilica that I have begun to construct in honour of St Mary, Mother of the Lord, where many of our sisters are already gathered in repose, whether it is finished or unfinished. If anyone shall attempt, or even think, to do otherwise, let him suffer divine vengeance by the power of the Cross of Christ and the Blessed Mary.

The dedication of a church to the Blessed Virgin may be thought to require no special explanation. But the particular interest in Mary's burial and transfer to heaven by St Michael within the convents of Poitiers and Arles certainly calls attention to the common dedication of these two churches to the Mother of Christ, especially since they were constructed as burial sites for the nuns.

The curse that Radegund included in her letter referenced the mutual power of Mary, who brought Christ into the world, and the Cross, upon which he departed. That relationship was echoed by Fortunatus in his poem *In Honour of the Holy Cross*: 'On the Cross the Virgin's lamb rescues his sheep, who were once prey to the fierce, ravenous wolf.'[21] Elsewhere, Fortunatus described Mary's womb as 'the temple built for Christ by the Holy Spirit'.[22] When Radegund obtained fragments of the Cross for her convent, which had originally been dedicated to Mary, she turned the religious house into such a temple. Like the womb of the Blessed Virgin, the convent, as the abode of the True Cross, served as the vessel through which Christ's salvific power flowed into the world. This arrangement was replicated in the Convent of St John once Rusticula had received her shard of the Cross and constructed a suitable temple to house it. Though the relationship between the convents in Arles

---

[19] Cyprian, *Life of Caesarius*, 57; Messianus and Stephanus, *Life of Caesarius*, 50. See Février, *Le Développement urbain en Provence*, pp. 67–69.

[20] On the church, see Kneepkens, 'À propos des débuts de l'histoire de l'église-funéraire'; and Favreau and Camus, 'Le Chapitre et l'église de sainte Radegonde'.

[21] Fortunatus, *Poems*, 2.3, lines 5–6.

[22] Fortunatus, *Poems*, 11.1, §17.

and Poitiers had begun when Radegund took inspiration from Caesaria, it clearly became one of mutual exchange in which influence flowed in both directions.

Radegund offered to the Convent of St John what she had obtained from the East, allowing the nuns of Arles to partake in the sacred objects she had discovered, and the sacred knowledge she had learned, from her envoys to Jerusalem and its surrounding regions, as well as Constantinople. She also looked beyond Arles when she sought one further quality, essential to her monastic project, that the nuns of St John were themselves unable to provide: a model of sanctity for Radegund that fit her status as queen. Neither Caesaria, nor Rusticula, nor the other abbesses of Arles had so prestigious a background, high ranking though they may have been. Radegund wished to model herself on an exemplary figure of the highest social station, ideally one personally connected to the True Cross and to Holy Jerusalem, and one who represented the particular form of spirituality that she sought to cultivate as a holy queen and monastic leader. This model Radegund found in Helena, the mother of the first Christian emperor, Constantine I.

> Just like the blessed Helena, who was imbued with wisdom, filled with the fear of God, and glorious in her good deeds, [Radegund] sought to honour the wood where the Ransom of the World was hung for our salvation, so that we might be delivered from the power of the Devil.[23]

When Baudonivia wrote these words, she had in mind the Helena of legend, who was believed to have discovered the True Cross during her journey to Jerusalem, and to have constructed the Church of the Holy Sepulchre—a grand ecclesiastical complex that marked the Empty Tomb (with a rotunda, known as the Anastasis) and the site of the Crucifixion (with a great basilica, joined to the rotunda by a courtyard).

* * *

Helena had not, in fact, discovered the Cross of the Crucifixion. The notion of such an event is simply too difficult to reconcile with the information provided by contemporary sources.[24] She did, however, journey to Jerusalem, sometime between 324 and 328, during her eighth decade of life. Helena

[23] Baudonivia, *Life of Radegund*, 16.
[24] Heid, 'Die gute Absicht im Schweigen Eusebs'.

distributed gifts, freed prisoners, and restored exiles to their homes. She also built two grand constructions in the Holy Land that marked the places where Jesus had entered and left this world: the Church of the Nativity in Bethlehem and the Eleona Church on the Mount of Olives. But not the Church of the Holy Sepulchre. These details appear within the *Life of Constantine*, written by Eusebius, bishop of Caesarea (d. 339). His account already bears the marks of pious embellishment, particularly his assertion that Helena undertook this journey as an act of devotion, inspired by a desire to walk in the footsteps of Christ.[25] Whatever her personal motivation, the trip took the form of an official imperial tour (i.e. an *iter principis*) designed to increase support for Constantine's rule in several key cities throughout the eastern provinces of the Empire.[26] Even so, Eusebius made no mention of the discovery of the True Cross, and he credited the construction of the Church of the Holy Sepulchre to Constantine alone. Admittedly, some sort of discovery must have occurred before 351, when the first reference to the veneration of wood from the Cross in Jerusalem was made by Cyril, bishop of Jerusalem (d. 386).[27] But none of the sources from Cyril's lifetime that mentioned the True Cross credited Helena with its discovery, and they also indicated that Jerusalem possessed nothing like a complete crucifixion cross.[28]

Radegund, however, had not read the *Life of Constantine*, which was not translated from the original Greek into Latin for several centuries, and which had little circulation even among Grecophone communities at the time.[29] Her information derived, instead, from Rufinus of Aquileia (d. 411), who produced a Latin version of another work by Eusebius, his *Ecclesiastical History*—or, more precisely, a version of the *continuation* of Eusebius's text by one of his successors, Gelasius of Caesarea (d. 395).[30] Eusebius had not actually mentioned Helena himself; Gelasius thus deserves credit as, in all likelihood, the first author to associate Helena with the discovery of the Cross.[31] Other versions of the legend did appear, and these may have

[25] Eusebius, *Life of Constantine*, 3.41.2–3.47.2.

[26] Holum, 'Hadrian and St Helena'.

[27] Hunt, 'Constantine and Jerusalem'.

[28] Drijvers, *Helena Augusta*, pp. 81–93, suggested a plausible scenario: pieces of wood that turned up during the excavation and construction work for the Church of the Holy Sepulchre were hailed as part of the True Cross and authenticated by clerical authorities in Jerusalem.

[29] On the limited knowledge of Eusebius's *Life of Constantine*, see Winkelmann, 'Die Beurteilung des Eusebius von Cäsarea'.

[30] Rufinus, *Ecclesiastical History*, 10.7–8. See Ewig, 'Das Bild Constantins des Grossen'. Note also the contrary views of van Nuffelen, 'Gélase de Césarée'.

[31] See Drijvers, *Helena Augusta*, pp. 95–100; and Drijvers, 'Promoting Jerusalem'.

reached Radegund as well. As discussed below, there is perhaps a hint of the Judas Cyriacus legend (also called the *Inventio crucis*) in Baudonivia's *Life of Radegund*, though the allusion is far from certain. But the version of the Helena legend found specifically in Rufinus's *Ecclesiastical History* is distinct, because it explains Radegund's behaviour to an extent unmatched by any other source.[32] The seventh-century abbess of Laon, Sadalberg, also took Rufinus's story to heart, as her hagiographer apparently declared by writing the following:

> The blessed Sadalberg imitated Helena Augusta, the mother of Emperor Constantine. The *Ecclesiastical History* narrates how she mortified her fleshy limbs and disregarded the pomp of the world, serving God in daily obedience.[33]

According to the legend as it appeared in Rufinus's work, Helena was inspired by divine visions to travel to Jerusalem to search for the site of the Crucifixion. Once she had arrived, Helena received a sign from heaven that pointed out to her the location she sought, unvisited and very nearly unremembered by the local population. Helena removed an idol of Venus, placed there in years past by the persecutors of the Church. She then excavated rubble from the site until she uncovered, to her great delight, three crosses and the inscribed panel that, according to the Gospel of Luke, 23:38, had declared Jesus 'king of the Jews' in Latin, Greek, and Hebrew. The panel proved that these crosses were authentic relics of the Crucifixion. But in order to identify which one belonged to Jesus, rather than the men crucified alongside him, Helena sought divine assistance. She had an ill woman brought to Macarius, the bishop of Jerusalem, who prayed for God's guidance, and who then touched the woman's hand to each cross, until she was cured by the third cross—proof that it had once carried the body of Jesus. Helena ordered the construction of a church over the site where she had discovered this great relic (the Church of the Holy Sepulchre). She placed part of the wood from the Cross in a silver reliquary, which she left in Jerusalem, and brought the rest to Constantine in Constantinople. Helena also discovered the nails of the Crucifixion, which she presented to her son, who placed them in the bridle of his horse and in his helmet, for protection in battle.

---

[32] On this point, see Whatley, 'An Early Literary Quotation from the *Inventio s. Crucis*'.

[33] *Life of Sadalberg*, 25. Presumably the *Ecclesiastical History* mentioned here is that of Rufinus.

The Helena of Rufinus's narrative offered Radegund an exemplar, a holy woman who sought out the True Cross, and who built a grand ecclesiastical complex to house this sacred relic. But Rufinus also added a detail to his story of equal importance for Radegund, because it presented Helena as a person of the highest social standing who embraced asceticism and honoured women dedicated to the religious life. Rufinus concluded his account of Helena by adding that, before she left Jerusalem, the empress hosted a meal for those women in the city who lived under religious vows. Helena humbled herself before these handmaidens of God: she dressed as a servant, set the table, offered refreshments, and washed the women's hands; she thus became 'a servant of the servants of Christ'.[34] In his Life of Radegund, Fortunatus described Radegund serving others in a very similar manner.[35] So did Baudonivia, even though her presentation of Radegund often differed from that of her literary counterpart.[36] Neither author, it must be admitted, made the connection to Helena here explicit, and a commitment to service is common in monastic literature, including in the Rule of Caesarius, which was used in Holy Cross. But it is not difficult to imagine that Radegund might have taken particular interest in Helena's humble service, in addition to her more noteworthy discovery of the True Cross, precisely because, as an empress, she provided a model suitable for a queen.

One suspects that, if Radegund had know the full details of Helena's life, and not just a legend about her time in Jerusalem, she might not have so readily used her as a model.[37] Helena never formally married Constantine's father, Constantius, for example, at least not in a manner that might be recognized by those who, in keeping with prevailing attitudes in the late Roman world, considered a union between an honourable man and a woman of humble birth to be a type of concubinage.[38] As Constantius's military career progressed, he seized upon the opportunity to marry the daughter of the emperor Maximian and sent the now inconvenient Helena away.[39] Only the remarkable and unforeseeable achievement of his son Constantine, who battled his way into becoming emperor himself, secured Helena's place in the upper echelons of Roman society. Ambrose, bishop of Milan (d. 397), candidly wrote that Helena had risen 'from manure to royalty', and that she had

---

[34] Rufinus, Ecclesiastical History, 10.8.
[35] Fortunatus, Life of Radegund, 24.
[36] Baudonivia, Life of Radegund, 8.
[37] On Helena's early life, see Hillner, Helena Augusta, pp. 15–54.
[38] McGinn, 'The Augustan Marriage Legislation', pp. 49–57.
[39] For a discussion of the sources, see Drijvers, Helena Augusta, pp. 9–76.

once been a *stabularia,* a 'woman of the tavern', by which he probably meant to imply a prostitute.[40] The description might even suggest that Helena had once been enslaved, as were most such tavern workers.[41] The details of her life, therefore, more closely matched those of the lowborn women who became concubines to Merovingian kings. These women included Ingund, the mother of Sigibert—the very king who helped Radegund to secure the fragments of the Cross for Poitiers (as discussed in Chapter 4), and who perhaps considered himself to be a new Constantine. But these details appeared only in texts that had little circulation in sixth-century Gaul.[42] The comparison to Helena thus fell, not to Ingund, but to Sigibert's stepmother, the highborn but humble Radegund.

* * *

Many years before she sent envoys to Constantinople to enquire about the Cross, Radegund showed a keen interest in relics, which she had begun to collect perhaps even while she reigned as Chlothar's queen. Her long-standing interest is implied in a dream she later had, reported by Baudonivia, in which she received divine confirmation that all the relics she had once gathered in Athies had been successfully transferred to her villa in Saix.[43] Radegund had apparently worried about the fate of these relics following her separation from the king, which prevented her from visiting Athies to retrieve them herself. The same passage in Baudonivia's *Life of Radegund* also mentioned, in a separate event, that she sent a priest named Magnus to bring her the relics of St Andrew, along with those of 'many other saints', to be placed above the altar in Saix.[44] The tomb of St Andrew, famed for its miracles, was located in Patras, in the northern Peloponnese, and it is not beyond possibility that Radegund dispatched Magnus across the Mediterranean. But there were options closer to home: the cathedral in Agde, along the Mediterranean coast in Languedoc, possessed relics of the saint, as did a church in the village of Neuvy-le-Roi, just 30 km north of Tours, though these examples were surely not as impressive.[45] Whether or not Magnus travelled as far as

---

[40] Ambrose, *On the Death of Theodosius,* 42 (*de stercore ad regnum*). See Leyerle, 'Mobility and the Traces of Empire', pp. 117–118.

[41] Hillner, *Helena Augusta,* p. 30.

[42] On the circulation of Ambrose's oration *On the Death of Theodosius* in particular, see Liebeschuetz, *Ambrose of Milan,* pp. 43–46 and 174–177.

[43] Baudonivia, *Life of Radegund,* 13.

[44] Baudonivia, *Life of Radegund,* 13.

[45] Gregory of Tours, *Glory of the Martyrs,* 30 and 78.

Greece, Radegund certainly sent other missions to eastern regions, including Constantinople and Jerusalem, once she was residing in Poitiers.[46]

Baudonivia provided the details of one such mission, which predated Radegund's acquisition of the relics of the Cross, though her account is not without its problems.[47] She wrote that Radegund learned of the martyr Mammes, whose body rested in Jerusalem, and she dispatched her physician, Reovalis, to obtain relics of the martyr. The bishop of Jerusalem, agreeing to put the request to the saint himself, went to Mammes's tomb and touched each finger on his right hand, until he felt the little finger pull away. Reovalis returned to Poitiers with this fingerbone, which Baudonivia later saw herself. Yet she must have been confused about the details of this story, even though she wrote while Reovalis still lived. The tomb of St Mammes was not located in Jerusalem, but in Caesarea—and not Caesarea Maritima, to the south of Haifa, nor Caesarea Philippi, in the Golan Heights, but the Caesarea in Cappadocia (present-day Kayseri) 1000 km north of Jerusalem.[48] This confusion has led to doubts that Reovalis set off to find relics of St Mammes at all, but instead that the original objective may have been the fragments the True Cross itself, and that Reovalis returned with St Mammes's fingerbone as a poor replacement only once he had learned that Jerusalem had no desire to part with any part of its shard of sacred wood.[49]

It seems difficult to believe, however, that Radegund had failed to confirm the location and availability of her desired relic beforehand, especially given the extensive preparation required for such a mission. Presumably some members of the expedition had prior experience travelling in the region, and some local knowledge. Reovalis had himself studied medicine in Constantinople, and he therefore must have known Greek, two attributes that made him well suited for the task.[50] Perhaps Baudonivia's confusion might instead be thought to lie in the identity of 'Mammes', a name borne by more than one martyr and similar to the names of others, including that of St Marinus. The martyrdom of Marinus had been described by Rufinus, who located it in Jerusalem (though Eusebius had set it in Caesarea Maritima).[51] Marinus might easily be misread as a variant of 'Mammes', with the medial letters 'rin' mistaken for the letter 'm'. Since Baudonivia claimed that she

---

[46]   Gregory of Tours, *Glory of the Martyrs*, 5.
[47]   Baudonivia, *Life of Radegund*, 14.
[48]   Delehaye, *Les Origines du culte des martyrs*, pp. 174–175.
[49]   Moreira, 'Provisatrix optima', p. 298.
[50]   Gregory of Tours, *Histories*, 10.15.
[51]   Rufinus, *Ecclesiastical History*, 7.15.1.

had seen the saint's fingerbone herself, she may have read the name from a label attached to a reliquary, written in small, partly legible letters. Examples of such relic labels from the Holy Land, known as *eulogia*, have survived from five monasteries in Gaul (though not from Poitiers).[52] This interpretation means that Baudonivia misidentified the saint whose relics Reovalis obtained, but not the objective of the expedition itself.

Reovalis returned with knowledge of the ecclesiastical lore and liturgical practices of Jerusalem.[53] Gregory of Tours, when describing a visit he made to Holy Cross, provided a hint that Radegund may have replicated the liturgical celebrations of the Church of the Holy Sepulchre within her convent. The nuns told him about a miracle that had occurred on Good Friday, in the oratory that housed the fragments of the Cross within their convent.[54] While they kept vigil in the darkness of the night, the nuns witnessed a light appear before the altar. Just a spark, at first, that grew in size and rose in height until it illuminated those in ceaseless prayer. There it remained, until dawn brightened the sky and the beacon faded against the coming daylight. Although clearly intended as a story about a singular miracle, Gregory's description has parallels with a liturgical ceremony, first reported by the pilgrim Egeria, that occurred every evening in the Church of the Holy Sepulchre.[55] Fire was taken from an inextinguishable lamp hanging above the tomb of Christ, which served as the source of light for all the other churches in Jerusalem. This practice may well have been the origin of a later phenomenon, known as the 'Holy Fire', in which a flame miraculously descended upon the Church of the Holy Sepulchre every Holy Saturday, kindling the lamps that hung above the sacred tomb. Radegund occupied the chronological midpoint between these two distant reports, with Egeria writing in the fourth century, and the Holy Fire first appearing in the eighth century *Life of Theodore the Sabaite*.[56] Although a lack of further information prevents firm conclusions, it is difficult to escape the idea that ceremonies associated with the Church of the Holy Sepulchre at Easter, concerning light and lamps, echoed in the paschal miracle of Holy Cross reported by Gregory of Tours.

Gregory opened his account by describing Radegund as 'comparable to Helena in her faith and merit', and he paired Helena's discovery of the Cross

[52] Hen, 'Les Authentiques des reliques de la Terre Sainte en Gaule franque'. I would like to thank Jessica Hodgkinson for her insights into such relic labels.

[53] See Rotman, *Hagiography, Historiography, and Identity*, pp. 97–99.

[54] Gregory of Tours, *Glory of the Martyrs*, 5.

[55] Egeria, *Itinerarium*, 24–25.

[56] Wilkinson, *Jerusalem Pilgrims*, p. 142, n. 16.

with Radegund's reception of it in pieces sent by Justin II and Sophia. Gregory also included information about the nails of the Crucifixion. Helena ordered two nails to be placed in the bridle of the emperor, to increase his power in battle, a third affixed to the head of a statue of her son in Constantinople, to protect the city from harm. Here Gregory followed established stories that appeared in older written sources, including (in variant forms) in Rufinus of Aquileia and Ambrose of Milan.[57] But Gregory also mentioned a fourth nail, which Helena threw into the Adriatic Sea, to forever calm its dangerous waters. Unique in the Latin literature of the period, this claim was so unusual that Gregory even felt compelled to explain why a crucifixion might require four nails at all. He had presumably learned about the fourth nail from the same source that provided him with the other information that he presented in this passage—the nuns of Holy Cross. Although one can only guess how the nuns themselves obtained this information, the most likely origin must be the men Radegund dispatched to Jerusalem, who were surely keen to hear a story of such relevance for travellers and pilgrims headed to the other side of the Adriatic.

The nuns in Holy Cross also believed that Radegund had the power to calm turbulent seas, in what seems to be another parallel with the legacy of Helena. Baudonivia wrote that a miracle had saved the envoys dispatched by Radegund to Constantinople to give thanks to Justin II and Sophia for their generous gift of the Cross. Threatened by violent storms and adrift on rough waters for forty days and nights, the group prepared for death and prayed in despair:

> Our lady Radegund, rescue your servants! Do not let us sink and die while we are in your service. Free us from the peril of death, for the sea is ready to swallow us alive. Whenever you have been invoked in faith, you have been merciful. Show us your mercy now. Save us, lest we perish.[58]

After this supplication, a dove rose from the waters and circled the ship three times. One of the imperilled envoys plucked three tail feathers, dipped them into the sea, and calmed the tempest. Baudonivia wrote that she had seen these feathers herself, which were kept in Holy Cross. The appearance of the dove, together with the duration of forty days and nights, evoked the biblical

---

[57] Ambrose, *On the Death of Theodosius*, 40–51; Rufinus, *Ecclesiastical History*, 9.8. (Also the eastern authors Socrates of Constantinople, Sozomen of Bethelia, and Theodoret of Cyrus.)

[58] Baudonivia, *Life of Radegund*, 17.

story of Noah (Genesis 8:6–12).[59] Baudonivia's account also recalled similar miracles by other holy intercessors who rescued seafarers from storms, including St Martin.[60] But in this example, the sailors called not upon a saint in heaven, but upon the living Radegund, who somehow heard their prayer from her cell in Poitiers.[61] She was therefore more like Jesus, who saved his disciples by dispersing a storm that threatened their boat (Matthew 8:23–27, Mark 4:35–41, and Luke 8:22–25), than other saints who calmed turbulent seas from beyond the grave.

These envoys had offered thanks to Justin II and Sophia for the gift of the Cross, and had presented the imperial couple with a poem, written by Fortunatus, that compared them to Constantine and Helena (even though Justin II and Sophia were husband and wife, rather than mother and son):

> The man resembles Constantine. You, pious woman, Helena. Alike in honour, alike in your love of the Cross. Helena discovered this treasure; you distribute salvation everywhere. What was at first of the East now fills the West.[62]

The inspiration for this somewhat forced comparison seems to have originated in Poitiers itself, rather than in Constantinople, or in any tradition within the literature associated with the imperial court. Other than the association of the emperor Marcian and his wife, Pulcheria, to Constantine and Helena at the Council of Chalcedon in 451, there is little trace of this comparison at work in Byzantine propaganda.[63] The court poet Corippus had made no mention of the emperor and his mother in his poem *In Praise of Emperor Justin the Younger*, which Fortunatus had used as his model. It may be that certain details about their lives, and in particular Constantine's controversial religious policies, made the pair an awkward fit for aggrandizing comparisons to later emperors and empresses. Helena's legacy on its own seems to have fared better as a useful model for imperial women, but even she was not unequivocally described in eastern sources as a saint, and no intercessory miracles were attributed to her.[64] And although local devotion

[59] A similar miracle appears in Fortunatus, *Life of Radegund*, 31.

[60] An example concerning St Martin and his relics appears in Gregory of Tours, *The Virtues of St Martin*, 2.17.

[61] Other examples of Radegund curing people at remove include Baudonivia, *Life of Radegund*, 11; and Fortunatus, *Life of Radegund*, 32.

[62] Fortunatus, *Poems*, appendix 2, lines 67–70.

[63] Whitby, 'Images for Emperors in Late Antiquity', pp. 86–88.

[64] The possible instances of emulation are assembled in Hillner, *Helena Augusta*, pp. 339–346.

at Helena's tomb had started to develop in Rome at least by the close of the sixth century, Radegund's early initiatives, and their subsequent memorialization in Poitiers, clearly contributed, perhaps decisively, to the veneration of Helena as a saint worthy of emulation.[65]

* * *

Maroveus, the bishop of Poitiers, apparently had little desire to assist Radegund in her efforts to become a new Helena. He refused her request to install the fragments of the Cross in her convent, and instead made himself unavailable, riding away to a villa.[66] To Radegund's great embarrassment, the relic had to be kept at a monastery in Tours, until Sigibert arranged for Euphronius, the bishop of Tours, to transfer it to her convent. The nuns in Poitiers probably waited a few months, assuming the relic arrived in the summer, since Euphronius seems to have transferred the relic on 19 November (the date when the event was later celebrated annually). The wait greatly troubled Radegund, who committed herself to extreme fasts and lengthy vigils, while her whole community lamented the insult shown to them by Maroveus. Baudonivia described the episode with indignation:

> The wood, upon which the salvation of the world once hung, came to the city of Poitiers, with a congregation of saints. The bishop of this area should have wished to receive it devoutly, together with all the people. But the Enemy of Humanity acted through his accomplices, so that they wished not to receive the ransom of the world into the city, but to drive it away, which sent Radegund into a state of profound suffering.[67]

In a final rebuke, Baudonivia quoted from II Timothy 2:19, which condemned false teachers as hypocrites who acted wickedly while claiming to know God; they might fool others, but they could not fool Christ. *Dominus novit qui sunt eius*, she wrote, 'the Lord knows his own', in a passage that alluded to John 10:14: 'I am the good shepherd; I know my sheep, and my sheep know me.' Maroveus might wear the ornaments of a bishop, a shepherd of God's flock, but he was, in fact, an agent of the Devil.[68]

---

[65] Hillner, *Helena Augusta*, p. 343.

[66] Gregory of Tours, *Histories*, 9.40.

[67] Baudonivia, *Life of Radegund*, 16.

[68] It is also possible to explain Baudonivia's brief remark, that the bishop of Poitiers 'played the role of the Jews' in this episode, by reference to biblical material alone, although her remark might also indicate her familiarity with the Judas Cyriacus legend (also called the *Inventio crucis*) and its

Maroveus probably found Radegund's presence in Poitiers disruptive of his own authority.[69] She had built her convent in the very heart of the city, next to the cathedral and baptistry.[70] The bishop had little desire to install so great a relic in a convent that cast its shadow over his episcopal complex. The sacred object also risked stealing attention away from another important site, the shrine of St Hilary, located outside the old boundaries of Poitiers, about 500 m west of the ancient amphitheatre.[71] As bishop of Poitiers, Maroveus derived much of his prestige from his association with St Hilary, who (as the local clergy proudly memorialized) had miraculously aided the Frankish victory over the Visigoths at the Battle of Vouillé in 507.[72] Even more troubling, Radegund controlled access to Holy Cross and everything within, and she intended to display the fragments of the True Cross to the public only on special days of celebration, otherwise showing it exclusively to her own nuns and guests of her choosing.[73] Radegund's independence ran counter to ecclesiastical legislation that made bishops responsible for the monasteries located within the walls of their cities.[74] While others might be prepared to accept Radegund's authority as a sign of her sanctity, Maroveus seems to have interpreted it more as an expression of sanctimony.

Gregory of Tours may have regarded Maroveus's plight with some sympathy, even though, in his account of the arrival of the fragments of the Cross, he explicitly blamed Maroveus for the disgraceful treatment of the relic. Gregory had his own personal experience with a particularly troublesome convent in Tours, founded in the atrium of St Martin's basilica by Ingitrude, a woman with connections to the Merovingian dynasty.[75] Gregory expressed the importance of St Hilary for the bishop of Poitiers in his account of a miracle that occurred in Tours during the Feast of St Martin, which Maroveus attended.[76] Elsewhere in his *Histories*, Gregory presented Maroveus as a dedicated pastor who served his flock well.[77] On

distinctively anti-Jewish details. See Drijvers, *Helena Augusta*, pp. 165–185; and, more generally, Drake, *A Century of Miracles*, pp. 115–134.

[69] Bailey, 'Leadership and Community in Late Antique Poitiers', pp. 53–56.
[70] Wood, 'Topographies of Holy Power', p. 153.
[71] Brennan, 'St Radegund', pp. 352–354. On the veneration of St Hilary, see Van Dam, *Saints and Their Miracles*, pp. 28–41.
[72] Gregory of Tours, *Histories*, 2.37.
[73] Rosenwein, 'Inaccessible Cloisters', pp. 192–194.
[74] Scheibelreiter, 'Königstöchter im Kloster', pp. 1–5.
[75] Gregory of Tours, *Histories*, 5.21, 8.2, 9.33, and 10.12.
[76] Gregory of Tours, *The Virtues of St Martin*, 2.44.
[77] Gregory of Tours, *Histories*, 7.24 and 9.30.

a visit to Poitiers, Gregory made sure to first pay his respects at the tomb of St Hilary, before he entered Holy Cross to speak with the nuns and to venerate the fragments of the Cross.[78] He also let an admission slip: he had initially doubted reports that the oil lamps placed before the relics of the Cross bubbled over as a result of the divine power pulsing through the oratory. When he noticed one of the lamps dripping onto the floor, he even chided Abbess Agnes for failing to replace what he presumed to be a cracked vessel, before he realized his error. 'Astonished into silence,' he wrote, 'I then proclaimed the power of the venerable Cross.'

Gregory was in no sense naturally disposed towards scepticism about such matters. His extensive efforts to record the miracles of the saints and the wonders of God included an account of the Sleepers of Ephesus, who awoke after a slumber of nearly two hundred years, and a description of the Lighthouse of Alexandria, held upright by four crabs so large that a man might easily fit within their claws.[79] Gregory's initial incredulity about the miraculous power of Radegund's most prized relic is, therefore, remarkably conspicuous. He cannot have been the only one to regard the claims about the bubbling lamps with some initial suspicion. Indeed, he probably acquired his reservations from others more predisposed to doubt than he was.[80] These sceptics were presumably to be found among the factions in Poitiers that opposed Radegund and her convent, including the clergy of the Basilica of St Hilary, and of course Maroveus himself. Sigibert also had his enemies in the city, who had every reason to question the authenticity of a relic acquired through his support. Even the imperial court in Constantinople suffered from a tarnished reputation in Gaul, especially among the clergy, following the doctrinal disputes that had troubled the middle decades of the sixth century.[81] The presence of such doubts may even have inspired the claim that demons, when faced with the fragments of the Cross, testified to the relic's authenticity before fleeing their hosts—proof intended to silence vocal doubters.

It is also possible that Maroveus expected Radegund to ask for his assistance in authenticating the fragments of the Cross. Quite reasonably so, it should be added, since bishops routinely assumed this role when confronted

[78] Gregory of Tours, *Glory of the Martyrs*, 5.
[79] Gregory of Tours, *Glory of the Martyrs*, 94; Gregory of Tours, *The Passion of the Seven Holy Sleepers*; Gregory of Tours, *On the Course of the Stars*, 8.
[80] See Veneskey, 'Jerusalem Refracted', pp. 64–66.
[81] Most notably the Three Chapters Controversy, on which see Wood, 'The Franks and Papal Theology'.

with an object or site invested with otherworldly power of uncertain origin. Gregory of Langres, for example, instructed the locals around Dijon not to venerate a grand sarcophagus on the assumption that it contained the body of a pagan from Antiquity. He reversed his decision after he learned in a dream that the tomb contained an early Christian martyr.[82] Euphronius of Tours initially refused the request of a local man to bless an oratory that he had constructed over a pair of ancient tombs on a hill. But Euphronius later agreed, after the inhabitants of the graves, the avowed virgins St Maura and St Britta, appeared to him in a dream and urged him to bless the site.[83] (In both instances, the bishops in question likely acquiesced to popular practices.) In Rufinus's account of Helena's journey to Jerusalem, the local bishop, Macarius, authenticated Jesus's cross from among three candidates.[84] Maroveus might have felt that, if Radegund wished to be a new Helena, then he deserved to be a new Macarius. His refusal to install the fragments of the Cross may have resulted in part because Radegund denied him this role.

* * *

Gregory of Tours considered Radegund's clash with Maroveus over the relics of the Cross to be a decisive moment that altered the practices within her convent, and her relationship with the world beyond its walls. In his interpretation, the fallout had led her to obtain and implement the Rule of Caesarius and to enjoin its distinctive regulations:

> After this event, Radegund often sought the good grace of her bishop, but she was not able to obtain it. Moved by necessity, she and Abbess Agnes, whom she had appointed, sought out the city of Arles. They received the Rule of the holy Caesarius and the blessed Caesaria, and they protected themselves under the aegis of the king, undoubtedly because they were unable to find any concern for their protection from the man who ought to have been their pastor.[85]

Gregory's interpretation raises several questions concerning the timing, purpose, and means by which Radegund received the Rule of Caesarius,

<hr/>

[82] Gregory of Tours, *Glory of the Martyrs*, 50 (St Benignus).
[83] Gregory of Tours, *Glory of the Confessors*, 18.
[84] Rufinus, *Ecclesiastical History*, 10.8.
[85] Gregory of Tours, *Histories*, 9.40.

especially since other evidence (detailed below) suggests that she had acquired the Rule long before her clash with Maroveus. Written for the convent of St John, at the behest of its first abbess, Caesaria the Elder, the Rule
enjoined an uncompromising form of seclusion upon the nuns by greatly
restricting both the entry of outsiders and the egress of inmates across the
convent's enclosure.[86] The eventual triumph of strict seclusion as a standard
characteristic of female monasticism ought not to obscure its novelty in
sixth-century Gaul. Gregory, contrary to what might be assumed, probably
thought that strict seclusion was less than ideal. In his writings about exemplary ascetics, he showed remarkably little enthusiasm for the practice,
at least when it restricted lay access to a site of divine intercession located
behind a monastic enclosure.[87] Because of these feelings, Gregory might
have been more comfortable with the idea that Radegund had adopted
strict seclusion in Holy Cross as a result of Maroveus's pastoral failings,
rather than that she had done so as an expression of her own vision for the
institution per se.

Yet her vision it was. Probably before Maroveus even became bishop.
In her letter *Dominis sanctis*, Radegund listed her accomplishments in
Poitiers, placing the adoption of the Rule between the foundation of Holy
Cross and her selection of Agnes as abbess. She certainly considered the
Rule essential to the character of the institution, and her list, though not
chronologically precise, suggests in its sequence of events that Gregory
erred when he dated the adoption of the Rule so much later than the foundation of the convent. Caesaria the Younger, the second abbess of St John's
in Arles, who died around the year 560, wrote a letter to Radegund and
mentioned that she was sending her a copy of the Rule 'so that you may see
how you can keep it'.[88] Unless the letter is considered a forgery, Radegund
must have received the Rule many years before her clash with Maroveus,
which occurred in 569. When several bishops wrote to Radegund in 567
(as detailed in Chapter 4) and pledged to excommunicate any nun who left
her convent in order to marry, they cited her use of the Rule as a justification.[89] Admittedly, Radegund's reception of the rule need not entail her full

---

[86] See Smith, 'Women at the Tomb'.
[87] Dailey, 'Confinement and Exclusion'.
[88] Caesaria the Younger, *Letter to Richild and Radegund*, 1. On the authenticity of the letter, see
Labande-Mailfert, 'Les Débuts de Sainte-Croix', pp. 43–44.
[89] Gregory of Tours, *Histories*, 9.39.

implementation of it in Holy Cross.[90] But an earlier date for the use of the Rule there aligns better with the available evidence, including points of detail not mentioned here, which must otherwise be made to fit an unwieldy (though not impossible) chronology.[91]

Gregory may have misunderstood, intentionally or otherwise, the sequence of events in Holy Cross that unfolded before he arrived in Tours in 573 (after a long clerical career in distant Lyon). Nor would this chronological imprecision be the only such example: on several other occasions in his *Histories*, Gregory reordered events to achieve a desired narrative, carefully curating the relationship between cause and effect to better align with his own authorial agenda.[92] His literary strategies, however, rarely took the form of crude fabrication, and it is unlikely that he wholly invented Radegund's journey to Arles, even if he was wrong about its purpose when he claimed that she had travelled there to obtain the Rule only after her clash with Maroveus. (Nor is there any reason to interpret his words as a merely metaphorical 're-orientation' towards Arles, rather than a physical journey, a reading that is at odds with the overall sense of the passage.[93]) It must be noted that this trip does not conflict with an early adoption of the strict enclosure espoused in the Rule itself, which granted the abbess leeway in applying exceptions to its general strictures, including those concerning egress.[94] Agnes herself travelled across Sigibert's kingdom on multiple occasions, and made stops in Metz and Tours, which cannot all be fitted into the time before the adoption of the Rule in Holy Cross (even if this is thought to have occurred after the clash with Maroveus).[95]

[90] Fortunatus, *Life of Radegund*, 24, described how Radegund adopted several ascetic practices enjoined by Caesarius 'even before she took up the Rule of Arles'.

[91] Fortunatus, *Poems*, 8.1, for example, stated that Radegund took the Rule as her guide. Although of uncertain date, this poem has been associated with the materials sent to Constantinople. See Hen, 'The Church in Sixth-Century Gaul'. The presence of a *posticiaria* in Holy Cross (Baudonivia, *Life of Radegund*, 8), a distinctly Caesarian office, suggests that the convent had long been organized along the lines stipulated in the Rule of Arles (although a later reorganization along such lines remains possible). See Diem, *The Pursuit of Salvation*, pp. 309–310.

[92] The classic example is the sequence of events in the reign of Clovis, on which see Wood, 'Gregory of Tours and Clovis'.

[93] Aigrain, 'Le Voyage de sainte Radegonde à Arles'.

[94] Caesarius, *Rule for Nuns*, 41. The abbess held the keys to the doors (59). The more plentiful evidence from the later medieval period indicates that abbesses left the convent to administer properties and to perform other necessary duties, and that the nuns participated in religious processions and visited the tomb of Radegund, just outside the sacred confines of Holy Cross, on specified holy days. See Edwards, *Superior Women*, pp. 201–228 and 246–247. Although this evidence concerns a later period, it nevertheless cautions against a simplistic interpretation of practices in the sixth century.

[95] Gregory of Tours, *The Virtues of St Martin*, 4.29. The reference to 'Austrasia' in this passage, which clearly includes Tours, indicates a time after the death of Charibert, in late 567 or early 568, when Sigibert ruled the city and Poitiers.

If an alternative reason for the journey is to be identified, it may be that Radegund had been prompted to travel to Arles upon the death of Liliola, the third abbess of St John's. Her successor, Rusticula, was only eighteen years old at the time, and she surely stood to benefit from the queen's support.[96] Indeed, this journey may even be the context in which St John's received its shard of the Cross. Whatever the case, it seems likely that Gregory knew about this journey and its timing, but misunderstood its purpose, substituting his own assumptions about the acquisition of the Rule of Caesarius that were based on a misreading of the consequences of Radegund's clash with Maroveus.

Gregory thought that the Rule, together with the support offered by Sigibert, placed Holy Cross beyond the reach of Maroveus. Royal protection was clearly crucial to the independence of the convent, as Baudonivia also emphasized in her account.[97] But it is not immediately apparent how the Rule prevented the bishop of Poitiers from interfering with the institution. The Rule listed several exceptions to its practice of strict seclusion that allowed men entry, and bishops headed the list (even though the Rule envisioned visits of limited scope and duration).[98] Radegund seems to have avoided the need for outside clergy by recruiting her own priests, who were affiliated to the church dedicated to the Virgin Mary that she constructed just outside the convent's walls.[99] But there was no avoiding Maroveus.

The reason Gregory thought otherwise might be found in a letter, written by Hormisdas, bishop of Rome (r. 514–523).[100] Caesarius of Arles had asked the pope for favours on behalf of the Convent of St John, his sister's foundation, out of concern that future bishops might not regard the institution with a brother's love. Hormisdas agreed that none of Caesarius's successors should be allowed to exercise power over the convent or to disturb the nuns in any way. The future bishops of Arles were granted entry to St John's only in order to fulfil the pastoral needs of the congregation. The letter thus stipulated the precise arrangements that Radegund wished for Poitiers, and that Maroveus seemingly opposed: the obligation to supply pastoral care, without the concomitant authority usually enjoyed by a bishop over the

---

[96] Florentius, *Life of Rusticula*, 7.
[97] Baudonivia, *Life of Radegund*, 16. Weaver, 'The Legacy of Caesarius of Arles'.
[98] Caesarius, *Rule for Nuns*, 36–40.
[99] This statement assumes that practices known from later centuries traced their origins back to Radegund's era. A possible early reference is found in Baudonivia, *Life of Radegund*, 27, which mentions an *abbas basilicae beatae regina*, i.e. the head of the clergy affiliated to Radegund's funerary church.
[100] Hormisdas, *Exulto in domino*.

monastic houses within his diocese. The letter was intended for Arles, of course, and not Poitiers; nor did it comprise part of the Rule itself.[101] But it may have been treated as such, at least by those who stood to benefit. The manner in which the letter survives, at least, suggests that this might have been the case: it exists in a single copy, contained in a ninth-century manuscript, where it appears as an appendix to the Rule.[102] It is tempting to speculate that this arrangement may trace back to Radegund herself, who associated the two documents with each other to strengthen her position in Poitiers. Perhaps Radegund even returned from her visit to Arles with a copy of this very letter—which might well have contributed to Gregory's confusion about the purpose of the journey.

* * *

When the reliquary containing the fragments of the Cross finally arrived in Poitiers, Radegund had the sacred object placed into a larger container, described by Gregory of Tours as a 'silver ark' (or box), and as the 'Ark of the Holy Cross'.[103] This container also held the relics of martyrs and confessors, which Radegund's envoys had obtained on their journeys in the East. It was kept within the oratory used to display the fragments of the True Cross. Like so much in Radegund's convent, it points to the influence of Helena, as she was depicted by Rufinus, who wrote that she had placed part of the wood from the True Cross in a silver box that she left in Jerusalem. Perhaps Reovalis had seen this very object, or a replacement version, during his visit to the Holy City. If so, Radegund may have commissioned the production of her own Ark of the Holy Cross prior to dispatching her envoys to Constantinople. It is impossible to reconstruct how this object may have appeared, but a parallel might be found in a silver box (Figure 5.2) discovered in Chersonesos Taurica on the Crimean Peninsula, which dates to the later part of the reign of Justinian (the predecessor of Justin II). It is decorated with bust medallions of Christ between Peter and Paul on its front, and of the Virgin Mary between two archangels on its back, which recall the medallions that decorate the cross reliquary sent by Justin II and Sophia to Rome (discussed in Chapter 4).[104] In her

[101] Benoit, 'Topographie monastique d'Arles'.

[102] Troyes, Médiathèque Jacques Chirac (bibliothèque municipale), MS 1248, a copy of Benedict of Aniane's *Codex regularum*.

[103] Gregory of Tours, *Glory of the Martyrs*, 5 (*arca argentea*); Gregory of Tours, *Histories*, 10.15 (*arca santae crucis*).

[104] Noga-Banai, 'Architectural Frames for Relics of the True Cross', pp. 65–66.

Figure 5.2 Silver casket (front and back) from Chersonesos Taurica on the Crimean Peninsula. Byzantine production of the early 560s. St Petersburg, State Hermitage Museum, inventory number x-249.

efforts to imitate Helena, Radegund overlooked no detail, and missed no opportunity to reproduce the pious endeavours of the empress in Jerusalem. Radegund had found her model, one fit for a holy queen.

6

Veil of Veils, Holy of Holies

> When her holy, diminutive body came to the end of its life—that ex-
> tended martyrdom for the love of the Lord—the whole of the blessed
> congregation wept and wailed sorrowfully around her deathbed,
> striking their chests with tight fists and stones. They raised their
> voices to heaven and cried, 'Let us not endure so great a loss, O Lord,
> for you are taking our light. Why are you leaving us in darkness?'
>
> Baudonivia, *Life of Radegund*, 21.

Radegund died on 13 August 587, at the age of perhaps sixty-five, in
circumstances that received no special remark from Baudonivia, who
narrated her deathbed scene. Maroveus was not in Poitiers, and Agnes feared
that he might repeat his behaviour from years earlier (when he refused to
install the fragments of the Cross in the convent) and decline to conduct
Radegund's funeral.[1] She turned to Gregory of Tours and urged him to help.
He fulfilled the request, but with greater reserve than Agnes perhaps expected. He waited for three days, in the hope that Maroveus might return and
reconcile with the nuns—a considerable delay in the heat of August. When
he finally gave up waiting and interred Radegund in her funerary church,
he left the tomb unsealed as a gesture of respect for Maroveus, who could
complete the task on his return. Gregory's behaviour indicates the new uncertainty confronting the nuns of Holy Cross now that Radegund no longer
conferred her influence and prestige upon the institution. Perhaps for this
reason, Gregory reassured the nuns that they remained under Radegund's
protection, because the departed queen had now become their advocate at
the celestial court. 'The blessed Radegund left the convent in body, but not in
power; she has been taken up (*adsumpta*) from the world and ensconced in

---

[1] On the ensuing events, see Gregory of Tours, *Histories*, 9.2; Gregory of Tours, *Glory of the
Confessors*, 104; and Baudonivia, *Life of Radegund*, 23–24.

Radegund. E. T. Dailey, Oxford University Press. © Oxford University Press 2023.
DOI: 10.1093/oso/9780197656105.003.0007

heaven.' His words recalled his account of the Assumption of Mary, when the Apostles gathered for the Blessed Virgin's death in the knowledge that 'she must be taken up (*adsumenda*)', before Jesus appeared and entrusted her soul to St Michael the Archangel.[2]

Gregory also told the nuns that he had observed a sign that proved Radegund's soul had entered heaven. When he first saw her body on her funeral bier, 'her holy face shone so brightly that it surpassed the beauty of lilies and roses', a reference to a literary tradition that associated these flowers with Paradise.[3] Elsewhere in his works, Gregory wrote that the scent of roses and lilies miraculously adorned the tombs of saints, marking them as places where heaven encroached upon the fallen world.[4] Jerome, in a work likely available in Holy Cross, had also deployed a floral metaphor that associated specific flowers with types of female saints, the white lily signifying the virgin, the red rose signifying the martyr.[5] By mentioning lilies and roses, Gregory suggested that, even though Radegund had been married and died a natural death, she had attained the honour of a virgin and a martyr through her deeds. In describing the same scene, Baudonivia went a step further and wrote that, in addition to the fragrant smell, Radegund's body also 'seemed to have the appearance of an angel in human form'. She added that, when Gregory saw this angelic visage, he was 'struck with fear and trembling, as if he were standing in the presence of the blessed Mother of the Lord herself'.[6] Her words recalled the biblical Letter to the Philippians, in which St Paul told his audience to obey him in his absence, and then warned them to *work out your salvation with fear and trembling* (Philippians 2:12). Radegund's absence provided no reason for the nuns to obey her instructions or example any less.

Baudonivia also reported that, on the day Radegund died, stonemasons at work on a mountain quarry overheard a conversation among several angels, who had descended to the lower reaches of the sky, and who were tasked with carrying Radegund's soul to heaven. 'What are you doing?', asked one angel of the others, who were apparently idling, 'bring her to me'. Concerned that this rebuke might reach the 'ears of the Lord', they replied: 'It has already been done, so what are we to do? Paradise has received her, where she is glorified

---

[2] Gregory of Tours, *Glory of the Martyrs*, 4.
[3] Brennan, 'Deathless Marriage and Spiritual Fecundity'.
[4] Gregory of Tours, *Glory of the Confessors*, 40.
[5] Jerome, *Letters*, 54.14. Fortunatus, *Poems*, 8.6, repeated this imagery.
[6] Baudonivia, *Life of Radegund*, 23.

with God.'[7] Radegund had entered the celestial realm already, taken into heaven immediately like the biblical figures Enoch (Genesis 5:24) and Elijah (II Kings 2:11). Baudonivia then declared:

> We believe that we are not separated from her, even though she reigns with the one whom she wished to please. For us, her death is a source of awe rather than anguish. We have lost our mother and *domina* in this present world, but we have gained an intercessor in the kingdom of Christ.[8]

Radegund now reigned in heaven alongside Christ, her celestial bridegroom, the King of Kings and Lord of Lords.[9]

Baudonivia had already presented this marriage with Christ to her audience, in the form of a vision Radegund received in the year before her death. A youthful, wealthy, and beautiful man asked Radegund why she sought to grow nearer to him through so many prayers, tears, and punishments, when he was already by her side: 'You, my precious gem, must know that you are the prime jewel in the crown upon my head.'[10] The man, of course, was Christ himself, who revealed to Radegund the union he planned for her in the life to come. An object of devotion believed to mark this event, a stone bearing the footprint of Christ known as the Pas de Dieu, survives. Baudonivia made no mention of the object, a clear indication that it represents a much later development, when the imprint (itself formed in prehistoric times) must have been uncovered in the later Middle Ages and associated with this moment in Radegund's life.[11] The growth of this legend, however, reflects the expectations of those who read Baudonivia's *Life of Radegund*, including her contemporaries in the early seventh century, who surely wished for reasons to believe that their holy queen had been crowned in heaven and sat alongside Christ enthroned. Baudonivia's claim noticeably outdid the assertion of Venantius Fortunatus, who presented Radegund, in the aftermath of her death, as something like the eternal bride of St Martin, in the poem he offered to Brunhild and Childebert II (discussed in Chapter 4).[12] Baudonivia's story represents an answer to the question, posed to the nuns of Holy Cross upon

---

[7] This rendering applies a different punctuation to the text than what is found in the *Monumenta Germaniae historica* edition.

[8] Baudonivia, *Life of Radegund*, 22.

[9] This title was applied to Jesus in I Timothy 6:15 and Revelation 17:14 and 19:16.

[10] Baudonivia, *Life of Radegund*, 20.

[11] The classic study is Baudouin, 'Le Pas de Dieu'.

[12] Fortunatus, *Poems*, 10.7.

Radegund's death, as to whether or not life in the convent could continue unchanged in the absence of the holy queen. She emphasized that Radegund remained present in spirit, precisely because the manner in which she had guided her institution in life was particular to her, dependent upon her unique status and her distinct vision. In asserting that Radegund need not be replaced, Baudonivia admitted that she was irreplaceable.

* * *

After placing Radegund in her tomb, Gregory returned to Holy Cross, where Agnes and her nuns showed him the departed queen's monastic cell, her prayer mat, a book she read, and the spindles she used for weaving.[13] Gregory used his account of this experience, in his *Glory of the Confessors*, to memorialize certain aspects of Radegund's character by choosing to mention objects that held significance in the context of the Rule of Caesarius. The mat and book, for example, signified Radegund's devotion and contemplation, which recalled the Rule's instructions to pray ceaselessly and read frequently.[14] The textile instruments demonstrated Radegund's humble piety, a reference to the Rule's stipulation that nuns spin and weave wool, and produce their own simple clothing.[15] By making such comparisons, Gregory provided an image of Radegund as a devout adherent to her Rule, and suggested that her nuns ought to follow her example. But his portrayal masked the more complex relationship Radegund had with her Rule, replacing her genuine example with a version more easily, and less controversially, replicable by her followers. Several hints within the sources indicate that Radegund regarded the Rule of Caesarius as a set of guidelines from which she might exempt herself, as befit a queen.[16] Some of these hints appear between the lines of Fortunatus and Baudonivia's hagiographies, while others emerge from a report produced by the bishops who investigated the practices within Holy Cross two years after Radegund's death, in the aftermath of a scandalous uprising (detailed in Chapter 7).

Radegund wove clothing not only for herself and her nuns, but also for the emperor Justin II, when she sent him a garment as a gesture of gratitude for the fragments of the Cross.[17] Baudonivia described this garment as

---

[13] Gregory of Tours, *Glory of the Confessors*, 104.
[14] Caesarius, *Rule for Nuns*, 15, 17, 18, 21.
[15] Caesarius, *Rule for Nuns*, 16 and 27.
[16] Scheibelreiter, 'Königstöchter im Kloster', pp. 20–27 and 32–37.
[17] Baudonivia, *Life of Radegund*, 17. The passage seems to imply that Radegund wove the *simplex vestimentum* herself, though that is not expressly stated.

'simple' and implied that its value came from the person who made it, rather than the material from which it had been made. Nonetheless, Caesarius had never envisioned nuns producing clothing for the emperor, an act that changed their weaving from a sign of humility to one that also emphasized their proximity to worldly power. Caesarius also stipulated that no one in the monastery, the abbess included, was permitted to have her own slave (*ancilla propria*) in her personal service (although the convent itself might own slaves), and that any acts of personal service were to be fulfilled by the younger nuns instead.[18] Radegund, who had enjoyed a full entourage of servants as Chlothar's queen, apparently established similar arrangements at her villa in Saix.[19] In describing the arrangements in Holy Cross, Baudonivia mentioned female domestic slaves, *famulae*, who served Radegund, though perhaps in a manner technically distinct from the *ancillae* forbidden in Caesarius's vision.[20] Radegund had allowed those who served the convent, including the *famulae*, to use a newly constructed bathhouse, because she feared the toxic fumes of the fresh mortar might harm her nuns.[21] After Radegund died, one of these enslaved women, Vinopergia, made the mistake of sitting on 'the throne of the blessed queen' (*cathedra*, a word that referred to a 'chair' invested with authority). She suffered the 'judgement of God' and burned for three days, until she was forgiven by the departed saint and restored to health.[22]

It may be that these enslaved women were not the personal attendants of Radegund herself, and therefore fell outside the category of slaves specifically forbidden by the Rule of Caesarius, perhaps in the same way that baths were also allowed for the purpose of treating illness, but not for mere pleasure.[23] Such technical distinctions, however, seem less satisfying an explanation for these exceptional practices than Radegund's own extraordinary status as queen, a point that recurs in numerous examples. Thus Radegund hosted laypersons within her convent and set banquets for noblemen, though she did not partake in the luxurious food herself.[24] This approach displayed her

---

[18] Caesarius, *Rule for Nuns*, 7. See Clark, *Women in Late Antiquity*, pp. 102–105; and Bailey, 'Handmaidens of God'.

[19] Fortunatus mentioned *puellae* (a term that literally meant 'girls', but often applied to enslaved women) who helped Radegund dress in his *Life of Radegund*, 9, while a *puella* appears in Saix in chapter 18. Baudonivia, *Life of Radegund*, 2, mentioned domestic slaves who travelled with Radegund when she reigned as a queen.

[20] Baudonivia, *Life of Radegund*, 2.8.

[21] Gregory of Tours, *Histories*, 10.16.

[22] Baudonivia, *Life of Radegund*, 12.

[23] Caesarius, *Rule for Nuns*, 31.

[24] Effros, *Creating Community with Food and Drink*, pp. 45–54.

elite status, as the host, alongside her other-worldliness, as an ascetic who declined the lavish food and wine on offer.[25] The poetry of Fortunatus reveals that Radegund served lavish food, including chicken, beef, goose, and seafood; vegetables accompanied with butter and honey; cheese and thick cream; and fruit presented in decorated baskets, served with nuts.[26] The Rule of Caesarius expressly forbade the nuns from providing such meals to outsiders, including ecclesiastical figures and secular authorities, male and female alike. The exception, 'unless they happen to be great in their pursuit of a holy life', can hardly have served as a sufficient justification, though for Radegund no justification was apparently required.[27]

This image of Radegund setting feasts for invited guests calls to mind the meals of the secular elite and, indeed, those of royal courts.[28] Avitus of Vienne satirized the meals celebrated at the court of Sigismund of Burgundy (d. 524), to which guests arrived with extreme expectations, such as their hope to dine on peacock wrapped in mince meat. They also displayed extreme gluttony, consuming more than what two mules might carry on their backs, before boasting of their experience to others.[29] In describing the royal court of Theodoric II (d. 466), the aristocrat Sidonius Apollinaris noted that such heavy meals were accompanied by even weightier discussion: they held important political value, not only to display status, but also to exert influence and nurture relationships.[30] Sidonius added that Theodoric played table games with his guests, who found this to be the best time to request favours. Radegund is also known to have played table games in Holy Cross, an activity that was continued after her death by Leubovera, Agnes's successor as abbess, who struggled to defend the practice in the face of criticism.[31] This form of entertainment, though not expressly forbidden by the Rule, certainly went against its spirit. Caesarius himself had preached against table games in the sermons he directed at his congregation in Arles.[32]

[25] For examples of holy ascetics declining food in courtly contexts, see Wood, 'The Development of the Visigothic Court'. I wish to express my sincere gratitude to Ian Wood for providing me with a copy of this article in draft.

[26] Tyrell, *Merovingian Letters and Letter Writers*, pp. 149–155.

[27] Caesarius, *Rule for Nuns*, 39.

[28] Rossiter, 'Convivium and Villa in Late Antiquity'.

[29] Avitus of Vienne, *Letters*, 86 (with the notes of Shanzer and Wood on pp. 279–281).

[30] Sidonius Apollinaris, *Letters*, 1.2.4–9.

[31] Gregory of Tours, *Histories*, 10.16 (*ad tabulam ipsa luserit*).

[32] Caesarius, *Sermons*, 116A.2, 193.1.

Radegund received a gift of silk skeins for weaving from one of her few surviving relatives in Constantinople.[33] The Rule of Caesarius forbade nuns from weaving silk, not only when producing their own clothing, but even when making altar cloth.[34] Rather than reject this gift, however, Radegund instructed Fortunatus to offer thanks in a poem that he sent to the imperial court.[35] Her actions set a precedent that survived her death. When Leubovera received a purple mantle made of silk, she had some of the fabric made into clothing for her niece, and the rest turned into an altar cloth.[36] Purple, a favourite colour of the emperors, signified wealth and status because the dye came from the secretions of the Murex snail, harvested only at great expense.[37] Unsurprisingly, the Rule forbade its use.[38] In his sermons, Caesarius repeatedly referred to purple cloth as a symbol of luxury and excess, an assertion he repeated in a letter to the nuns of St John's convent.[39] Purple also appeared in the biblical parable of Lazarus, a beggar who ate crumbs from the table of a rich man clothed in the colour. When they both died, the rich man suffered torment in the underworld, while Lazarus enjoyed the blessing of Abraham's embrace. The rich man pleaded for forgiveness, but Abraham told him that his contrition had come too late. *A great chasm has been placed between you and us, so that those who want to go to you from here cannot, nor can you come from there to here* (Luke 16:19–31). Undoubtedly Radegund had refused to wear the colour herself, but perhaps, like Leubovera, she too had adorned the altars of Holy Cross with purple cloth. This ornamentation signified the sovereign grandeur of God, yet any such association with royal majesty also reflected upon the convent itself and its inhabitants.[40]

Fortunatus sent Radegund a bouquet of crocuses and violets, in the colours of gold and purple, and included a message that interpreted the gift as a representation of the wealth she had rejected in her efforts to secure greater riches in heaven.[41] Fortunatus was certainly right to believe that Radegund had renounced her personal wealth, but his message overlooked

---

[33] Fortunatus, *Poems*, appendix 3, lines 17–18. Silk production began in the Byzantine Empire during the reign of Justinian. See Procopius, *History of the Wars*, 8.17.1–8.

[34] Del Fiat Miola, 'Permitted and Prohibited Textiles', pp. 100–101.

[35] Fortunatus, *Poems*, appendix 3, lines 17–18.

[36] Gregory of Tours, *Histories*, 10.16.

[37] Matteo, 'Alchemical Textiles'.

[38] Caesarius, *Rule for Nuns*, 55 and 60.

[39] Caesarius, *Sermons*, 5.4, 27.2, 31.4, 51.2, 97.4, 144.2, 151.8, 164, 165, 208.1, 215.4, 224.2. Caesarius, *Letters*, 21.8, 21.10.

[40] Radegund kept an altar in her own monastic cell, according to Gregory of Tours, *Glory of the Confessors*, 104.

[41] Fortunatus, *Poems*, 8.8. Curta, 'Merovingian and Carolingian Gift Giving', p. 680.

how she had endowed much of that wealth to Holy Cross. The convent itself, of course, remained very much hers in every practical sense. In her letter *Dominis sanctis*, Radegund discussed the convent's vast resources, which included the donations of pious benefactors, the personal wealth handed over by each nun upon entry, and the properties given to her by Chlothar and his sons (Radegund transferred these properties to the ownership of the convent). If Fortunatus felt justified in describing this transfer of wealth as a renunciation, it was because Radegund personally adhered to an austere way of life. But even though she lived like Lazarus, she still shared the anxieties of the rich man. The letter Radegund received from Caesaria the Younger noted her abundant resources and urged her to help the poor as much as possible, in order that she 'store up treasure in heaven' for herself.[42] This phrase echoed Jesus's admonition in the Gospels: *Lay up for yourselves treasures in heaven, where neither moth nor rust destroy, where thieves do not break in and steal. For where your treasure is, there your heart will be also.* (Matthew 6:19–21). Gregory of Tours quoted this biblical verse in his rebuke of Empress Sophia, when she filled up the imperial coffers at the expense of the poor. That Radegund faced the same temptation as a Byzantine empress, however more charitable she may have been, suggests that her convent functioned rather like her own royal treasury.

Radegund kept an *archiatrus*, or personal physician, in Holy Cross—a man named Reovalis, the same official she dispatched to the East in search of relics, who later became a priest. Both Gregory of Tours and Baudonivia described Reovalis with this term, derived from the Greek *arkhiatrós* (literally, 'chief physician') and applied to the physicians of the royal court. Reovalis had studied medicine in Constantinople, where he witnessed procedures that included castration, an operation he subsequently performed on a man in Poitiers at Radegund's instruction. This procedure led to accusations, at least after Radegund's death, that Holy Cross housed eunuchs in a manner that mimicked the arrangements of the Byzantine court.[43] Reovalis insisted that the man had suffered from a disease of the testes, and that the operation had a medical justification. Although there is no reason to doubt his explanation, it does not entirely account for why the eunuch maintained an association with the convent in subsequent years. Indeed, the mere fact that Holy Cross

[42] Caesaria the Younger, *Letter to the Holy Ladies Richild and Radegund*.
[43] Gregory of Tours, *Histories*, 10.15 (*imperialis ordo*).

possessed a physician, trained in Constantinople and capable of rendering a man into a eunuch, was itself enough to evoke the idea of imperial pomp.

Whether or not Radegund wholly shunned such associations is unclear, and she may well have not. It is entirely possible that she felt the presence of a eunuch befit the particular nature of Holy Cross. In his poem *In Praise of Emperor Justin the Younger*, Corippus described the eunuch Kallinikos, the grand chamberlain of the emperor Justinian, in a manner that echoed the imagery in the Book of Isaiah, which linked the eunuch's imperial court service to the celestial service of the heavenly court.[44] This poem was known to Fortunatus, and presumably also to Radegund and her nuns, and there is no reason to assume that they were necessarily unreceptive to such a comparison. *For thus the Lord says to eunuchs, who observe my Sabbath, who choose as I wish, and who uphold my covenant: 'I will give him a place within my temple and its walls and [. . .] an everlasting name that shall never perish* (Isaiah 56:4–5). In another important passage of scripture, found in the Acts of the Apostles, Philip the Evangelist was dispatched by an angel to an Ethiopian eunuch, the treasurer to the Queen of the Ethiopians, whom he found on the road to Gaza, sitting next to his chariot and reading the Book of Isaiah. The eunuch listened to Philip's preaching about Jesus and asked to be baptized, rising from the waters and departing in a spirit of joy (Acts 8:26–40). This passage cannot have escaped the attention of Radegund and her nuns, and it may well have even served to encourage her to elevate the eunuch in Poitiers to a position of importance in the administration of Holy Cross, just as it also influenced practices within the imperial court.[45]

The position held by Fortunatus merits attention as well. The unusual aspect of his presence in Holy Cross is easy to overlook, since he has become so closely associated with Radegund in modern scholarship as a source of information about her life. But his activity reveals that Radegund kept her own poet in her service, whom she had originally received as a gift from the royal court of Sigibert and Brunhild.[46] Like Reovalis, Fortunatus became a priest (and in the years after Radegund's death, bishop of Poitiers), which perhaps afforded him greater access to the sacred confines of the convent.[47]

---

[44] Corippus, *In Praise of Emperor Justin the Younger*, 1.86–88. See Sidéris, 'Eunuchs of Light', pp. 165–166.

[45] See Ringrose, *The Perfect Servant*, pp. 206–209; and more generally, Tougher, *The Eunuch in Byzantine History and Society*, pp. 36–53. Kuefler, *The Manly Eunuch*, pp. 258–260, discussed the connection between the two passages, but confused Philip the Evangelist with Philip the Apostle.

[46] Brennan, 'The Career of Venantius Fortunatus'.

[47] George, *Venantius Fortunatus*, pp. 212–214.

In one of his poems, he described himself as an 'agent' (*agens*) for the abbess, Agnes, which might mean that he acted on behalf of the institution in an official manner.[48] He wrote poems to further the interests of Radegund and her nuns, in a capacity much greater than that of a mere amanuensis, a personal secretary often kept by elite patrons to draft correspondence according to either dictation or set formulae.[49] The poems Fortunatus composed on Radegund's behalf, including those he wrote in her name and voice, were literary productions that featured his own distinctive vocabulary and style, even though they aligned with her perspective and received her approval.[50] They were, in a sense, the result of what might be described as a collaboration between Radegund and Fortunatus, one in which she actively participated, as a superior holding her court poet to a set of expectations.[51]

Fortunatus developed a friendship with Radegund, even though he never used the word 'friendship' (*amicitia*) to describe their relationship, since that term might wrongly imply an equal status between himself and the queen.[52] An extensive collection of what might be described as his personal correspondence to Radegund and Agnes has survived.[53] These poems reveal a close relationship that included time spent in one another's presence and the exchange of gifts, interactions that eventually gave rise to rumours about Fortunatus and Agnes. (No one dared accuse Radegund.) He reassured Agnes that he regarded her as a sister and felt only a 'divine affection' for her, uncorrupted by any desires of the flesh.[54] Fortunatus added that these 'hurtful words' had caused him distress, and he seems to have been excluded from their company for a time, although he was eventually allowed back.[55] His denial offers the only indication in the sources that he may have had

---

[48] Fortunatus, *Poems*, 11.4.3. Tardi, *Fortunat*, p. 85; Brennan, 'The Career of Venantius Fortunatus', pp. 69–70. Fortunatus, *Life of Radegund*, 34, identified a certain Andered as Radegund's *agens*. Baudonivia, *Life of Radegund*, 7, described Proculus as Radegund's *agens*. This interpretation of Fortunatus as Agnes's 'agent' has somewhat fallen out of favour, though it has much to commend it.

[49] Ferrante, 'What Really Matters', pp. 180–181.

[50] Brennan, 'The Disputed Authorship of Fortunatus'. The poems written by Fortunatus in Radegund's name were not, in fact, written by the queen herself, as has occasionally been asserted (e.g. Cherewatuk, 'Germanic Echoes in Latin Verse'). For a definitive refutation of this view, see Williard, 'Friendship in the Works of Venantius Fortunatus', pp. 144–151.

[51] Stevenson, *Women Latin Poets*, pp. 87–89; Wasyl, 'An Aggrieved Heroine in Merovingian Gaul', pp. 64–67.

[52] On the friendship between Fortunatus, Radegund, and Agnes, see Williard, 'Friendship in the Works of Venantius Fortunatus'; and Roberts, *The Humblest Sparrow*, pp. 283–315.

[53] Roberts, 'Venantius Fortunatus and Gregory of Tours', p. 35.

[54] Fortunatus, *Poems*, 11.6.

[55] Fortunatus, *Poems*, 11.7, appendix 10 and appendix 24. Roberts, *The Humblest Sparrow*, p. 307.

any romantic feelings towards her.[56] But the rumours, whatever their basis, call attention to the dissonance between Agnes's behaviour and the Rule of Caesarius, which never envisioned such close ties between a nun and a man who was not her relative. Any man admitted into the sacred confines of the convent operated under clear restrictions—even priests, who were allowed access only to perform strictly necessary liturgical functions. The Rule instructed nuns to guard their reputation and to select men for this purpose who were of a sufficient age and reputation as to be beyond suspicion.[57] Fortunatus's access to Holy Cross not only exceeded these limitations, but his presence alone, as a court poet and personal agent, represented a luxury more befitting a royal palace than a secluded monastery.

A royal physician, a court poet, feasts and banquets, table games, notable guests, slaves and attendants, a throne, and perhaps a eunuch—Holy Cross, though a monastery, had all the features of a royal court. There is no reason to believe that such arrangements, in the eyes of Radegund and her nuns, detracted from the holiness of the institution itself. Indeed, Radegund clearly imbued Holy Cross with a deep sense of sacrality, which elevated the convent above even other religious houses in Gaul. Precedent for this union of sacred and secular prestige might be found, somewhat surprisingly, in the imperial palace of Constantinople itself. In his poem *In Praise of Emperor Justin the Younger*, Corippus presented the abode of the emperor and empress as 'another heaven', which featured its own inner sanctum concealed by veils.[58] Visitors fortunate enough to be invited into the imperial presence prostrated themselves as the veils were pulled back to reveal the emperor, crowned with a diadem and seated on a bejewelled throne of purple and gold.[59] The empress also seems to have unveiled herself in a similar way, as suggested by two surviving diptychs that show tied veils alongside a figure usually thought to be the empress Ariadne (d. 515), but who might instead be identified as Sophia, the wife of Justin II who dispatched the fragments of the Cross to Radegund.[60] Deeply sacralized, secluded from the pollution of the wider

---

[56] Bezzola, *Les Origines et la formation de la littérature courtoise*, vol. 1, p. 60, was prepared to consider the question. The novel *Women in the Wall* by Julia O'Faolain fully embraced the possibility. I would like to thank Neil Christie for calling this novel to my attention and kindly gifting me his copy.

[57] Caesarius, *Rule for Nuns*, 36.

[58] Corippus, *In Praise of Emperor Justin the Younger*, 3.194–259.

[59] Corippus, *In Praise of Emperor Justin the Younger*, 3.255.

[60] The diptychs are Florence, Museo Nazionale del Bargello, inventory number 24; and Vienna, Kunsthistorisches Museum, inventory number X.39 of the Antikensammlung. McClanan, *Representations of Early Byzantine Empresses*, pp. 168–178. Corippus, *In Praise of Emperor Justin the*

world, and evocative of heaven itself, the imperial court served as a model for Radegund as she sought to define the character of her convent and, indeed, the very nature of monastic space.

* * *

Euphronius of Tours carried the fragments of the Cross into Radegund's convent and placed them in an oratory, a shrine dedicated to the imperial gift, in a liturgical procession that featured burning incense, glowing tapers, and chanted psalms. The pageantry expressed not only the solemnity due a holy relic, but also the regality befitting the kingship of Christ.[61] Fortunatus set his *Pange lingua*, a poem almost certainly composed for this occasion, to a meter associated with the marching chants of the Roman legions.[62] It described the Cross as a *tropaeum*, a wooden pillar adorned with the weapons of a vanquished enemy, in a metaphorical reference to Jesus's victory over death, which he had won through his Crucifixion.[63] In another poem, the *Vexilla regis*, Fortunatus described the Cross as a pole holding aloft a royal banner: 'O glorious and glittering tree, adorned with the purple of a king, chosen worthy to touch so holy a body with your trunk.'[64] The symbolism recalled the biblical narrative in which Pontius Pilate ordered a panel to be affixed to the Cross that read, 'Jesus of Nazareth, King of the Jews'. The procession itself likewise evoked a Roman *adventus* ceremony, in which the emperor was greeted and escorted into a city in great honour—a ritual that had, since the days of Constantine, acquired a distinctly Christian character, melding elements of the old Roman triumph with Jesus's entry into Jerusalem.[65] *The crowd of disciples began to praise God rejoicefully, in a loud voice, for all the miracles they had seen, saying: 'Blessed is the king who comes in the name of the Lord.'* (Luke 19:37–38).

No complete description of the oratory of the True Cross survives, although incidental references mention oil lamps, altar cloth, and wreaths of flowers in gold, violet, blue, green, white, and red.[66] The Rule of Caesarius

Younger, 1.158, expressly described senators prostrating themselves before the emperor and empress alike. See also Radle, 'The Veiling of Women in Byzantium'.

[61] Gregory of Tours, *Histories*, 9.40.
[62] Fortunatus, *Poems*, 2.2. Norberg, 'Le *Pange lingua* de Fortunat'.
[63] Fortunatus, *Poems*, 2.2, lines 1–3.
[64] Fortunatus, *Poems*, 2.6, lines 17–20. Szövérffy, 'Venantius Fortunatus'.
[65] Liverani, 'Saint Peter's and the City of Rome'.
[66] Gregory of Tours, *Glory of the Martyrs*, 5 (oil lamps). Gregory of Tours, *Histories*, 10.16 (altar cloth). Fortunatus, *Poems*, 8.7 (wreaths of flowers).

stipulated that oratories were to be decorated simply, though there is no guarantee that this regulation was followed for a space containing so sacred a relic.[67] Radegund apparently adorned the oratory with a remarkable feature: two large woven hangings, or 'veils' (*vela*), on which acrostic poems written by Fortunatus in honour of the Cross were displayed.[68] One poem, *On the Sign of the Cross*, featured lines of poetry that emerged from the field of the poem to form the shape of a *Prankenkreuz*, a straight-sided cross that terminated in wider feet (or 'paws', to borrow from categories used to describe later heraldic designs).[69] The other poem, which is untitled and incomplete in the surviving manuscripts, presented two perpendicular lines of readable text that intersected to form a simple cross. These large veils presumably concealed the fragments of the Cross and were pulled back to reveal the relic as occasion required. Gregory of Tours wrote that the fragments of the Cross were displayed on Wednesdays and Fridays.[70] In arrangements likely inspired by those in Holy Cross, Gregory hung white veils embroidered with purple and adorned with crosses in an oratory in Tours, which housed a silk cloth that had been used to wrap the wood of the True Cross in Jerusalem.[71] Occasional references in the sources indicate that veils were used similarly elsewhere in Gaul.[72]

Excavations at the site of Holy Cross in 1962 uncovered a space identified as the oratory of the Cross: a 5.5 m square room with an eastern apse that connected to a smaller room, 1.9 × 1.8 m, which had its own entrance on its southern side (Figure 6.1).[73] The smaller room has been interpreted as the shrine that housed the fragments of the Cross, with the larger space representing the oratory dedicated to the veneration of the great relic. Although it is impossible to reconstruct the precise arrangements of this space from the surviving foundations, it is not difficult to imagine an opening between the two rooms, concealed by veils, with oil lamps (mentioned by Gregory) hanging along the curved wall of the apse, and an altar beneath. Although an unusual (perhaps even unique) layout for a holy shrine in Gaul,

---

[67] Caesarius, *Rule for Nuns*, 45.

[68] Fortunatus, *Poems*, 2.4 and 2.5. This attractive hypothesis was advanced by Brennan, 'Weaving with Words'.

[69] Oswald, *Lexikon der Heraldik*, p. 312.

[70] Gregory of Tours, *Glory of the Martyrs*, 5.

[71] Gregory of Tours, *Glory of the Martyrs*, 5; Fortunatus, *Poems*, 2.3.

[72] Such veils appear in Gregory of Tours, *Glory of the Martyrs*, 22; and Gregory of Tours, *The Virtues of St Martin*, 2.60. Similar references, of a later date, also appear in the *Liber pontificalis*.

[73] Eygun, 'Circonscription de Poitiers'. On this and earlier excavations, see Labande-Mailfert, 'Poitiers: abbaye Sainte-Croix'.

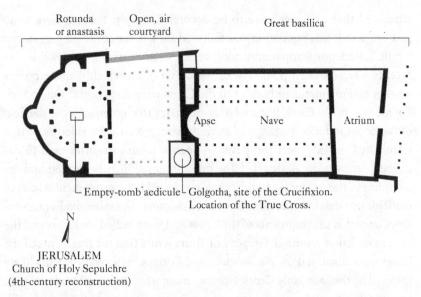

Figure 6.1 The Church of the Holy Sepulchre, Jerusalem. Produced by Erik Goosmann, with reference to Kelley, *The Church of the Holy Sepulchre*, and Ousterhout, 'Architecture as Relic', from the excavations of Virgilio C. Corbo.

the design of the oratory has important parallels with two other shrines associated with veneration of the Cross: a church in Rome dedicated to 'Holy Jerusalem' (*sancta Hierusalem*, later known as Santa Croce in Gerusalemme) (Figure 6.2);[74] and a church in Ravenna, built in the fifth century and also known as *sancta Hierusalem* (and later, Santa Croce) (Figure 6.3).[75] The similar architectural arrangements in these two churches, and in the oratory in Holy Cross, resulted from their shared intention to represent the spatial relationship (if not the precise layout) within the Church of the Holy Sepulchre in Jerusalem (Figure 6.4). In this ecclesiastical complex, a courtyard joined two sites of profound significance, the Empty Tomb (contained in an aedicule, surrounded by a rotunda, known as the Anastasis), and Golgotha, the site of

---

[74] Noga-Banai, 'Relocation to the West'. *Liber pontificalis*, 34.22, mentioned this church when it claimed that Constantine I had converted part of Helena's Sessorian Palace into a basilica as a *memoria* for the Cross. See de Blaauw, 'Jerusalem in Rome'. A version of the *Liber pontificalis* was known to Gregory of Tours, and perhaps also to Radegund.

[75] Noga-Banai, 'Architectural Frames for Relics of the True Cross', p. 67. Fortunatus unquestionably knew this church from his time in Ravenna.

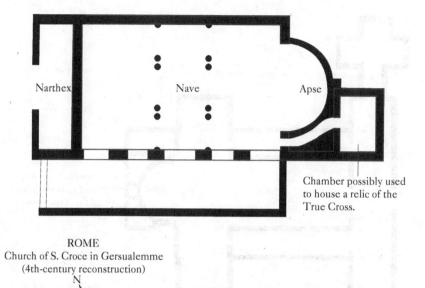

ROME
Church of S. Croce in Gersualemme
(4th-century reconstruction)

Figure 6.2 The Church of Santa Croce in Gerusalemme, Rome. Produced by Erik Goosmann, with reference to Krautheimer, *Early Christian and Byzantine Architecture*.

the Crucifixion, located within a great basilica, behind the southern wall of the apse.[76]

The fourth-century pilgrim Egeria reported that silken veils were hung in the Church of the Holy Sepulchre in front of the site of the Crucifixion, and in front of the empty tomb, located across an enclosed courtyard (and possibly represented in Holy Cross by Radegund's cell, discussed below).[77] Within Radegund's convent, the significance of the Crucifixion was expressed in the acrostic poems woven onto the veils that concealed the fragments of the Cross. Fortunatus's poem *On the Sign of the Cross*, for example, began with the creation of Adam and Eve, their sin, and their expulsion from Paradise, before it turned to the Incarnation, the sacrifice of the Cross, and the redemption of humanity. The text that formed the prominent *Prankenkreuz* concluded: 'We place our true hope in the wood, in the blood of the lamb, in the nails, in the sweet tree of the field. With you we are provided a new

[76] Kelley, *The Church of the Holy Sepulchre*.
[77] Egeria, *Itinerarium*, 25.8.

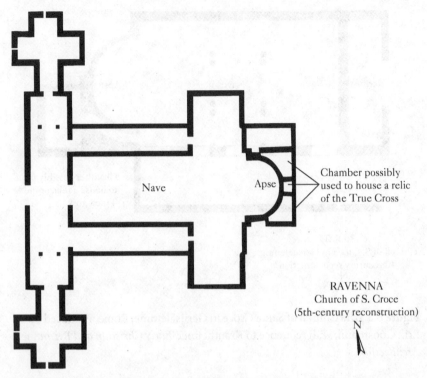

Figure 6.3 The Church of Santa Croce, Ravenna. Produced by Erik Goosmann, with reference to David, 'Potere imperiale'.

life' (Figure 6.5). The other (untitled) acrostic poem mentioned, in the vertical text on its left and right borders, the salvation of believers and the forgiveness of sins. The two lines on its horizontal and vertical axes formed a cross through the intersection of the words 'lamb' (*agnus*) and 'cross' (*crux*). The horizontal line mentioned the faith of Abraham, a reference to the biblical patriarch's acceptance of God's command to sacrifice his son, which was interpreted as prefiguring the Crucifixion. The vertical line referenced 'the temples of God, enriched with the Cross and adorned with the veil' (Figure 6.6).

The phrase 'temples of God' (*templa Dei*) might apply to any shrine or church, but in this context the reference invited the reader to contemplate the biblical *Templum Dei*, the Temple of Jerusalem, and the unique place this building had in the history of salvation. It also called to mind other buildings that intentionally invoked the biblical Temple, including the Church of the Holy Sepulchre and the oratory in Holy Cross itself. According to the

POITIERS
Speculative Reconstruction of Structures within Holy Cross
(Produced with reference to the excavation map by Eygun, 'Circonscription de Poitiers', p. 470)

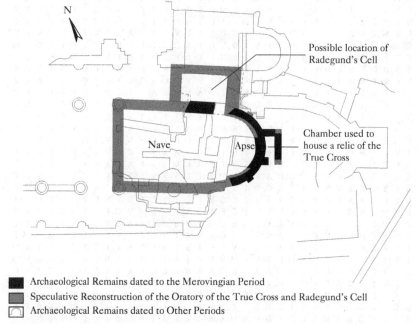

Figure 6.4 The oratory of the True Cross and adjacent cell in Radegund's convent, Poitiers. Produced by Erik Goosmann, with reference to Eygun, 'Circonscription de Poitiers'.

Hebrew scriptures, the inner sanctum of the Temple, i.e. the Tabernacle, contained a scared space known as the Holy of Holies, which was concealed by a veil woven of blue, purple, white, and red thread (II Chronicles 3:8–14). Behind this barrier stood the Ark of the Covenant and its gold cover, the Mercy Seat, described as an 'altar' in the Latin text, upon which the presence of God appeared. On the Day of Atonement, the high priest entered the Holy of Holies to sprinkle the blood of sacrificed animals upon this altar, in the presence of God, a ritual that cleansed the people of their sins. In the biblical Book of Hebrews, this ritual was metaphorically associated with the Crucifixion of Christ, interpreted as the blood sacrificed for the atonement of sins that forever replaced the practices in the Temple (Hebrews 9:1–28). The moment Jesus died on the Cross, the veil of the Temple was torn in two, symbolizing this new reality (Matthew 27:50–51). Radegund thus presented

```
D I V S A P E X C A R N E E F F I G I A N S G E N E T A L I A L I M I
V I T A L I T E R R A E C O N P I N G I T S A N G V I N E G L V T E N
L V C I F E R A X A V R A S A N I M A N T E S A F F L V I T I L L I C
C O N D I T V R E N I X A N S A D A M F A C T O R I S A D I N S T A R
E X I L V I T P R O T O P L A S M A S O L O R E S N O B I L I S V S V
D I V E S I N A R B I T R I O R A D I A N T I L V M I N E D E H I N C
E X M E M B R I S A D A E V A S F I T T V M V I R G I N I S E V V A E
C A R N E C R E A T A V I R I D E H I N C C O P V L A T V R E I D E M
V T P A R A D Y S S I A C O B E N E L A E T A R E T V R I N H O R T O
S E D D E S E D E P I A P E P V L I T T E M E R A B I L E G V T T V R
S E R P E N T I S S V A S V P O M I S V C O A T R A P R O P I N A N S
I N S A T I A T R I C I M O R T I F A M E S A C C I D I T I L L I N C
G A V I S V R V S O B H O C C A E L I F L V I S A R C E L O C A T O R
N A S C I P R O N O B I S M I S E R A R I S E T V L C E R E C L A V I
I N C R V C E C O N F I G I T A L I M A L A G M A T E I N V N C T I S
V N A S A L V S N O B I S L I G N O A G N I S A N G V I N E V E N I T
I V C V N D A S P E C I E S I N T E P I A B R A C C H I A C R I S T I
A F F I X A S T E T E R V N T E T P A L M A B E A B I L I S I N H A C
C A R A C A R O P O E N A S I N M I T E S S V S T V L I T H A V S T V
A R B O R S V A V I S A G R I T E C V M N O V A V I T A P A R A T V R
E L E C T A V T V I S V S I C E C R V C I S O R D I N E P V L C H R A
L V M E N S P E S S C V T V M G E R E R I S L I V O R I S A B I C T V
I N M O R T A L E D E C V S N E C E I V S T I L A E T A P A R A S T I
V N A O M N E M V I T A M S I C C R V X T V A C A V S A R I G A V I T
I M B R E C R V E N T A P I O V E L I S D A S N A V I T A P O R T V M
T R I S T I A S V M M E R S O M V N D A S T I V V L N E R A C L A V O
A R B O R D V L C I S A G R I R O R A N S E C O R T I C E N E C T A R
R A M I S D E C V I V S V I T A L I A C R I S M A T A F R A G R A N T
E X C E L L E N S C V L T V D I V A O R T V F V L G I D A F R V C T V
D E L I C I O S A C I B O E T P E R P O M A S V A V I S I N V M B R A
E N R E G I S M A G N I G E M M A N T E M E T N O B I L E S I G N V M
M V R V S E T A R M A V I R I S V I R T V S L V X A R A P R E C A T V
P A N D E B E N I G N A V I A M V I V A X E T F E R T I L E L V M E N
T V M M E M O R A D F E R O P E M N O B I S E G E R M I N E D A V I D
I N C R V C E R E X F I X V S I V D E X C V M P R A E E R I T O R B I
```

Figure 6.5 *On the Sign of the Cross,* acrostic poem by Fortunatus (*Poems,* 2.4), as it appears in Paris, Bibliothèque nationale de France, MS Lat. 8312, fol. 21ᵛ.

her convent as a metaphorical Temple, her oratory as a Tabernacle, her veiled shrine as a Holy of Holies, her Ark of the Holy Cross (described in Chapter 5) as that of the Covenant. Pulling back the two sides of the veil revealed the fragments of the Cross, the symbol of this eternal sacrifice.

Holy women appeared in scriptural descriptions of both the Temple and the Crucifixion, which must have encouraged Radegund in her efforts to unite and embody these realities within Holy Cross. The Gospel of Luke mentioned a 'prophetess' who dwelled in the Temple in fasting and prayer (2:36–38).[78]

[78] Caesarius, *Sermons,* 6.7, presented Anna as an exemplary figure. See the comments by Coon, *Sacred Fictions,* p. 129.

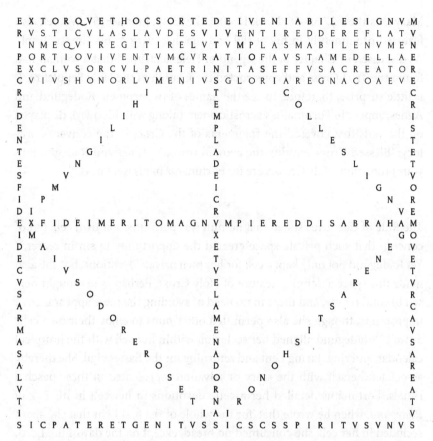

Figure 6.6 Untitled (and incomplete) acrostic poem by Fortunatus (*Poems*, 2.5), as it appears in Paris, Bibliothèque nationale de France, MS Lat. 8312, fol. 22ʳ.

The apocryphal *Protoevangelium of James*, which circulated in a Latin version in Merovingian Gaul, claimed that Mary had been sent as a young child to live in the Temple, where she was fed by an angel.[79] Mary was later selected to spin the purple and red thread used in the veil of the Holy of Holies.[80] During the Crucifixion, Jesus was surrounded by his female disciples and his mother,

<hr />

[79] *Protoevangelium of James*, 4–7. The Latin translation is no longer extant, but it must have existed, since the text was known to the author of the *Decretum Gelasianum* in the early sixth century. The text also served as a source for the *Infancy Gospel of Matthew*, produced in Merovingian Gaul in the seventh century. Elliott, *The Apocryphal New Testament*, pp. 48–51.

[80] *Protoevangelium of James*, 10.

Mary (Matthew 27:55–56; Mark 15:40; Luke 23:49; John 19:25). Women also featured prominently in his burial and the discovery of his Empty Tomb. As discussed in Chapter 5, the legend of Helena claimed that a woman had found the True Cross and constructed the Church of the Holy Sepulchre. It is little surprise, therefore, to see the names of two women, Radegund and Agnes, appear in Fortunatus's acrostic poem (along with his own), displayed on the veils that covered the fragments of the Cross in the convent's oratory: 'Blessed Cross, envelop the avowed women, Agnes and Radegund, in your protection. Holy Cross, care for Fortunatus in his weakness.'[81]

* * *

The Rule of Caesarius stated that no nun was permitted her own cell, out of concern that such private space created the opportunity to sin in secret.[82] Yet Radegund not only kept a cell for her own private devotions, but she also made this space a defining feature of Holy Cross. Perhaps she thought herself beyond repute, and there in no need of avoiding the mere appearance of impropriety, though she also permitted other nuns to enjoy their own cells as well.[83] Radegund aligned her seclusion within her cell with the liturgical calendar, entering during Lent and returning for the Easter vigil. She thereby associated herself with the story of salvation represented in these paschal rituals. Fortunatus detailed her ascetic devotions in her cell in his *Life of Radegund*, when he wrote that 'for the whole of the first Lent that she spent secluded in her cell, she consumed no bread, except on the day of the Lord', before he added that she drank so little water during this time 'she was barely able to recite the psalms through her parched throat'.[84] He also described Radegund sleeping on cinders and wearing a hair shirt, in imitation of the biblical sackcloth and ashes.[85]

During one Lent, Radegund placed iron bands around her neck and arms and chained them together. So tightly were these chains bound that, after forty days, her skin had swollen over the iron itself. When the fetters were finally removed, 'blood flowed out from her diminutive body, to its very limit'.[86] On another occasion, Radegund brought into her cell a metal plate, which

[81] Fortunatus, *Poems*, 2.4.
[82] Caesarius, *Rule for Nuns*, 9 and 51.
[83] Gregory of Tours, *Histories*, 6.29 and 9.40.
[84] Fortunatus, *Life of Radegund*, 22–23.
[85] For an analysis of Radegund's Lenten devotions in her cell, see Kroll and Bachrach, *The Mystic Mind*, pp. 129–145.
[86] Fortunatus, *Life of Radegund*, 25.

she had ordered to be made 'in the sign of Christ', presumably a cross, but perhaps a Chi Rho. She heated this plate to a glow and pressed it deeply upon her body in two places until her flesh was fully seared, permanently branding herself in the process. 'Her spirit aflame', Fortunatus wrote, 'she made her very limbs burn.'[87] Fortunatus referred to the plate itself as a *lamina*, a word that, though applied to various flat metal objects, often indicated a specific type of plate heated and pressed into the skin of slaves as a form of torture. He also described the metal as *orichalcum*, an alloy particularly associated with Roman and Byzantine coinage. These words might suggest that Radegund had reforged this metal plate from imperial coins, perhaps to symbolize her renunciation of wealth, which were now repurposed and deployed in her un-compromising pursuit of sanctification and self-abasement.

During another Lent, Radegund carried a basin (*aquamanile*) filled with hot coals in her arms, then pressed its white hot metal to her body, which sizzled her skin and left an impression that resembled a trench.[88] Putrid blood seeped out of abscesses to reveal the corporal mortification that she had oth-erwise attempted to perform in secret, like the wounds of Christ exposed to a doubting Thomas after the Resurrection (John 20:27).[89] Fortunatus expressly described the harm Radegund did to herself as torture, which she undertook 'so that she might be a martyr, since these were not times of persecution'. Her self-torture reproduced the martyrdoms of women in Christian antiquity, gruesome events known in full detail to the nuns of Holy Cross.[90] In addition to hagiographic texts kept in the convent's library, the *Ecclesiastical History* of Rufinus also recounted martyrdoms that featured iron chains, heated plates, and hot coals.[91] Gregory of Tours recorded several miracle stories in which devout believers embraced objects heated by coals to prove the truth of their virtue or faith.[92] The accuracy of such stories is, of course, less important than their relevance for the nuns of Holy Cross.[93]

---

[87] Fortunatus, *Life of Radegund*, 26.

[88] The term *aquamanile* here likely referred to the basin, rather than the pitcher.

[89] Fortunatus, *Life of Radegund*, 26. Kitchen, *Saints' Lives and the Rhetoric of Gender*, pp. 116–121. See also Bikeeva, 'Secrecy in the Asceticism of St Radegund'.

[90] Fortunatus, *Poems*, 8.1, references Eugenia (beheaded in Rome) and Thecla (fed to the beasts in Antioch, but miraculously saved) in a manner that assumed the nuns in Holy Cross knew about them already.

[91] Rufinus, *Ecclesiastical History*, 5.1.34, 5.1.52, 5.2.2, 7.10.25, 8.3.1, 8.6.3, 8.12.2, 8.12.6, 8.14.13.

[92] Gregory of Tours, *Histories*, 2.1; Gregory of Tours, *Glory of the Confessors*, 14 and 75; Gregory of Tours, *Glory of the Martyrs*, 9 and 80.

[93] Wehlau, 'Literal and Symbolic'; Wittern, 'Frauen zwischen asketischem Ideal und weltlichem Leben'.

Fortunatus's account of Radegund's self-torture might also be questioned, on the grounds that it fit his greater literary theme, which portrayed her as a martyr.[94] He certainly wrote within a broader hagiographic tradition that presented ascetic deeds, in the absence of any persecution, as a form of martyrdom.[95] 'If anyone mentioned everything that the most holy woman had zealously achieved—her fasting, service, humility, compassion, work, and suffering—they declared her to be both a confessor and a martyr', Fortunatus wrote, before he described Radegund's torments.[96] Yet the inescapable impression of these passages is, in fact, quite the opposite: that Fortunatus laboured to make sense out of stories that he feared might disturb his audience.[97] He certainly did not himself consider such extreme acts to be a necessary condition of 'martyrdom' via holy asceticism. In his *Life of Germanus*, he wrote that the bishop of Paris had attained 'martyrdom' simply through fasting, vigils, and the mild discomfort of a hair shirt.[98] Neither does it seem that his contemporaries believed anything similar, since there are no clear parallels for Radegund's extreme asceticism in hagiographic works written about the holy men and women of Merovingian Gaul.[99] If Radegund's behaviour has any equal, it is to be found in the monastic literature of the East, which featured stories about holy ascetics like the beautiful Zacharius, who bathed in natron to destroy his skin and turn himself into a leper; or Anthony, who told a young man to cover his naked body in meat so that, when his flesh was torn apart by dogs and birds, he might learn the importance of renouncing all worldly goods.[100] It seems unlikely, therefore, that Fortunatus fabricated stories about Radegund's extreme asceticism in pursuit of a literary theme. Instead, he deployed various literary strategies to provide Radegund's behaviour with a context and rationale.

Fortunatus alluded to the purpose of Radegund's self-torment within a series of poems that expressed his sense of loss upon her seclusion during Lent, and his joy upon her return at Easter. 'Now you are torturing yourself, to be recreated in the light that is to be.'[101] Her absence meant the withdrawal

---

[94] Pon, 'Un corps martyrisé'.
[95] Markus, *The End of Ancient Christianity*, pp. 70–72.
[96] Fortunatus, *Life of Radegund*, 21.
[97] Fortunatus, *Poems*, 11.4, expresses concern for Radegund's extreme fasting.
[98] Fortunatus, *Life of Germanus of Paris*, 75.
[99] Kitchen, *Saints' Lives and the Rhetoric of Gender*, p. 117.
[100] *The Alphabetical Collection*, The sayings of Carion (§2) and Anthony the Great (§20). See also the remarks of Coon, *Sacred Fictions*, p. 129.
[101] Fortunatus, *Poems*, 8.8.

of her light from the world, resulting in a darkness that touched Fortunatus's very soul.[102]

> Today you keep your yearly vows and return to seclusion. I pray that the joys of Easter restore you to us unharmed, and that your light returns to us twice as bright.[103]

In the meantime, Fortunatus looked for the first shoots of spring, a sign that 'the Lord has conquered the underworld'.[104] He found one such sign in the flowers that bloomed upon an altar, contained in wreaths made by Radegund herself.[105] When she returned from seclusion, Fortunatus had 'a second reason to celebrate Easter Day'.[106] His language, which deployed images of light and dark, echoed the paschal liturgy, which interpreted the resurrection of Christ as the restoration of light to the world.[107] 'Through your return, all is full and bright'.[108] Fortunatus thereby presented a cosmic analogy between Radegund's confinement and Christ's entombment.[109]

Enclosed within the narrow confines of her cell during Lent, Radegund embraced suffering and mortality, so that she might conqueror death and reign with Christ. More than a mere space for contemplation and tribulation, Radegund's cell represented nothing less than the tomb that Christ inhabited before his Resurrection. This interpretation seems to lurk behind a passage in Gregory's account of Radegund's funeral. When Agnes took Gregory to Radegund's empty cell, she declared: 'Behold, we are entering her cell, yet we have not found our missing mother'.[110] Her words evoked the sentiment of the disciples when they found Jesus's tomb empty: *They have taken the Lord out of the tomb, and we do not know where they have put him* (John 20:2). As a theme that appears across multiple works, the association mostly likely originated with the nuns of Holy Cross, rather than Radegund's hagiographers. Together with the oratory of the Cross, which represented the

---

[102] Fortunatus, *Poems*, 11.2.

[103] Fortunatus, *Poems*, 8.9, lines 3 and 15–16.

[104] Fortunatus deployed a term, *tartarus*, found in the Second Letter of Peter (2:4), which described the 'underworld' as a place of 'torment' (*cruciatio*).

[105] Fortunatus, *Poems*, 8.7.

[106] Fortunatus, *Poems*, 8.10.

[107] Coon, 'Merovingian Meditations on Jesus', p. 1097, compares the imagery of light in Fortunatus's poems to the *Exsultet*, an ancient Christian prayer, chanted during the Easter vigil.

[108] Fortunatus, *Poems*, 8.10.

[109] Roberts, *The Humblest Sparrow*, p. 289.

[110] Gregory of Tours, *Glory of the Confessors*, 104.

site of the Crucifixion, Radegund's cell combined to recreate the landscape of biblical Jerusalem. Although the precise arrangement of the two structures within Holy Cross is not known, the metaphorical significance alone is sufficient to call to mind the Church of the Holy Sepulchre, which marked both sites, that of the Crucifixion and the Empty Tomb. Architecture followed the ideals and practices of Radegund and her nuns, who considered Holy Cross to be a new Jerusalem.

* * *

When Radegund emerged from her cell, she performed miracles that echoed those of Jesus in the Gospels, including exorcisms. She expelled the agents of the Devil from the eyes of a carpenter's wife, forced a possessed woman to vomit up her demon when she stomped on her neck, and cured another woman 'greatly troubled in her back by the Adversary' with a prayer that expelled a 'worm' from the skin of her shoulders, which she then crushed with her foot.[111] The expulsion of this worm (*vermis*), a biblical symbol for death, signified Radegund's power over mortal flesh and its inevitable decay. Biblical passages described how Antiochus IV Epiphanes, for example, suffered from worms that rotted his bowels, because he intended to make Jerusalem 'a graveyard for the Jews' (II Maccabees 9:9). Herod Agrippa was struck dead by an angel and consumed by worms, because he allowed others to praise him as a divine manifestation (Acts 12:13). Other passages referred to a similar creature, a serpent (*serpens*), as a symbol of evil, most notably the Book of Genesis, in which Eve ate from the forbidden tree under the influence of a serpent, leading to her expulsion from Paradise. God cursed the serpent: *I put enmity between you and her, between your seed and her seed; she will crush your head, and you will lie in wait for her heel* (Genesis 3:15). The Book of Revelation addressed this prophecy when it characterized the Devil as the 'old serpent' and described his defeat, in the form of a mythical snake, at the hands of a woman crowned with twelve stars and her son, the Messiah (Revelation 12:1–17 and 20:1–15).

Fortunatus included several instances in which Radegund healed a person who was dead or dying back to life.[112] These miracles included the resuscitation of a baby girl, deceased but still warm to the touch. As the grieving family made preparations for the funeral, Radegund took the child into her

---

[111] Fortunatus, *Life of Radegund*, 28, 30, and 33.
[112] Petersen, 'The Spirituality and Miracles of St Radegund', p. 41.

cell. Although the family thought that she was simply washing the body and offering final prayers, Radegund spent seven hours invoking the power of God, until the baby was fully restored to life.[113] On another occasion, she brought into her cell a nun who had been unable to move for six months, and who had reached such a state of deterioration that she had become entirely unresponsive. Radegund placed the woman into a warm bath, ran her hands over her body for two hours, and miraculously restored her to health. The nun arose, reinvigorated, from the waters. 'The next day, although she was expected to leave this world, she went forth in public, healed.'[114] The word translated as 'healed', *salva*, might equally be rendered as 'saved', conferring a dual sense of physical and spiritual healing that called to mind the question of salvation. Another nun, who lay dying from a disease, experienced a vision in which Radegund ordered her to descend into an empty bath, then rubbed oil on her head and clothed her in a new garment. The woman awoke, cured of her ailment, with her head still smelling of oil.[115] Fortunatus described this miracle as a *mysterium*, by which he likely meant a 'sacred ritual', rather than an incomprehensible occurrence (even if the vision contained unusual details), and specifically the ritual of baptism, with its power to confer salvation upon Christian neophytes.[116]

The ancient Church practised baptism by immersion, in which neophytes were brought to a baptismal pool on the Easter vigil.[117] They renounced the Devil, in what represented an exorcism, removed their clothes, and received an anointing with oil, as though they were corpses awaiting burial. They then descended into the water, as if entering a tomb.[118] They were submerged three times, professing their belief in the Father, the Son, and the Holy Spirit, before they arose, reborn. The state of undress meant that deaconesses provided assistance during the baptism of women, which recalled Radegund's unusual status (discussed in Chapter 3).[119] This ritual pointed to the scriptural comparison between baptism and resurrection:

> Are you not aware that those baptised in Christ Jesus were baptised in his death? We were buried together with him through baptism into death, so

---

[113] Fortunatus, *Life of Radegund*, 37.
[114] Fortunatus, *Life of Radegund*, 29.
[115] Fortunatus, *Life of Radegund*, 35.
[116] De Nie, 'Fatherly and Motherly Curing'.
[117] Coon, *Sacred Fictions*, p. 129.
[118] Kelley, *Early Christian Creeds*, pp. 30–61.
[119] Barcellona, 'Lo spazio declinato al femminile', p. 34.

that, just as Christ has risen from the dead through the glory of the Father, we too might walk in the newness of life. (Romans 6:3–4)

Fortunatus positioned these stories, in which Radegund restored the dead and dying to life, immediately after his description of her self-mortification in her tomb. He thus implied it was these torments, which brought Radegund close to death, that also empowered her, through her deep union with the crucified and entombed Christ, to expel demons and to even raise the dead.

* * *

When he conducted Radegund's funeral, Gregory brought her body outside the walls of Holy Cross, and then paused before he continued into the funerary church dedicated to the Virgin Mary (a building discussed further in Chapter 8). He wished to give the nuns, confined to their convent, a final moment to mourn. Watching from the walls, they witnessed a final sign of Radegund's holy power:

> As soon as we had begun the procession with the singing of psalms, those who were possessed let out a cry and testified that Radegund was a saint of God, and that they were being tortured by her.[120]

The fact that Radegund possessed the power to torment demons, and to force them to testify to her sanctity, recalled a power that Jesus wielded in the Gospels. *Two men possessed by demons came up to Jesus from the tombs. They were so exceedingly fierce that no one was able to pass that way. And they cried out, declaring: 'What do you want from us, Son of God? Have you come here to torture us before the appointed time?* (Matthew 8:28–29). Radegund's body now rested in its tomb, where it awaited the Resurrection on the Last Day, but her soul had already entered in to a union with Christ.

Gregory claimed that Radegund's body gave off the scent of roses and lilies, which, as explained above, symbolized the glorious state of martyrs and virgins in a tradition apparent within the writings of Jerome. Interestingly, Gregory made no mention of violets in his description of the departed Radegund, flowers that, according to Jerome, symbolized the widow. Perhaps Gregory thought that such a comparison was inappropriate because

---

[120] Gregory of Tours, *Glory of the Confessors*, 104. Baudonivia, *Life of Radegund*, 27, also described the expulsion of demons from two women at Radegund's tomb, though she placed this exorcism after the funeral.

Radegund had now found her celestial husband. She reigned as a queen in heaven, alongside Christ, the King of Kings and Lord of Lords. To achieve this lofty status, and to acquire her heavenly inheritance, however, Radegund had left Holy Cross behind. She had governed the institution as if both a royal court and a godly convent. Her legacy was not easily continued. She had imposed the strict confinement of the Rule of Caesarius, but exempted herself as necessary, not to reduce her ascetic devotions, but to retain and display her royal status. The nuns of Holy Cross, though committed to the success of Radegund's unique monastic project, found her style of leadership difficult to replicate. In the years that immediately followed her death, Radegund's ability to protect her institution, as an intercessor in the celestial court, was put to the test in the face of turmoil that resulted from a previously unthinkable crisis of leadership. Less than two years after Gregory had laid her body to rest within her funerary church, Radegund watched from her heavenly perch as a revolt broke out among the nuns of Holy Cross, an uprising that threatened to destroy her life's work.

Note on Figures 6.1–4: These images display the floorplans of the four churches described above (in Jerusalem, Rome, Ravenna, and Poitiers). They are not produced to scale and not intended to provide highly precise depictions of each structure. Instead, they offer reconstructions of the schema of each building intended to demonstrate their structural and spatial similarities. The floorplan for Radegund's oratory in Poitiers is the most hypothetical.

7

Like Eve Driven from Paradise

As February turned to March in the year 589, a group of forty disgruntled
nuns left the convent of Holy Cross in Poitiers and headed north for Tours.
They travelled the 100 km journey on foot. A deluge soaked them and made
the roads a quagmire, extending what might normally have taken twelve
hours into a much longer journey, perhaps a full day and night, which they
completed without provisions or rest. Tired, cold, sodden, shivering, the nuns
arrived without anything but an expectation: they assumed that Gregory, the
bishop of Tours, would support them as they pursued their dispute against
their new abbéss, Leubovera. Nor was such an expectation unreasonable.
Although these women might not have looked like it in their dishevelled state,
they belonged to the upper echelons of Gallic society, and they were led by
two princesses: Chlothild, a daughter of Charibert, and Basina, a daughter of
Chilperic I (both kings now deceased).[1] These two leaders counted Chlothar
as their grandfather, and their illustrious names recalled two great women
of the Merovingian past: Chlothild's name echoed that of Clovis's wife, and
Basina's that of Clovis's mother. When Chlothild asked Gregory for support,
she referenced her membership to the royal family, even as she spoke the language of humility:

> I pray, holy bishop, that you deign to offer your protection and provide food
> for these women, who have been reduced in profound degradation by the
> abbess of Poitiers, while I take myself to our royal kinspeople and explain to
> them what we have suffered, and then return.[2]

Chlothild expected Gregory to intervene, even though Poitiers fell within
the metropolitan jurisdiction of the bishop of Bordeaux, over 300 km to the
south, presumably because of the special relationship that Radegund had

---

[1] On the relationship between Chlothild and Basina, and their representation in the sources, see
Singer, 'Gregory's Forgotten Rebel'.
[2] Gregory of Tours, *Histories*, 9.39.

Radegund. E. T. Dailey, Oxford University Press. © Oxford University Press 2023.
DOI: 10.1093/oso/9780197656105.003.0008

established with the bishops of Tours in the days of Euphronius's episcopate (discussed in Chapter 5). Gregory thought it best not to refuse the princess's request.

He later wrote an account of the affair in his *Histories*, in which he narrated the series of events that grew into a great scandal—an armed conflict that captured public attention, consumed the energies of bishops and kings, and caused the convent itself to be plundered by thugs.[3] Gregory attempted to justify his involvement in this episode, as he likely felt embarrassed that he had initially provided support to the nuns after they left their convent.[4] He also addressed the perception that he could have done more to resolve the crisis, which affected him personally because his own niece, Justina, was a nun in Holy Cross who served as the *praeposita* (a kind of deputy to the abbess), and who remained loyal to Leubovera. After the hostilities had ended, Gregory sat alongside his episcopal colleagues in a tribunal that adjudicated the dispute, chastised Chlothild and Basina, and issued a report to the reigning kings, Guntram and Childebert II. This report, which Gregory copied into his *Histories*, represents a second source of information about the rebellion—the only other source, but for two poems written by Fortunatus that mentioned the scandal without providing any details.[5] Referred to here (and in Gregory's text) as the *Iudicium*, or 'Judgement', this document contains additional details that broadly overlap, but occasionally disturb, the narrative of the *Histories*. Together, these two entwined texts provide an opportunity to understand how the arrangements established by Radegund in Holy Cross unravelled so quickly after her death.[6]

* * *

Not long after Radegund's death, Maroveus gained oversight of Holy Cross by royal consent. Gregory of Tours presented this outcome, implausibly, as the fulfilment of Radegund's long-standing desires. He portrayed her as an obedient and humble woman who had submitted herself to the authority of her local bishop from the very beginning.[7] Even after her conflict with

---

[3] Gregory of Tours, *Histories*, 9.39–43, 10.15–17, and 10.20. See Dailey, *Queens, Consorts, Concubines*, pp. 64–79.

[4] Dailey, 'Misremembering Radegund's Foundation of Sainte-Croix'.

[5] Fortunatus, *Poems*, 8.12 and 8.12a. Gregory of Tours, *Histories*, 10.16, reproduces the *Iudicium*, apparently verbatim; see Flierman, 'Gregory of Tours and the Merovingian Letter', p. 138.

[6] In what follows, information from Gregory's narrative and the *Iudicium* is presented in single account, with the precise source of information specified only as and when relevant. It is beyond the scope of this analysis to detail the divergences between these two texts, but it will suffice to say that the discrepancies can largely be explained by the different purposes and audiences of each text.

[7] Casias, 'Rebel Nuns and the Bishop Historian', pp. 18–19.

Maroveus (detailed in Chapter 5), Radegund wished to reconcile, until her dying breath.

> After Radegund passed away, the abbess [Agnes] again begged her own bishop [Maroveus] to place the nuns under his authority. At first he was inclined to refuse, but, on the advice of those around him, he promised to be a father to the nuns, as was right and proper, and to protect them when need arose. He therefore went to King Childebert and obtained an order placing the monastery under his regular governance, like everything else in his diocese. Nevertheless, I think something that I cannot understand lingered in his heart, and this stirred up the scandal, as the nuns claimed.[8]

Gregory's interpretation is doubtful. Throughout his works, he consistently upheld the authority of bishops as the cornerstone of the social order in Gaul.[9] Radegund, in contrast, had clearly expressed her desire for Holy Cross to remain independent, under the protection of the king, in her letter *Dominis sanctis*, which (as discussed in Appendix 1) she very likely wrote shortly before her death. Radegund feared that, after her passing, Agnes might be removed by a scheming individual, 'the local bishop, a royal official, or anyone else', who wished to seize 'authority over the monastery or the property belonging to it'. Radegund clearly saw Maroveus as a potential threat, not a trustworthy pastor.

In an unforeseen development, Agnes died not long after Radegund, and she was replaced by Leubovera. The precise timing is difficult to discern, beyond the obvious chronological boundaries of Radegund's death (on 13 August 587) and Chlothild's departure (at the end of February 589). But even these extreme *termini* indicate that the communal life within Holy Cross had deteriorated quickly, in a year and a half. Although no source described Agnes's death or Leubovera's accession, the *Iudicium* contains incidental details that help clarify this picture. Leubovera admitted to the tribunal of bishops that she had allowed workers affiliated with the convent to access the baths during Lent and Eastertide, which must refer to 588, a year in which Lent began on 8 March. Thus, Agnes died fewer than seven months after Radegund—not nearly enough time for Holy Cross to stabilize itself. The *Iudicium* also revealed that Leubovera celebrated the betrothal of her

[8] Gregory of Tours, *Histories*, 9.40.
[9] Leyser, 'Divine Power Flowed from His Book'; Bjornlie, 'Gregory of Tours and the *Decem libri Historiarum*', pp. 182–184.

orphaned niece by receiving a payment (the *arrha sponsalitia*, presented by the groom's side) in the presence of witnesses that included Maroveus and his clergy, as well as other leading figures in Poitiers. The betrothal, which also certainly dates to 588, suggests that the new abbess had wasted little time in aligning herself with Maroveus, whose attendance cannot have been well received by many of the nuns in Holy Cross.

Fortunatus may have responded to these developments himself. According to a generally accepted reconstruction of events, he travelled with Gregory to the royal centre of Metz in the latter part of 588, and subsequently accompanied Childebert and his mother, Brunhild, by boat to Andernach (near Koblenz).[10] Fortunatus delivered a poem to the king and his mother on the feast day of St Martin, 11 November. The work depicted Radegund as a saint in the heavenly court alongside St Martin (as discussed in Chapter 4).[11] It is tempting to connect this trip to the recent disruptions in Holy Cross. Fortunatus clearly wished to remind Childebert and Brunhild of the power that the late queen retained in the afterlife. He may also have wished to emphasize the close relationship that Radegund had established with the bishops of Tours (represented by St Martin), in the hope that the king and his mother might rescind their decree and remove Holy Cross from Maroveus's oversight.[12] But if this was indeed his plan, it was not successful. The special arrangements established during the reign of Sigibert (Childebert's father and Brunhild's husband) were apparently regarded by the new king and his mother as a personal concession made to Radegund herself, rather than a general privilege conferred upon her institution in perpetuity. Fortunatus's diplomatic failure may have contributed to the decision made by the disgruntled nuns to abandon Holy Cross at the first signs of spring in 589, and to champion their own cause by taking their grievances to King Guntram instead.

* * *

As a member of the royal family, Chlothild planned to use her influence to remove Leubovera from office and to acquire control of the convent herself. Although little is known about Leubovera's background, she was clearly of lower social standing than Chlothild.[13] Not only is her inferiority implied

---

[10] Meyer, *Der Gelegenheitsdichter*, pp. 21–22; Koebner, *Venantius Fortunatus*, pp. 108–109.

[11] Brennan, 'The Career of Venantius Fortunatus', pp. 75–77.

[12] Fortunatus, *Poems*, 10.7. On Maroveus's intentions at this time, see Mineau, 'Un évêque de Poitiers au vi[e] siècle', pp. 371–372.

[13] Scheibelreiter, 'Königstöchter im Kloster', pp. 36–37.

by the very nature of Chlothild's plan, but it was also implied in words that Gregory put into Chlothild's mouth, when she rebuked Leubovera for a final time before she left Holy Cross:

> I am going to my royal kin, because I want them to know about our humiliation. For we are abased in this place as though we were not the daughters of kings, but the spawn of pernicious slave girls.[14]

Gregory may have indulged in his own subtle insult here, since it is likely that Chlothild and Basina were indeed born to women who had been enslaved.[15] Nonetheless, Chlothild was right to claim that she deserved respect as the daughter of a king. By the conventions of the Merovingian royal family, paternity alone conferred royal status, just as Chlothild asserted, even though certain moralists were unimpressed with this custom.[16]

Gregory thought that the revolt resulted from the personal failings of the nuns who abandoned their convent. He wrote, for example, that Chlothild suffered from excess pride. She was a 'frivolous malcontent' who lacked Radegund's 'humility', and she 'kept boasting that her father was King Charibert'.[17] In a manner reminiscent of the Fall of Man, Chlothild had been 'lured in her heart by the Devil' to abandon the sacred confines of Holy Cross. Gregory thus implicitly associated Chlothild with 'Eve driven out of Paradise', a phrase found in a letter, *Dominae beatissimae*, that he copied into this part of his *Histories*, written to Radegund by several bishops (most likely in 567, as discussed in Chapter 4), who pledged to excommunicate any nun who left Holy Cross in violation of the Rule of Caesarius. The association was unfair, because this letter envisioned nuns who forsook their religious vows for marriage. Chlothild had no desire to abandon the monastic life, and she intended instead to return to Holy Cross and lead the institution herself. On her journey back from Guntram's court, she left one of her followers, a nun named Constantina, in a convent in Autun, a clear indication that she

---

[14] Gregory of Tours, *Histories*, 9.39.

[15] Hartmann, '*Reginae sumus*: Merowingische Königstöchter', pp. 2–3, suggested that Theudogild was probably Chlothild's mother. Basina was the daughter of Audovera. See Gregory of Tours, *Histories*, 4.26 and 4.28.

[16] Gregory of Tours, *Histories*, 5.20. See Dailey, *Queens, Consorts, Concubines*, pp. 96–99.

[17] This passage has been read by some historians as revealing doubts about Chlothild's paternity, in the sense that she kept 'asserting' (*asserere*) that she was Charibert's daughter, e.g. Widdowson, 'Merovingian Partitions', p. 4. This interpretation is difficult to reconcile with the rest of Gregory's account, in which the authenticity of her assertion is not doubted, and in which the kings themselves clearly accepted her paternity without question.

was not rebelling against institutional monasticism.[18] She might also have used the reassignment of Constantina to strengthen her connections with Brunhild, the founder of the convent in Autun, in a further sign that she planned to use the existing religio-political system to her advantage, rather than challenge it outright.[19]

When Chlothild later faced the tribunal of bishops, in the aftermath of the uprising, she justified her decision to leave the sacred confines of her monastery on the grounds that it had become impossible to stay true to the Rule of Caesarius under the inept governance of Leubovera. Rather than complain about the difficulties of strict monastic enclosure, Chlothild complained that Leubovera failed to adhere to the Rule consistently, accusing her of both laxity and hypocrisy. Although this approach might be interpreted merely as a useful defence, given that the bishops were committed to upholding the Rule, it is notable that they did not reject Chlothild's position outright, even though they thought that her decision to leave Holy Cross was itself an unjustified violation of monastic seclusion. Neither did Leubovera question Chlothild's commitment to her religious vows, presumably because her two decades of service within Holy Cross undermined such a line of attack. It is even possible that Chlothild regarded herself as something of a monastic reformer, a perception that, while certainly not the result of any personal humility, nonetheless expressed a different type of pride than what Gregory had in mind.[20] But Gregory had no interest in presenting Chlothild as anything other than a wayward daughter of Eve, to which purpose he added the claim that she had left Holy Cross as a result of Maroveus's 'deceit' (*dolus*)— an odd and unexplained remark that served his literary purposes by further associating her revolt with the Fall of Man. *And the Lord said to the woman, 'What is this you have done?' And the woman said, 'The serpent, he deceived me, and I ate'* (Genesis 3:13).

This interpretation is not intended to exclude the possibility that many of the nuns who followed Chlothild and Basina out of Holy Cross had started to reconsider their religious vows, or perhaps had never wished to take them in the first place.[21] High-status women entered convents for reasons that might

---

[18] The fictional exploration of other motives, such as a desire to oppose a patriarchal clerical order and to restore a lost, protofeminist paganism, features in a novel by Charlier, *The Rebel Nun*.

[19] Hartmann, '*Reginae sumus*: Merowingische Königstöchter', p. 10.

[20] Dailey, 'Misremembering Radegund's Foundation of Sainte-Croix', pp. 122–123.

[21] On this issue compare the perspectives of Hartmann, '*Reginae sumus*: Merowingische Königstöchter', pp. 2–3; Rütjes, *Der Klosterstreit in Poitiers*, p. 6; and Götsch, 'Der Nonnenaufstand von Poitiers', p. 13.

lose their relevance over time, such as a desire to avoid a particular marriage arrangement, or as a matter of political expediency. Others may have been forced into monastic seclusion, the clearest example of which occurred when Guntram rejected Theudogild's offer of marriage, confiscated her wealth, and sent her into a convent in Arles.[22] No similar example can be found to indicate with certainty that Radegund accepted women into Holy Cross against their will, but the complex pressures that influenced each woman to adopt a religious life meant that some of the nuns in Poitiers had likely chosen to take their vows in circumstances of restricted personal agency.[23] During Radegund's lifetime, an anchoress, who had apparently changed her mind, descended from the walls of Holy Cross and sought refuge in the Basilica of St Hilary, where she made accusations against Abbess Agnes, before she subsequently repented and returned to the monastic community (for a time, at least, as discussed below).[24]

Chlothild and Basina themselves might have entered Holy Cross in less than ideal circumstances. As discussed in Chapter 4, Chlothild adopted the monastic life after the death of her father in 568, as part of what seems to have been a broader strategy to remove the women of the old regime from political relevance. Basina had apparently found refuge in Holy Cross after a sexual assault at the hands of Fredegund's agents, a dreadful experience that Gregory described sympathetically in the years before the rebellion had erased the pity he once felt toward her.[25] However conflicted Chlothild and Basina may have felt upon entering Holy Cross, however, they had remained for the better part of their lives. Basina even resisted her father's attempt to remove her so that she might marry into the Visigothic royal family.[26] By

---

[22] Gregory of Tours, *Histories*, 4.26. On the identification of the convent, see Chapter 4. See also Hillner, 'Female Crime and Female Confinement'.

[23] On the difficulty of theorizing the idea of monastic confinement, see de Jong, 'Monastic Prisoners or Opting Out?'.

[24] Gregory of Tours, *Histories*, 9.40. See also the incident in Jonas, *Life of Columbanus*, 2.19.

[25] Gregory of Tours, *Histories*, 6.34. This interpretation follows the established view that Gregory wrote the *Histories* over many years, and that it is sometimes possible to discern his changing opinions in the text, which he had not finished editing at the time of his death in 594. For the schema, see Buchner, *Gregor von Tours*, vol. 1, pp. xx–xxv. Because I am not able to provide detailed arguments here, I can only assert that I do not agree with the alternative view expressed by Murray, 'Chronology and the Composition of the *Histories*', that the work is best understood as consistently expressing the opinions Gregory held in the early 590s. I therefore cannot agree with the criticism of Singer, 'Gregory's Forgotten Rebel', p. 193, that my interpretation of Gregory's changing opinion of Basina (which I also expressed in earlier publications), 'falls afoul of the persuasive arguments of A. C. Murray that Gregory composed the *Histories* in or around 590, after the rebellion had ended'. Neither is this an accurate reflection of Murray's view about the *Histories*, which he said were 'unlikely to have been written from scratch in a short period of time prior to Gregory's death in 594' (p. 195). See also Murray, 'The Composition of the *Histories*'.

[26] Gregory of Tours, *Histories*, 6.34

rejecting this opportunity to abandon her vows, she indicated that she had no desire to return to the world.[27] Basina always intended to go back to Holy Cross after the rebellion, an ambition that she eventually fulfilled (in circumstances discussed below).

When the nuns arrived in Tours, Gregory offered to go with them and speak to Maroveus in person, and to determine if Leubovera had indeed mistreated them. 'Certainly not', Chlothild replied, 'we shall go to the kings.' According to the *Iudicium*, Maroveus had offered to adjudicate the dispute, a proposal that the nuns rejected, shoving him aside and trampling over him as they broke through the convent's doors. Gregory found their response outrageous:

> How can you oppose my plan? On what grounds do you ignore this priestly instruction? I fear that an assembly of bishops might remove you from communion.[28]

He then read out *Dominae beatissimae*, the letter that threatened excommunication upon any nun who abandoned Holy Cross, but to no avail. 'Nothing will hold us back from appealing, without delay, to the kings, whom we know to be our kin,' Chlothild declared, clearly expecting special treatment on account of her status. Although Gregory did not admit it, this attitude was not entirely different from that displayed by Radegund herself on occasion.[29] And what Chlothild expected, she received. However unimpressed Gregory may have with the nuns, he declined to excommunicate them, and instead offered to host them in Tours through the spring and summer, while Chlothild travelled in better weather to Guntram's royal court in Chalon-sur-Saône.

Chlothild's uncle gave her a warm welcome. Guntram presented her with gifts, listened to her grievances, and promised to call an assembly of bishops to investigate Leubovera's conduct. Chlothild then returned to Tours and waited for the king's promised ecclesiastical council. But these bishops did not arrive in good order, or at least not quickly enough for her. Gregory provided no explanation for the delay, but political circumstances may have played a role. When Guntram's army suffered a disastrous defeat in

---

[27] Compare this interpretation to Scheibelreiter, 'Königstöchter im Kloster', pp. 35–36.

[28] Gregory of Tours, *Histories*, 9.39.

[29] Casias, 'Rebel Nuns and the Bishop Historian', pp. 23–28. Bailey, 'Leadership and Community in Late Antique Poitiers', p. 60, wrote insightfully: 'One could argue that, rather than undermining Radegund's legacy, the rebelling nuns were working out some of the consequences of her disruptive acts.'

Visigothic Septimania, he closed the roads in his kingdom to restrict travel across the territories ruled by Childebert and Brunhild, whom he suspected of betrayal (since Brunhild hailed from the Visigothic royal house).[30] These territories included Poitiers, which had been transferred to Childebert's jurisdiction a year earlier. Such disruption may have caused the bishops to delay their plans to travel. But Chlothild had reason to be impatient. When she returned from Guntram's court, she discovered that many of her nuns had been, in Gregory's words, 'taken in marriage, deceived by twisted men'. Gregory offered this information as a warning about what might happen to any nun who left the protection of her convent. Yet this development also helps to explain why Chlothild needed to move quickly, before these nuns abandoned the cause, willingly or otherwise.[31]

The remaining nuns returned to Poitiers and set themselves up in the Basilica of St Hilary, a fact that deepens suspicions (expressed in Chapter 5) that the site had long been a centre of opposition to Radegund and her monastic project. They were joined by an anchoress from Holy Cross, who, not for the first time, abandoned her monastic cell and sought refuge with the rival congregation. Chlothild and Basina may have hoped that their return to Poitiers might inspire other disgruntled nuns to leave. But their most important recruits were armed men who formed a makeshift military retainer— soldiers of fortune whom Gregory characterized as 'killers, criminals, bastards, runaway slaves, and every other sort of outlaw'.[32] A contingent of senior clerics also arrived in Poitiers, intent on resolving the dispute. Led by Gundegisel, the metropolitan bishop of Bordeaux, the clerics summoned Chlothild, Basina, and their nuns to Holy Cross. When this request was refused, Gundegisel and his entourage went to the Basilica of St Hilary and confronted Chlothild and Basina directly, demanding that they and their followers return to the convent. Gundegisel read to them the same letter, *Dominae beatissimae*, that Gregory had previously read out when they first arrived in Tours, and he too threatened excommunication. But Gundegisel followed through with the ecclesiastical sanction and removed the wayward nuns from communion. In response, Chlothild ordered her armed men to attack:

---

[30] Gregory of Tours, *Histories*, 9.31–32.

[31] See the important reflections of Orlinski, 'Lost in Translation', p. 66.

[32] This translates *adulteri* as 'bastards', rather than 'adulterers' or 'fornicators', and *fugitivi* as 'runaway slaves', rather than 'fugitives', in contrast to other translations.

This band of imbeciles [. . .] rose up against the clergymen and showered them with blows within the church of St Hilary itself. The bishops collapsed upon the paving stones and barely managed to return to their feet. The surviving deacons and clerics escaped the church with fractured skulls, covered with blood.

Chlothild capitalized on this moment and seized estates that belonged to Holy Cross, forcing workers associated with the properties to provide their service to her instead, and appointing officials to administer her new possessions. She also threatened that, 'if she was able to enter the monastery, she would throw the abbess down from the walls flat upon the earth.'

For Chlothild to act so boldly, she must have thought she had Guntram's support. Others seem to have believed that as well. Gundegisel discovered, for example, that several of his fellow bishops were reluctant to give him their unequivocal backing. When he wrote to a meeting of eleven bishops, who had by coincidence recently gathered on Guntram's orders to address unrelated matters, describing the abuse he had suffered at the hands of Chlothild's armed men, he received a lacklustre reply. Although these bishops expressed regret for his suffering and accepted the excommunication he issued, they did so only as a temporary measure. They told Gundegisel that the matter would be addressed at a major council already scheduled to be held on 1 November, which had been convoked to address the question of Brunhild's suspect loyalties. Until then, Gundegisel was advised to pray for the wayward nuns, to reach out to them as a shepherd to his lost sheep, and to coax them to reconcile with their religious sisters in Holy Cross. This response surely fell short of Gundegisel's expectations, and there is no indication that he subsequently acted as a compassionate pastor to the wayward nuns. Leubovera also seems to have worried that the dispute might be not be resolved in her favour, as she circulated anew Radegund's letter, *Dominis sanctis*, which condemned anyone who seized the properties or revenues of Holy Cross, and which emphasized the inviolability of the Rule of Caesarius and its strict injunction of monastic enclosure.

With many bishops already en route, Guntram unexpectedly cancelled the November council, after Brunhild proved her innocence through the swearing of oaths. With winter approaching, the dispute in Poitiers now needed to wait until the following year to be resolved. Chlothild's sense of urgency turned into one of desperation. Heavy rain and flooding had led to a poor harvest, and the rebel nuns now suffered from a lack of food—and even firewood—through the season's cold, long nights. Many abandoned the cause. Some returned to their families. Others entered different convents. Only the most committed remained, a self-selecting group of malcontents who were prepared to undertake the most extreme course of action to achieve their desired ends. When spring arrived, Chlothild ordered her armed men to enter Holy Cross at night and capture Leubovera by force. With a candle in one hand and a weapon in the other, the men searched the convent for the abbess until they found a group of nuns praying in the oratory of the Cross. In the confused melee that followed, one of the assailants stabbed another, who lay bleeding to death as his fellow henchmen seized the woman they believed to be Leubovera and dragged her out of the monastery and toward the Basilica of St Hilary. But the first light of dawn made clear that their now unveiled hostage was not the abbess but the *praeposita*, Justina. The men returned to Holy Cross, identified Leubovera properly, and carried her away, dragging her, naked and humiliated, by her hair through the streets of Poitiers, now in full daylight. The following night they returned to Holy Cross, lit a bonfire, and took away anything they could carry. They may have done worse as well: the *Iudicium* alluded to sexual violence suffered by the nuns, in a vague statement (discussed below) that might be best associated with this moment.

This headlong descent into bottomless perdition occurred on Psalm Sunday, the start of Holy Week. The nuns who had remained in Holy Cross, loyal to their abbess, surely hoped for divine intervention. They may well have known a story about the nuns of St John's in Arles, who were miraculously saved when they chose to escape a fire by taking refuge in the convent's cisterns, rather than contravene the Rule of Caesarius and abandon the convent altogether.[33] But no similar divine intervention rescued the nuns who stayed in Holy Cross from the chaos that enveloped them. A slave who sought the protection of Radegund's tomb was killed regardless; he received no mercy other than to die in the presence of the holy queen. 'Sacrilege had crept into the sacred confines of the holy community, such as has never before defiled eyes and ears', wrote Fortunatus, in a poem that expressed his sorrow over the scandal.[34] His style recalled that of a biblical lamentation. *Most wretched was this incursion of evil, grievous to all; for the Temple had been filled with the excess and ungodliness of the heathen* (2 Maccabees 6:3–4).

---

[33] Cyprian, *Life of Caesarius*, 26. Baudonivia copied from this text, indicating that it was known in Holy Cross in her lifetime.

[34] Fortunatus, *Poems*, 8.12.

Gregory also lamented these events: 'Pride surged through Chlothild more greatly with every passing day [...] and the transgressors committed murders and other assaults without ceasing'. Chlothild refused to release Leubovera, even when Maroveus threatened to withhold the celebration of Easter or the baptism of catechumens, which left him with no option but to gather the leading men in Poitiers and attempt to extract Leubovera by force.[35]

Events now began to turn against Chlothild. Flavianus, an agent of Queen Brunhild, rescued Leubovera from her armed guards, who had been given orders by Chlothild to kill their prisoner in the event of an escape.[36] Basina lost her resolve. Her relationship with Chlothild is difficult to understand. Gregory presented her as something of a deputy to Chlothild, even though he characterized both women as the ringleaders of the revolt. The *Iudicium*, making little distinction between the two, blamed both in equal measure. They may never have achieved a clear understanding themselves about their roles, and now the matter had become an unavoidable point of contention.[37] According to Gregory, the pride of Chlothild grew so large that 'she even looked down upon her cousin Basina from on high, until the latter began to have regrets'. Basina may well have thought that, if Chlothild had no desire to grant her any influence in the leadership of Holy Cross, then her condition was perhaps not very different to what she had experienced under Leubovera.[38] 'She switched sides, humbled herself before her abbess, and sought peace, and they were of one mind and one will,' Gregory wrote. The accord, however, became troubled almost immediately, when, in a confused melee, one of Basina's servants was struck and killed by the attendants of Leubovera. Although the two women managed to live in peace again, discord continued to erupt between their followers, mirroring the chaos Chlothild had brought into Holy Cross.

What had begun as a question of governance and discipline within the convent now became a public scandal and a violent affair. But violence

[35] On the terminology that indicated these men were leaders within the city, see Loseby, 'Lost Cities', p. 232.

[36] For Flavianus as an agent of Brunhild, see Gregory of Tours, *Histories*, 9.19 and 10.5. In the *Iudicium*, Chlothild claimed that she had ordered her guard to stand down, and therefore deserved credit for Leubovera's release.

[37] See, for example, Gregory's comments at the end of *Histories*, 9.43: 'Only a few nuns remained with Chlothild and Basina [through the difficult winter from 589 to 590]. There was a major disagreement between them, for each wished to place herself over the others.'

[38] Singer, 'Gregory's Forgotten Rebel', pp. 195–196, thought that Chlothild and Basina instead fell out over Leubovera's escape. Of course this event cannot have helped their relationship, but the friction between the two probably ran more deeply and concerned questions of leadership.

belonged to kings and those authorized to act on their behalf.[39] Chlothild had finally gone too far. Guntram and Childebert joined in a concerted effort to end the turmoil in Poitiers and to restore their reputation as the sole purveyors of legitimate violence. Macco, the *comes* of Poitiers, received the royal order to suppress the uprising, and he brought an overwhelming force with him to Holy Cross. He had already shown his loyalty to Leubovera in 588, when he had attended the betrothal payment for her orphaned niece and even contributed the considerable sum of twenty *solidi* himself. With such superior forces now arrayed against Chlothild, the unfavourable outcome of the rebellion must have been clear. But when Macco offered her the chance to surrender, Chlothild refused:

> She ordered her vile assassins to ready themselves, weapons in hand, before the entrance to the oratory, so that, if Macco wished to bring violence, they might certainly respond in equal measure and fight back against the commander.

Chlothild's men were beaten with cudgels and run through with spears. Those who survived were bound and dragged out of the monastery. Some were tied to posts and beaten severely. Others had their hands cut off, or their ears, noses, or scalps removed. Chlothild took possession of the fragments of the Cross and emerged from the oratory.[40] She reminded Macco and the gathered crowd of the consequences that faced anyone who harmed a member of the royal family:

> Bring no violence upon me, I ask, for I am a queen (*regina*), the daughter of one king and the first cousin of another. Desist, lest there come a time when I take vengeance upon you all.

The crowd mocked this final threat, and amidst the jeers Macco took Chlothild into custody.

* * *

[39] Compare this point to Bikeeva, '*Serente diabulo*: The Revolt of the Nuns'.

[40] Gregory's statement that Chlothild 'took the Cross of the Lord' (*accepta cruce dominica*) has been imagined as a dramatic display, holding the relic aloft or waiving it around (e.g. Edwards, *Superior Women*, p. 82). But Gregory claimed only that Chlothild took the holy object with her, not that she brandished it, and the *Iudicium* clearly stated that Chlothild had removed the relic 'secretly' (*occulte*). She was later made to hand it over to the tribunal.

A tribunal of bishops met in the cathedral of Poitiers to resolve the dispute and restore order to Holy Cross. Chlothild was made to explain her decision to leave the convent, as was Basina, whose earlier attempt to reconcile with Leubovera did not spare her from being questioned now. Leubovera was also summoned by the bishops to address Chlothild and Basina's accusations. The question at stake was simply the violation of the Rule of Caesarius, rather than the wider issue of crimes committed during the uprising, and punishment was limited to some form of ecclesiastical sanction, though this might include excommunication.[41] The bishops lacked the authority of a secular court, though they were able to make recommendations to Guntram and Childebert in their *Iudicium*. Without underestimating the spiritual and social consequences associated with excommunication, it can be said that Chlothild and Basina were not placed in serious jeopardy, at least not of the sort that they had visited upon Holy Cross through the course of their rebellion.

Chlothild and Basina claimed that they had no option but to abandon the enclosure of Holy Cross because they received such poor treatment from their abbess, who deprived them of sufficient food and clothing, and who treated them disgracefully. They also said that Leubovera had violated the Rule of Caesarius herself when she allowed workers to use the baths, entertained laypersons within the monastery's sacred confines, repurposed a silk altar cloth and its gold border to create adornments for her niece, and frivolously indulged in table games. Leubovera rejected these accusations as either exaggerations or outright lies, and she claimed that Radegund herself had set a precedent for the way in which she governed Holy Cross (as discussed in Chapter 6). In one remarkable accusation, Chlothild asked: 'Just what sort of holiness dwells in this abbess, who makes men eunuchs and keeps them in her presence, as per imperial custom?' A startled Leubovera claimed to have no knowledge of the matter, but Chlothild provided the name of the person in question. The 'chief physician' of the convent, Reovalis, rose to Leubovera's defence. He said that he had performed the operation himself, under instructions from Radegund, not Leubovera, and for a medical reason: the boy suffered from 'a disease of the groin'. This testimony confirmed Leubovera's claim that she had no knowledge of the eunuch's condition, but it also suggests that Chlothild, who clearly did know, might have been a closer confidant to Radegund than Leubovera herself.

[41] Scheibelreiter, 'Königstöchter im Kloster', pp. 27–32.

Chlothild also claimed that the abbess kept a man as her close associate, 'who dressed in womanly vestments and was held to be female'. It is clear in Gregory's account that this man was an entirely different individual to the eunuch, a point that must be emphasized because the matter has been confused by some scholars.[42] Chlothild even pointed the man out among the attendees who had come to observe the tribunal. Gregory described the dramatic moment:

'There he stands', she cried, pointing at him with her finger. He stepped forward, in front of everyone present, dressed in the clothing of a woman, as I have said. He now declared that he was unable to perform manly work, and for this reason he had taken on such attire. As for the abbess, he knew her only by name. He had never seen her or spoken to her, for he lived more than forty miles away.

Gregory had no doubt that this individual, despite his female attire, 'was most plainly a man', but it is impossible to know if everyone agreed with his assessment, or indeed what the self-perception of the individual in question might have been.[43] Neither is it clear just what Gregory meant by the phrase 'unable to perform manly work' (*se nihil opus posse virile agere*), which some scholars have interpreted to imply sexual impotence.[44]

With more confidence, it can be said that this accusation was not principally about sexual impropriety, even though Chlothild and Basina suggested that the man acted as Leubovera's domestic servant. The *Iudicium* clearly stated that Chlothild and Basina were directly asked by the bishops if they wished to accuse Leubovera of sexual misconduct (*adulterium*), or any other capital offence, such as murder or witchcraft, and they declined. 'They replied that they had no accusations other than those which they had made when they accused her of acting against the Rule.' But Chlothild and Basina, in an attempt to demonstrate that Leubovera had allowed illicit activity on her watch, did point the bishops to some of the nuns from Holy Cross who had recently become pregnant. The bishops, however, determined that these nuns had been left 'without the discipline of their abbess' because Chlothild

---

[42] For one example, see Bullough, 'On Being Male in the Middle Ages', p. 34.

[43] Partner, 'No Sex, No Gender', pp. 419–422.

[44] See Halsall, 'Material Culture, Sex, Gender', pp. 323–325. McNamara, 'Chastity as a Third Gender', pp. 202–203, imagined that it might refer to a failed act of revenge, the 'manliest of all activities'.

and Basina had disturbed the integrity of the monastic enclosure, and that they were 'innocent' in this regard, presumably because the pregnancies resulted from the sexual violence during the uprising.[45]

After listening to the arguments put forth by Chlothild and Basina, and the defence offered by Leubovera, the bishops concluded the tribunal by judging in the abbess's favour, though she received a 'paternal rebuke' for her naive conduct. Her mistakes did not excuse the appalling misdeeds committed by Chlothild and Basina, who were ordered to ask Leubovera for forgiveness, and to make restitution for the damages they had caused to Holy Cross. Indignant that the tribunal had ruled against them, Chlothild and Basina not only refused this request, but they even swore that they wanted to see Leubovera dead. The bishops excommunicated Chlothild and Basina and forced them to hand over the fragments of the Cross, which they had brought, concealed on their persons, to the tribunal. The bishops then dispatched the *Iudicium* to Guntram and Childebert, in which they asked for Chlothild and Basina to be compelled to restore to Holy Cross the property they had seized during their revolt. They also insisted that the two nuns be forbidden from ever having the pleasure of returning—'or even the hope of returning'—to the convent, 'the place that, in this ungodly and sacrilegious manner, they laid waste, lest even worse happen'.

Chlothild and Basina went immediately to Childebert and pleaded their case directly to the king. They clearly hoped for a royal decree that might overrule the judgement of the bishops. While they had previously avoided accusing Leubovera of a capital offence, now they maintained no such reservations, issuing charges of sexual misconduct and even high treason:

> Heaping evil upon evil, they denounced to the king certain persons whom they not only accused of committing adultery with the abbess, but also carrying messages every day to his enemy, Fredegund.

The burning feud between Fredegund and Brunhild, discussed in Chapter 4, bestowed an incendiary quality to these accusations. Childebert ordered the accused men to be brought to him in chains. It is remarkable that Chlothild and Basina, even after their calamitous uprising and their excommunication by the ecclesiastical tribunal, had found an audience with Childebert,

---

[45] On clerical attitudes towards sexual violence and personal culpability, see Vihervalli, 'Wartime Rape in Late Antiquity'.

and that he gave their claims due consideration. For a moment, it may have seemed that the downfall of Leubovera was imminent. After completing the interrogation, however, Childebert found the charges baseless and released the accused from custody. This decision by Childebert, rather than the judgement of the bishops, represents the true end of the affair, even though Gregory gave far less weight to it in his narrative. Gregory also declined to identify the men in question, but it might be assumed that they were significant individuals, holders of high office, since their pleas of innocence were taken seriously.

Chlothild and Basina at last discovered that they had overestimated their influence and overplayed their hand. They now knew that they had truly failed in their efforts to see Leubovera unseated as abbess and punished for refusing to defer to their superior status. Even so, the most noteworthy aspect of the whole affair is the absence of any serious consequences for these two princesses.[46] They had led a violent uprising that resulted in the desecration of Holy Cross, the deaths of several people, and the injury and humiliation of Gudegisel and his clerical entourage. Yet Chlothild and Basina were held to account only for violating their monastic Rule, and even here the kings showed little support for the ecclesiastical sanction. Childebert asked the bishops to forgive Chlothild and Basina and lift their excommunication, even though only Basina had even asked for forgiveness. She was allowed to return to Holy Cross, despite the express request to the contrary in the *Iudicium*. There Basina continued her life as a nun, though with a shamelessness particular to a princess. Chlothild did not return, but only because she had no desire to do so, and instead Guntram gave her an estate in Poitiers, which had formerly belonged to a high-ranking official at court, and which must have been of considerable size. Although nothing more is known of her, it is possible to imagine that she operated this estate as a religious centre, in a manner not altogether unlike how Radegund had run her villa in Saix.[47] The return of Chlothild and Basina to Poitiers reminded the city's inhabitants, and the nuns of Holy Cross, that power rested in the hands of the kings, and that members of the royal family were to be treated differently. Perhaps the crowd that mocked Chlothild in her moment of defeat had been too quick to laugh after all.

---

[46] Scheibelreiter, 'Königstöchter im Kloster', p. 28.
[47] Compare this point to Rütjes, *Der Klosterstreit in Poitiers*, p. 6.

* * *

The uprising of nuns in Holy Cross represented a failure for all involved. No one achieved their desired result. Not Chlothild or Basina, who failed to oust Leubovera. Not the abbess herself, who had to justify her governance of Holy Cross, and who emerged a diminished figure. Not the bishops, whose requests in the *Iudicium* were largely ignored by Guntram and Childebert. Not the kings, who were burdened with the responsibility of cleaning up the mess caused by their rebellious relatives. And, most of all, not Radegund. In her letter *Dominis sanctis*, she had expressed her desire to see Holy Cross continue as a privileged and independent institution after her death. She worried that the nuns might deviate from the Rule of Caesarius. She knew the estates and property affiliated with the institution might come under threat. She insisted that her vision for Holy Cross endure unchanged. And she threatened anyone who violated her wishes with 'the judgement of God, the Holy Cross, and the Blessed Mary', as well as that of St Hilary and St Martin. She clearly understood the challenges that her foundation might face upon her death. Within a mere three years of her passing, these fears had come true. Indeed, worse. Not even the threat of divine retribution had spared her convent from theft, abuse, violence, and desecration.

After Radegund's funeral, Gregory had told Agnes that the blessed queen had only 'left the convent in body, but not in power'. Though intended to offer reassurance, his statement tacitly admitted the new reality that Holy Cross faced: Radegund was an irreplicable feature of the institution; without her, it could not continue as it had before.[48] The only way to imagine otherwise was to believe in her enduring spiritual presence within the convent's sacred confines, a perspective that became a central theme in Baudonivia's *Life of Radegund* for this very reason. This belief also underpinned Fortunatus's depiction of Radegund as a divine intercessor, which he presented to Brunhild and Childebert in what might have been a failed effort to persuade them to respect the late queen's wish that her convent remain independent from her local bishop. Leubovera's principal mistake had been to think that she could govern Holy Cross in a similar manner as had prevailed in the days of Radegund. She hosted secular magnates, maintained an uncertain boundary between monastic and personal property, issued ad hoc exceptions to the Rule, and took a strict approach to fasting and other forms of ascetic devotion. That model of authority depended upon Radegund's unparalleled

---

[48] Gregory of Tours, *Glory of the Confessors*, 104.

standing in the realm. Leubovera stood little chance of implementing it her-self without facing insurmountable opposition. Chlothild and Basina, as the daughters of kings, perhaps thought that they were better positioned to fill the hole left by Radegund's departure; the opportunity to fulfil their birth-right proved to be their forbidden fruit. Leubovera accepted the support and authority of Maroveus instead, reopening wounds within the religious community that had yet to heal. Whether or not Holy Cross had not suffered from its own Eve, without Radegund it was certainly destined to become a paradise lost.

> Gather, gather the wheat of the Lord. For truly I say to you that there will not be long for the harvest. Consider what I say and gather it, because un-doubtedly one day you will be seeking more time. Truly, truly, you will be begging for such days as these, and you will wish that you had them again.
>
> (Radegund to her nuns, recorded in Baudonivia, *Life of Radegund*, 19)

8

Amen

On the day Radegund passed away, the royal official Domnolenus lay dying, after a respiratory illness stole his breath. In his delirium, he experienced a dream in which he saw Radegund approaching his town, and he ran out to greet her and ask the purpose of her visit. He was amazed to learn that she had come to see him and to inform him that it was his duty to build an oratory dedicated to St Martin, for the sake of the local population. As Domnolenus slept, Radegund stroked his mouth and throat, massaging away his illness. 'I have come so that God might improve your condition', she said, before issuing a final request that he also set prisoners free. Domnolenus awoke, cured of his ailment, and explained everything to his wife. He also dispatched a messenger to Poitiers, who confirmed that Radegund had died on the same day as his vision. Recognizing that his life had been restored for a reason, he freed seven prisoners from confinement. He then discovered the foundations and the paving stones of a ruined basilica, upon which he was able to begin building a shrine in honour of St Martin, as per Radegund's request. Fortunatus, who recorded this miracle at the end of his *Life of Radegund*, had perhaps acquired his information from Domnolenus's wife, whose incidental appearance in the story is difficult to explain otherwise.[1]

Fortunatus offered this miracle as proof that Radegund now dwelled with God. He certainly made the most of it, expressly connecting the details of this single miracle to three different aspects of Radegund's life (and themes with his work): her care for the sick, her construction of what he termed a 'temple', and her liberation of prisoners. Fortunatus described this threefold significance a 'triple mystery', as if this made the miracle all the more impressive. But in truth it seems that he had few other options. Fortunatus apparently had no miracles to report that had occurred after her funeral had finished and she had been entombed. The absence of such material is especially conspicuous in comparison to other hagiographic works, which are usually replete with posthumous signs and wonders, especially those performed at a

---

[1] Fortunatus, *Life of Radegund*, 38.

Radegund. E. T. Dailey, Oxford University Press. © Oxford University Press 2023.
DOI: 10.1093/oso/9780197656105.003.0009

saint's tomb. Perhaps to avoid embarrassment, Fortunatus quickly added that he had chosen to limit his record of miracles because he worried that the inclusion of too many 'might lead to contempt'.[2] A more likely explanation is found in the context in which he wrote, probably soon after the uprising of 589.[3] Fortunatus probably felt a sense of urgency to rescue Radegund's legacy from the recent chaos. Even if he had wanted to wait for posthumous miracles to occur at her sepulchre, he may not have believed that pilgrims were likely to return any time soon, when they had other shrines to visit that had not been tainted by the blood shed during the troubled events of 590.

It is perhaps no surprise that Fortunatus failed to mention the uprising in his *Life of Radegund*, especially since he was consistently discreet throughout his works about sensitive topics. But Fortunatus omitted many other important events relating to Holy Cross, including the arrival of the fragments of the Cross and the funeral of Radegund herself.[4] Fortunatus never mentioned Agnes in this work, for example, even though she was very important to him personally and appeared throughout his poetry. He obscured the very foundation of Holy Cross itself, which seems to have occurred around §21 of his text, though the matter is not entirely clear. In more than one later passage, Fortunatus recounted events that had probably taken place while Radegund still lived in her villa in Saix.[5] Holy Cross served only as a setting, not as an object of discussion in its own right.[6] Fortunatus probably sought to distance Radegund's legacy from the fate of the convent, which had come to define her reputation, and which now threatened to tarnish it. Instead, he gave equal weight to Radegund's whole life, with considerable detail about her early years, and he omitted key moments that related to the convent itself. The protagonist of his *Life of Radegund* would have been a saint even if she had never founded Holy Cross. Not that Fortunatus held any personal hostility towards the nuns. Quite the opposite. But in light of recent events, he thought it best to put Radegund's legacy on a new footing.

---

[2] Fortunatus, *Life of Radegund*, 39.

[3] It seems unlikely that Fortunatus had the time to finish his work before Chlothild and Basina started to cause trouble. Radegund died on 13 August 587. Chlothild left in late February 589. As discussed in Chapter 7, Fortunatus had likely journeyed to Metz and then travelled by boat to Andernach, in 588, a lengthy trip. He also spent time composing poems for the occasion. There is little opportunity here for Fortunatus to have completed his *Life of Radegund*, and no reason why he should have hurried such a project.

[4] Effros, 'Images of Sanctity'.

[5] Fortunatus, *Life of Radegund*, 24 and 28, for example, seem to reference her life before the foundation of Holy Cross.

[6] Bouchard, 'Reconstructing Sanctity and Refiguring Saints', pp. 107–109.

Baudonivia wrote in the early seventh century, several years after Fortunatus completed his work, by which time she had posthumous miracles to record, including those received by pilgrims who visited Radegund's tomb. Baudonivia recorded such stories proudly, without any concern that she might inspire contempt.[7] She even noted that the church containing Radegund's shrine had its own guardian, who attended to the needs of pilgrims, and who dipped the pall draped over her tomb into water for the ill and infirm to drink.[8] Radegund had dedicated this funerary church to the Virgin Mary, but Baudonivia described it as the 'basilica of the blessed queen' and the 'basilica of Lady Radegund'.[9] She wrote at the behest of her abbess, Dedimia, in full knowledge of Fortunatus's earlier work, and with the purpose of rectifying his noteworthy omissions. Her Life of Radegund detailed the foundation of the convent and the arrival of the fragments of the Cross. She also narrated Radegund's passing, surrounded by her tearful nuns. Baudonivia aimed to restore Holy Cross to prominence in the story of Radegund's life, undeterred by awkward details, such as Maroveus's refusal to install the relic of the Cross or to attend Radegund's funeral. Not only did Baudonivia mention these events, she attributed them, ultimately, to the scheming of the Devil.[10] But she kept silent about the uprising led by Chlothild and Basina, which seems to have been too sensitive to appear even in her more candid account. Like many of Dedimia's nuns, Baudonivia had lived through the experience herself, perhaps while still at an early age. 'I am the littlest of the little ones', she wrote, 'whom Radegund reared in this household from our very cradles as her own children at her feet'.[11]

Although the wounds from the uprising clearly remained, much had changed during the years when Fortunatus and Baudonivia wrote. Without any source providing a coherent narrative, these events cannot always be set in a proper sequence, let alone a precise chronology. But it is clear that Maroveus died not long after he attended the tribunal that condemned Chlothild and Basina. He was replaced by Plato, formerly an archdeacon in Tours. This selection restored the connection between the convent in Poitiers and the clergy of Tours, but in an informal way. It can be assumed that Plato's

---

[7] Brennan, 'St Radegund'.

[8] Baudonivia, Life of Radegund, 26 and 28.

[9] Baudonivia, Life of Radegund, 27.

[10] Wemple, Women in Frankish Society, pp. 181–185. Baudonivia did, however, spare Maroveus from personal ignominy by choosing not to refer to him by name when she called him an agent of the 'Enemy of Humanity'. Only Gregory of Tours named Maroveus outright.

[11] Baudonivia, Life of Radegund, preface.

appointment improved relations between the nuns and their local bishop. Fortunatus celebrated Plato's consecration to episcopal orders in a poem that also lauded the celestial alliance between St Hilary and St Martin, the premier saints of Poitiers and Tours.[12] When Plato died, sometime in the 590s, Fortunatus himself succeeded him as bishop. His poem *On the Bishop Plato* is, in fact, his last (that can be securely dated, at least), though he lived into the early seventh century.[13] Perhaps Fortunatus's responsibilities as bishop consumed all of his remaining time. Gregory of Tours died late in 594, at the age of fifty-five, with many of his works still incomplete.[14] His successor, a certain Pelagius, is known only from a letter he received in July 596, and from the appearance of his name on episcopal lists.[15]

Holy Cross eventually recovered from Chlothild's uprising and continued as a religious house throughout the Middle Ages, though not without moments of significant disruption.[16] Radegund's convent experienced the same cycles of decline and reinvention that can be found in the history of any enduring institution, monasteries included.[17] Some attacks came from outsiders, such as the Viking raids that troubled Poitiers in the ninth century.[18] Others came from closer to home, as when the Count of Paris, Hugh the Great, attacked Poitiers in 955 and set fire to the area of the city that surrounded the convent.[19] Natural disasters also necessitated the repair and reconstruction of Holy Cross, and of Radegund's funerary church, especially a series of earthquakes and fires that erupted during the eleventh century. Poitiers became a city of crucial importance during the Hundred Years' War (1337–1453), threatening Radegund's community, though greater harm occurred during the Wars of Religion, when in 1562 the Huguenots desecrated Radegund's tomb, as discussed below. Holy Cross itself was razed to the ground in the Revolution of 1789 (but not Radegund's funerary church, which survives today). The community of nuns reformed close to the original site, but in 1965 they relocated to Saint-Benoît, about 5 km to

---

[12] Fortunatus, *Poems*, 10.14.

[13] On the uncertain date for the death of Fortunatus, see de Gaiffier, 'Saint Venance Fortunat'.

[14] Edwards, *Superior Women*, p. 98.

[15] Duchesne, *Fastes épiscopaux*, vol. 2, p. 308. The letter was from Pope Gregory I, concerning the mission to Kent.

[16] For the later history of Holy Cross, and many of the details presented here, see Edwards, *Superior Women*.

[17] For a case study concerning a different monastic community, see Rennie, *The Destruction and Recovery of Monte Cassino*.

[18] Renaud, *Les Vikings de la Charente*.

[19] Flodoard, *Annals*, 37B.

the south, where they continue today. The nuns retain several treasures from the original convent, including a reading stand that likely dates to the sixth century.[20] They also preserve the fragments of the Cross, which are regularly displayed for veneration.

Excavations conducted in 1962 uncovered an inscription from the later Middle Ages that read 'Hail to the Cross', which indicates that devotion to the relic continued within the convent.[21] The fragments of the Cross and their small reliquary also apparently received a new, additional container in the ninth century. A large gold and bejewelled box of distinctly Carolingian appearance (Figure 8.1) can be seen in an anonymous painting, which dates to the seventeenth century, and which depicts Radegund receiving the relic.[22] Since the rest of the painting is conspicuously anachronistic, the artist presumably worked with this particular object in sight.[23] The production of this box may have occurred under Rotrude (d. 912), an abbess of Holy Cross and a daughter of Charles the Bald.[24] The relationship between the box, which is now lost, and the surviving reliquary that (as discussed in Chapter 5) dates to the eleventh century is unclear, but the box was apparently large enough to contain the smaller reliquary during the centuries in which they coexisted.[25]

The difficulty in establishing the history of the fragments of the Cross results in part from their status as a private object, kept within the sacred confines of Holy Cross, which became increasingly difficult to access for anyone other than the nuns themselves. Carolingian reforms led to a greater emphasis on monastic seclusion and the regularization of coenobitic life within all religious houses. During this period, the nuns of Holy Cross exchanged the Rule of Caesarius for the Rule of Benedict, which gained prominence in the Carolingian era.[26] Lay access to Radegund's tomb also suffered, even though it was contained within a funerary church located outside the monastic enclosure. The original building was replaced with a new construction in the ninth century, which cannot have been designed in a

[20] Germond, *Le Pupitre de Sainte Radegonde*.
[21] Eygun, 'Circonscription de Poitiers', pp. 471–472 (that is, O CRUX A[VE]).
[22] Hahn, 'Collector and Saint', pp. 268–270.
[23] The reliquary is likely that which appears on an inventory of Holy Cross taken in 1457. Skubiszewski, 'La Staurothèque de Poitiers', p. 66.
[24] Jones, 'Perceptions of Byzantium'
[25] On the eleventh-century date of the present reliquary, see Skubiszewski, 'La Staurothèque de Poitiers'.
[26] The community was eventually pressured into adopting the Rule of Benedict of Nursia, at least partially under the Carolingian reforms, and fully by the twelfth century. Edwards, *Superior Women*, pp. 97–98.

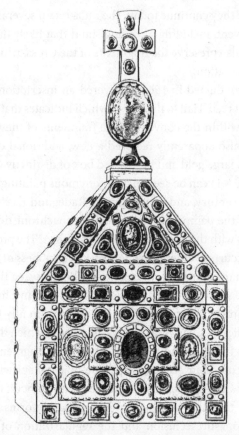

Figure 8.1 A sketch of the Carolingian reliquary (adapted from Conway, 'St Radegund's Reliquary at Poitiers'), produced from its depiction on an anonymous painting of the seventeenth century kept in the Abbaye Sainte-Croix, Saint-Benoît.

manner that improved access.[27] Carolingian reforms increased the standing of the clergy as mediators between pious believers and heavenly intercessors, diminishing pilgrimages to the tombs and crypts of the holy dead.[28] But these circumstances changed in the eleventh century, when in 1012 the

---

[27] Kneepkens, 'À propos des débuts de l'histoire de l'église-funéraire'.
[28] Fouracre, 'The Origins of the Carolingian Attempt to Regulate the Cult of Saints'. Smith, 'Rulers and Relics'.

Figure 8.2 The tomb of Radegund in the crypt of her funerary church in Poitiers.

abbess Béliarde made alterations to the church that improved lay access and encouraged pilgrimage again.[29]

Repeated efforts were made to repair the church when it suffered damage later in the century, which demonstrate that it had indeed become the means by which the wider public engaged with Radegund's legacy. The apse and choir of the church that stands today are the result of these eleventh-century efforts to revive the veneration of Radegund as an intercessor for the Christian faithful, while the other elements of the building were later replaced. The nave dates to the early thirteenth century and still features stained glass produced in the 1260s and 1270s, though the glass was damaged during the Huguenot attack of 1562 (and subjected to a heavy-handed restoration by Henri Carot in 1898).[30] Radegund's sarcophagus (Figure 8.2), broken and held together with metal pins, also appears to date to the eleventh century, though the base on which it sits, upheld by pillars, may be older. An inscription in the crypt of the church indicates that Abbess Béliarde restored the saint's tomb in 1012 and adorned it with lamps. According to a sixteenth-century report composed by the ambassadors of Venice, the Huguenots also damaged Radegund's tomb and discarded her body.[31] No record exists of its

[29] Edwards, *Superior Women*, p. 101.
[30] Edwards, *Superior Women*, p. 180, n. 32.
[31] Girolamo Lippomano, *Viaggio*, p. 315.

recovery, but when the tomb was last opened on 13 December 1988, the body of a woman was found inside.[32]

Perhaps the clearest sign of the extensive eleventh-century efforts to revive interest in Radegund's veneration is to be found in an artefact kept within the Médiathèque François-Mitterrand in Poitiers: an eleventh-century illuminated manuscript of substantial size—280 mm × 215 mm, roughly four times the size of the reliquary of the Cross—that contains Fortunatus's *Life of Radegund* (and probably once included Baudonivia's version as well).[33] Twenty-two illuminations depict scenes from Fortunatus's text, suggesting that the manuscript was intended to be displayed, at least on days in which the events of Radegund's life were celebrated locally.[34] Radegund's capture by Chlothar, her nocturnal prayers while the king slept, her consecration as a deaconess, and her entrance into her cell complement depictions of her powerful miracles. The images emphasize Radegund's other-worldly power; her embrace of monastic seclusion; and her humility, charity, and asceticism, while overlooking her extreme self-mortification and downplaying her queenly status once she had taken her religious vows. The manuscript, and the reliquary and the funerary church, identify the eleventh century as a turning point in the medieval veneration of Radegund, when her cult was reinvented for the benefit of the religious community in Poitiers and tailored for their contemporary needs.[35]

Radegund's legacy continued to be updated and redeployed, often with political purposes in view, across the following centuries. Some examples are readily apparent, such as the production of a new *Life of Radegund* by Hildebert of Lavardin (d. 1133) that clearly adapted the saint's image to better align with the religious reforms of Pope Gregory VII.[36] Others are less evident, such as the appearance of a figure thought to be Eleanor of Aquitaine (who governed the eponymous region while resident in Poitiers from 1168 to 1173) on a mural in a church dedicated to Radegund in Chinon, the settlement east of Saix where the saint had once sought the otherworldly intercession of the hermit John (as discussed in Chapter 3).[37] Vernacular versions of Radegund's life appeared in printed texts from the early sixteenth century,

[32] Edwards, *Superior Women*, p. 101, n. 64.
[33] Poitiers, Médiathèque François-Mitterrand (bibliothèque municipale), MS 250 (136). Favreau, *La Vie de sainte Radegonde par Fortunat*. Carrasco, 'Spirituality in Context'.
[34] Hahn, *Portrayed on the Heart*, pp. 259–281.
[35] Edwards, *Superior Women*, pp. 103–133.
[36] Von Moos, *Hildebert von Lavardin*, 208–239.
[37] Evans, *Inventing Eleanor*, pp. 150–155.

including an English *Lyfe of Saynt Radegunde*, most likely the work of the Benedictine monk Henry Bradshaw (d. 1513). Her life also remained important to the French monarchy well beyond the medieval period. The Valois king Charles VIII and his wife, Anne of Brittany, for example, commissioned a richly illuminated manuscript that recounted her life in image and text, produced in Poitiers in 1497.[38] Charlotte Flandrina of Nassau, a member of the House of Bourbon and an abbess of Holy Cross, encouraged the production of more than one version of the saint's life in the seventeenth century.[39] Radegund's legacy not only survived the turmoil of the Revolution of 1789, which destroyed her convent, but it even became central to French national identity during the Third Republic, evident most clearly in the celebration of the 1300th anniversary of her death in 1887, when she was hailed as *Mère de la Patrie Française*, 'Mother of the French Fatherland'.[40]

Although Holy Cross remained an important institution throughout the medieval and early modern periods, without its visionary queen the convent never recovered the prominence it had enjoyed in the sixth century. The frequent efforts to revitalize interest in Radegund over the centuries, however successful, fell short of the radical and dynamic impulses that Radegund herself expressed in her vision for the institution. She had been an altogether more disruptive force when she had founded a convent in order to create an environment that offered her what she had previously been denied: a place in which she, surrounded by her nuns and armed with the fragments of the Cross, might be valued in her own right. Within the sacred confines of Holy Cross, the effects of the trauma that she had suffered were seen, not as flaws, but as signs of virtue. Self-mortification and self-starvation brought Radegund closer to God and conferred upon her the power to exorcise demons, to cure the sick, and even to raise the dead. The Christ whom she and her congregation collectively envisioned had granted her a spiritual relationship with himself, which became both her daily pursuit and her ultimate purpose. As a holy queen, she fought the Devil and his agents to protect those in her care and, ultimately, to win a place of honour in the Kingdom of Heaven. In this sense, the most fitting tribute to Radegund was perhaps the legend of the *Grand'goule*, in which she vanquished the evil that menaced the denizens of Poitiers through her unique combination of virtue and authority.

---

[38] The manuscript is now held in a private collection in the United States. It was last displayed at The European Fine Art Foundation (TEFAF) fair in Maastricht in 2019.

[39] Van der Does, *Prinsessen*, pp. 97–106.

[40] Brennan, 'Piety and Politics'.

Radegund had overcome the threats posed by a hostile world to create a place in which she might win greater respect for herself through piety and charity than through the fear and terror used by many of her contemporaries.

* * *

Violence stalked Radegund throughout her entire life, and no more so than in her younger years. She became an orphan even before Chlothar and his half-brother slaughtered most members of her royal family. Her marriage placed her in a state of continuous anxiety through the many threats she faced: the hostility she encountered as queen from certain magnates, the constraints within which she lived, and the intertwined precariousness of her existence with that of her brother. Radegund's intimate life with Chlothar, whatever she may have experienced, can itself be considered a form of sexual violence in this context. Once she was cloistered within the protective walls of Holy Cross, some of these anxieties endured. Radegund feared that Chlothar might force her to return to his side, for example, in violation of her religious vows. Perhaps in response to this menace, she began to inflict violence upon herself, to torture her flesh so that she might purify her soul. Even after Chlothar died, Radegund and her nuns faced the threat of violence from marauding armies, and from the whims of Merovingian kings. Radegund also dealt with the obstinacy of her local bishop, who preferred to insult her and to publicly defy her wishes, rather than to share prominence with her. After Radegund died, violence was brought even to her tomb, and not for the last time, by the band of ruthless mercenaries assembled by Chlothild and Basina.

Radegund's most easily overlooked achievement was simply to survive within this system of violence, and to do so without inflicting violence upon others. She might easily have faced the same fate as Chalda, who was burned alive with her daughters, or Audovera, who was given a 'cruel death' after she fell out of favour.[41] Fredegund and Brunhild, in contrast, maintained their position at court for decades, but in large part because others feared them. Their ability to influence their husbands and to eliminate their enemies was respected, but they still faced moments of great peril.[42] Any attempt to opt out of this system also came with its own risks. When Galswinth tried to leave Chilperic, for example, she was denied her request and then murdered, even though she had offered to leave all her wealth behind.[43] Radegund had met

---

[41] Gregory of Tours, *Histories*, 4.20 (Chalda) and 5.39 (Audovera).
[42] Dailey, *Queens, Consorts, Concubines*, pp. 118–140.
[43] Gregory of Tours, *Histories*, 4.28.

with Galswinth upon her arrival in Gaul, and the two corresponded thereafter. Perhaps she had told her about the dangers and expectations that she
might face at Chilperic's court. The burdens of a queen included the need to
uphold the royal dynasty's honour. The elder Chlothild, Radegund's mother-
in-law, was asked to decide the fate of her grandchildren, and to choose between the scissors or the sword. She decided that death, if it affirmed the
inviolability of royal descent, was preferable to shorn hair and the disgrace of
disinheritance.[44] Brunhild, Fredegund, Galswinth, and Chlothild were, like
Radegund, outsiders who found themselves elevated to the highest echelons
of the Frankish elite—placed on a pedestal that also served as a precipice,
from which a great fall threatened. To inflict or receive violence was merely
the choice to push or be pushed from such a precarious pinnacle.

Radegund protected herself by inspiring awe and devotion from her
supporters. This strategy required her to impress others, and to do so on their
terms. Her supporters belonged to the same social order that, by its very nature, placed a great burden upon Radegund and threatened her standing.
Such relationships were hard to maintain without personal compromise.
Fortunatus, for example, considered virginity superior to any other state, and
he explicitly said as much in the poem he composed for the consecration of
Agnes as abbess. It can only be imagined how Radegund, who regarded herself as a bride of Christ, might have felt as Fortunatus recited his work to her
community, in which he declared, after recounting the virtue of the Virgin
Mary and her 'undefiled womb', that

> Christ esteems in the internal flesh of his bride what his sacred self previ-
> ously chose to value in his mother. He freely penetrates the inner cavities
> known only to him, happier to enter where no one has been before. He
> regards those parts which have not been deflowered and bruised to belong
> to him, since they have not been shared with any other man.[45]

Fortunatus never fully accepted Radegund's idea of a holy queen, through
which she had entwined her royal and righteous qualities to weave an image
of herself unique among her peers. In his *Life of Radegund*, he instead created
tension between her secular and otherworldly ties, and he theologized
the idea of sacred queenship into a meaningless abstraction.[46] Though a

[44] Gregory of Tours, *Histories*, 3.18.
[45] Fortunatus, *Poems*, 8.3, lines 107–110.
[46] De Nie, 'Fatherly and Motherly Curing'.

supporter and client of Radegund, Fortunatus placed his values above hers in his account of her life.

Gregory of Tours was another supporter who praised Radegund in his works, but without necessarily appreciating her own understanding of spiritual perfection. Radegund had influenced Gregory's appointment as bishop. But in his *Histories*, he devoted far more space to the uprising of Chlothild and Basina than to anything that she had accomplished in Holy Cross.[47] When he composed his collection of exemplary figures, which he titled the *Life of the Fathers*, he included only one woman alongside nineteen men— and this woman was not Radegund. In introducing Monegund, he wrote:

> God has provided us with models drawn not only from holy men, but also from those of the inferior sex who press on in a manly way rather than lazily. He grants a share of his heavenly kingdom not only to men, who fight in a legitimate way, but also to women, who sweat in these battles and win the field.[48]

It remains unclear whether or not Radegund (or Monegund, for that matter) also thought that femininity was by its nature unconducive to the pursuit of holiness. Such a perspective might help to explain her extreme fasting, which may have interrupted menstruation, and her embrace of a basin filled with hot coals, which may have severely disfigured her chest.[49] But these acts can also be explained without reference to a theory that triangulates gender, the body, and the soul. With more certainty, it can be said that, whatever her own personal feelings, Radegund must have taken such opinions into consideration when she presented herself as a holy queen, especially to those bishops and clergy who shared Gregory's views.[50]

Radegund found herself enveloped by the expectations of her society. Some of these constraints she was able to subvert, others to bypass or ignore, but many she internalized. They informed her identity and guided her actions. Radegund carved out an impressive degree of agency for herself, successfully

[47] A similar dynamic was at work in the treatment of St Geneviève by Gregory of Tours, *Glory of the Confessors*, 89, as is clear from a comparison with the *Life of Geneviève*. See Heinzelmann and Poulin, *Les Vies anciennes de sainte Geneviève*, pp. 132–133.

[48] Gregory of Tours, *Life of the Fathers*, 19. De Nie, 'Consciousness Fecund through God'.

[49] On extreme asceticism and the question of gender, see Rousselle, *Porneia*; Coates, 'Regendering Radegund?'.

[50] On the relationship between asceticism and clerical authority, see Cooper, *The Virgin and the Bride*, pp. 55–59.

creating room to manoeuvre in a world of obligations, within which her very sense of self took shape. Yet despite her many individual acts of resistance, when it concerned the system as a whole, Radegund adhered to the prevailing structures of her society and often reinforced them. Audacity was no substitute for autonomy. She had neither the power to break these chains, nor the scope to reconceptualize the social order in a radically different form. She might embrace the leper, clothe the poor, free the imprisoned, and show decency to slaves, but she could not cure leprosy, prevent poverty, end captivity, or abolish slavery. Or even contemplate such possibilities. To describe her as a visionary is not to suggest that her horizons were without limit. And for all that she lost to the social system that prevailed in sixth-century Gaul, she also benefitted; her achievements depended on her elite status, which informed her every experience. As a biographical subject, Radegund necessarily exists within the complex relationship between 'her life' and 'her times', between her shifting state of conflict and conformity with the prevailing attitudes that defined her worth, her potential, and her aspirations. Queen and saint are not mere descriptions of Radegund. They were her ambitions and her achievements, and inseparably so.

Dominis sanctis
Radegund's Letter to the Bishops

This letter appears within the *Histories* of Gregory of Tours, copied alongside other documents in his account of the uprising of nuns in Poitiers (discussed in Chapter 7).[1] Gregory provided no title for the letter, which I have referred to throughout this book as *Dominis sanctis* from its opening words. Another version, known from an eleventh-century manuscript and a (now lost) medieval parchment roll that contained documents from Holy Cross, was edited in the nineteenth century; it presents variant readings that, when not entirely trivial, are clearly later interpolations made in Poitiers.[2] The translation offered here, therefore, follows the text found in the *Histories*. This is, of course, not the first English translation of Radegund's letter. Earlier versions appeared in translations of the *Histories* and in scholarly articles, referenced in the Bibliography alongside the editions of the *Histories* (listed under 'Gregory of Tours') and *Dominis sanctis* (under 'Radegund'). The translation offered here prioritizes the meaning of Radegund's words over the grammatical structure of the Latin text, when it is not possible to clearly communicate both in English prose.

Although the letter contains no dating clause, its contents, and indeed its tone, strongly suggest the perspective of a mature Radegund, writing with hindsight about the foundation of Holy Cross, and with foresight about her own death. She clearly worried about the future of her convent in her absence. Her emphasis on the transient nature of temporal life, and on the need to preserve copies of the letter in episcopal archives, further implies that she wrote with a view to her own (potentially imminent) passing and the legacy that she hoped to leave behind. In a particularly revealing passage, Radegund explained to the bishops that she had chosen to compose the letter while she still lived (deploying a form of *superstare*, in the sense of 'to remain standing' or 'to survive'), rather than to appear before them in person, because she lacked the strength (*non valere*) to prostrate herself at their feet. This passage implies that she was too frail to travel, not (as often thought) that she was prevented from attending by the Rule of Caesarius. As explained in Chapter 5, the Rule was not interpreted in this manner in Holy Cross, where Abbess Agnes had the power to permit travel under circumstances of her choosing, and who consistently deferred to Radegund's wishes. This misunderstanding has contributed to the view that Radegund may have written this letter years earlier, an interpretation that sits uncomfortably with the content of the letter itself. The letter cannot be read as a letter of foundation, even it if has been described in such terms; it is, if anything, closer to a last will and testament.[3]

---

[1] Gregory of Tours, *Histories*, 9.42.

[2] *Diplomata regum Francorum*, number 7, pp. 8–11; and *Diplomata* (Pardessus), vol. 1, pp. 150–154. The manuscript is Poitiers, Médiathèque François-Mitterrand (bibliothèque municipale), MS 250 (136), fols 73^v–75^r. The parchment roll has been dated anywhere from the eleventh to the thirteenth century. A seventeenth-century copy survives. See Vezin, 'Étude paléographique et codicologique'.

[3] See Williard, 'Friendship in the Works of Venantius Fortunatus', p. 138; and Jeffrey, 'Radegund and the Letter of Foundation', p. 14.

* * *

To all the bishops, my holy lords and fathers in Christ, most worthy in your apostolic sees, Radegund, a sinner.

The start of a shared endeavour better achieves its result when brought to the ears, and commended to the good sense, of our collective fathers, our physicians and shepherds, who care for the sheepfold, and whose involvement will enable the venture's success, through generous counsel, powerful support, and prayerful petition.

In days past, I was loosened from my worldly ties by divine providence and unmerited mercy. I willingly turned to the mandate of religion and the command of Christ. With the passion of a focused mind, I considered how to advance other women so that—the Lord willing—my own desires might prove beneficial for others. At the order and expense of the most excellent lord, King Chlothar, a monastery for girls was established in the city of Poitiers. After its foundation, I endowed the monastery with however much wealth I had received from the generosity of the king.

For this community, which I assembled through Christ's provision, I adopted the Rule that the holy Caesaria had lived under, which had been compiled to suit her needs by the blessed Caesarius, bishop of Arles, from the example of the holy fathers. With the approval of the most blessed bishops of this city, and all of the others as well, and by the choice of our own community, I appointed as abbess my sister, Lady Agnes, whom I had loved and raised from a young age in the place of a daughter. I submitted myself in regular obedience to her authority, next to that of God. In keeping with the apostolic example,[4] my sisters and I, upon entering the monastery, handed over by deed the worldly resources that we had once thought belonged to us. Bearing in mind Ananias and Sapphira, we kept nothing for ourselves.[5] Because the cycles and circumstances of the human condition are uncertain, because the world hastens to its end, and because some people wish to serve their own interests rather than the divine will, I am sending this written entreaty while I still live, a devoted woman led by the zeal of God, to you who hold apostolic office, with my intentions, in the name of Christ.

Since at present I lack the strength to throw myself at your feet, I lay before you a letter in my place. I swear by the Father, the Son, and the Holy Spirit, and by the mighty Day of Judgement, that, if you who are present wish not to be tormented by the Tyrant, but to be crowned by the True King,[6] then may the following persons be kept outside your grace, as deprivers and despoilers of the poor, on account of the will of Christ and this request of mine, and in accordance with your holiness and the holiness of your successors next to God: any person—the local bishop, a royal official, or anyone else—who, as I am sure will never happen, tries to interfere with my community after my death, by evil enticements or legal procedures. Or anyone who attempts to break the Rule. Or anyone who promotes an abbess other than my sister, Agnes, consecrated through the benediction of the most blessed Germanus in the presence of his brethren.[7] Or this community, should it agitate to become something other than what it is, which cannot be allowed to happen. Or the local bishop, or anyone else, who desires to seize either authority over the monastery or the property belonging to it, through a new privilege that surpasses what earlier bishops held

---

[4] Acts 4:32.

[5] Acts 5:1–11. God struck Ananias and Sapphira dead for concealing wealth from the apostles.

[6] I have read the juxtaposition of *legitimus rex* and *tyrannus* to refer to Christ and the Devil, rather than to any specific ruler.

[7] Germanus, bishop of Paris (d. 576).

in my lifetime. Or anyone who tries to further transgress beyond the Rule. Or a prince, or a bishop, or a magnate, or anyone among the sisters who breaks a sacrilegious vow, and attempts to transfer into their own possession the property that the sisters handed over from their personal assets, or that others gave for the salvation of their souls, or that the most excellent lord Chlothar or his sons, the most excellent lord kings, conferred upon me. I transferred these possessions to the monastery with his express permission, and on the authority of the most excellent lord kings, Charibert, Guntram, Chilperic, and Sigibert, which was confirmed and publicly demonstrated by signatures from their own hands and by the swearing of an oath. Through your opposition, no aspect of our Rule, and no property of our monastery, will be reduced or changed.

I also pray that, when God wishes to remove our aforementioned sister, Lady Agnes, from this world, an abbess is ordained in her place from our community, one who will please God, preserve the rule, and in no way lessen the precepts of holiness. May she never, of her own will or that of anyone else, cast these aside. If anyone shall desire to go against the command of God and the authority of the kings, which is wholly improper, concerning the arrangement written above and entrusted to you in the presence of the Lord and his saints, or concerning the diminishment of a person or property, or if anyone shall try to bring about tribulation for my aforementioned sister, Abbess Agnes, let them face the judgement of God, and the Holy Cross, and the Blessed Mary. Let them have as enemies and persecutors the blessed confessors Hilary and Martin, to whom, after God, I have entrusted the protection of my sisters.

You too, holy bishop, and your successors, whom I have diligently adopted as patrons in God's cause, if anyone appears who, God forbid, wishes to soften these injunctions, show no reluctance to petition the king who at that time has purview over this place, or over the city of Poitiers, on behalf of the institution entrusted to you before the Lord. Show no reluctance to work in the pursuit and defence of justice against the injustice of others. Halt and drive back the enemy of God, so that no Catholic king in his own times allows in any way such an unholy violation, lest he permit the destruction of what has been firmly established by God's will and mine, and the will of those kings.

I likewise compel those princes whom God ordains to rule the people when I am gone—in the name of the King whose reign has no end, by the nod of whose head kingdoms endure, and indeed who gives them their very life and dominion—that they arrange under their care, and in one voice with Abbess Agnes, the management of the monastery that I envisioned to be built, ordered under a rule, and endowed, all with the consent and support of the lord kings, their fathers, and their grandfathers. May it never be allowed for our abbess, mentioned here so often, to be harassed or disturbed by anyone. May it never be allowed for anything pertaining to our monastery to be altered or diminished. Instead, for the sake of God, and together with the lord bishops themselves, let them give orders to defend and protect the monastery just as I have entreated, as I pray in the presence of the Redeemer of Nations, so that they may be forever united in the eternal kingdom with the Defender of the Poor and Bridegroom of the Virgins, in whose honour they protect the handmaidens of God.

I also compel you, holy bishops, and you, most excellent lord kings, and the entire Christian people, by the Catholic faith in which you are baptized and the churches you preserve, that, when God decides to take me from the light, my dear body ought to be interred in the basilica that I have begun to construct in honour of St Mary, Mother of the Lord, where many of our sisters are already gathered in repose, whether it is finished or unfinished. If anyone shall attempt, or even think to do otherwise, let him suffer divine vengeance by the power of the Cross of Christ and the Blessed Mary. Thus, through your intervention, I might be rewarded with a burial place in this basilica, surrounded by my sisters. Shedding tears, I pray that this supplication of mine, signed by my own hand, be preserved in the archive of the universal church.[8] And that, if it becomes necessary for my sister, Abbess Agnes, or her congregation to ask for your help and protection against any unscrupulous people, you will provide, in your pious compassion, the assistance of a good shepherd. As a result, they will not say that I left them helpless, when God has provided your kindness as protection.

All this I lay before your eyes, in the name of the one who, from his glorious Cross, entrusted his mother, the Virgin, to the blessed apostle John. As he fulfilled the Lord's instruction, so shall you fulfil what I, though unworthy and insignificant, have entrusted to you, my lords—apostolic men and fathers of the Church. If you uphold what I set forth, then you shall deserve to be partakers in the merits of the one whose will you implement, and you shall worthily renew the apostolic example.

---

[8] Radegund asked the bishops to preserve the letter within their own archives (rather than within the archives of the cathedral of Poitiers alone). See Flierman, 'Gregory of Tours and the Merovingian Letter', p. 140, n. 132.

APPENDIX 2

Family Tree of Select Merovingians

This family tree only identifies individuals named in the main text.
For a complete version, see Wood, *The Merovingian Kingdoms*, pp. 344–349.

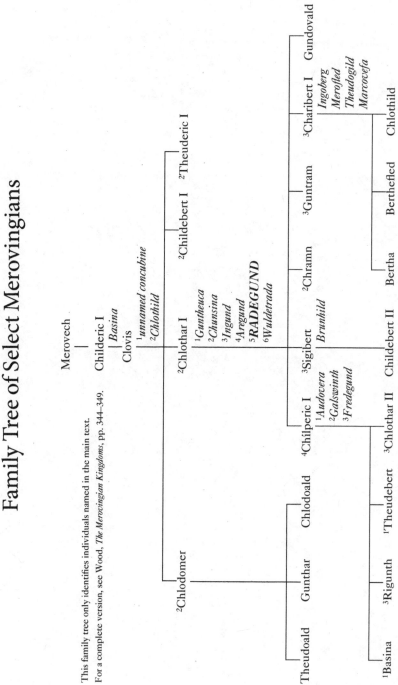

Bibliography

Primary Sources

The Alphabetical Collection, trans. by Benedicta Ward, *The Sayings of the Desert Fathers: The Alphabetical Collection*, rev. edn (Kalamazoo, MI: Cistercian Publications, 1984; orig. edn 1975)

Ambrose of Milan, *Concerning Virgins*, ed. by Franco Gori, *Sancti Ambrosii episcopi Mediolanensis opera*, vol. 14.2: *De virginitate, De institutione virginis, Exhortatio virginitatis* (Milan: Biblioteca Ambrosiana, 1989); trans. by H. de Romestin in *A Select Library of Nicene and Post-Nicene Fathers of the Christian Church*, ed. by Philip Schaff and Henry Wace, 2nd series, vol. 10: *St Ambrose: Select Works and Letters* (New York: Christian Literature Company, 1896), pp. 361–390

Ambrose of Milan, *On the Death of Theodosius*, ed. by Otto Faller, *De obitu Theodosii*, Corpus scriptorum ecclesiasticorum Latinorum, 73 (Vienna: Österreichische Akademie der Wissenschaften, 1955), pp. 369–401; trans. by John Hugo Wolfgang Gideon Liebeschuetz and Carole Hill, *Ambrose of Milan: Political Letters and Speeches* (Liverpool: Liverpool University Press, 2005), pp. 177–203

Ammianus Marcellinus, *Res Gestae*, ed. by Charles Upson Clark, 2 vols (Berlin: Weidmann, 1910–1915)

Augustine of Hippo, *The City of God*, ed. by Patrick G. Walsh, *De civitate Dei*, 6 vols (Oxford: Oxbow Books, 2005–2014); trans. by William Babcock (Hyde Park, NY: New City Press, 2012)

Augustine of Hippo, *Confessions*, ed. by James J. O'Donnell, 3 vols (Oxford: Oxford University Press, 2013); trans. by Maria Boulding, *The Confessions of Saint Augustine* (Hyde Park, NY, New City Press, 1997)

Avitus of Vienne, *Letters*, ed. by Rudolf Peiper, *Epistulae*, in *Monumenta Germaniae historica, Auctores antiquissimi*, vol. 6.2 (Berlin: Weidmann, 1883), pp. 1–102; trans. by Danuta Shanzer and Ian Wood, *Avitus of Vienne: Letters and Selected Prose* (Liverpool: Liverpool University Press, 2002), pp. 89–376

Baudonivia, *Life of Radegund*, ed. by Bruno Krusch, *De vitae sanctae Radegundis: Liber II.*, in *Monumenta Germaniae historica, Scriptores rerum Merovingicarum*, vol. 2 (Hanover: Hahn, 1888), pp. 377–395; trans. by Jo Ann McNamara and John E. Halborg, *Sainted Women of the Dark Ages* (Durham, NC: Duke University Press, 1992), pp. 86–105

Bede, *Ecclesiastical History of the English People*, ed. and trans. by Bertram Colgrave and R. A. B. Mynors, *Bede's Ecclesiastical History of the English People*, rev. edn (Oxford: Clarendon Press, 1992)

Biblia sacra iuxta vulgatam versionem, ed. by Robert Weber, Roger Gryson, Bonifatius Fischer, Jean Gribomont, and Hedley Frederick Davis Sparks, 5th edn (Stuttgart: Deutsche Bibelgesellschaft, 2003; orig. edn 1969)

Boethius, *On the Consolation of Philosophy*, ed. by James J. O'Donnell, *Boethius' Consolatio Philosophiae*, 2 vols (Indianapolis: Hackett, 1984); trans. by Patrick G. Walsh, *Boethius: The Consolation of Philosophy* (Oxford: Oxford University Press, 2008)

Cassiodorus, *Variae*, ed. by Theodor Mommsen, in *Monumenta Germaniae historica, Auctores antiquissimi*, vol. 12 (Berlin: Weidmann, 1894); trans. by M. Shane Bjornlie, *The Variae: The Complete Translation. Cassiodorus* (Oakland, CA: University of California Press, 2019)

Caesaria the Younger, *Letter to Richild and Radegund*, ed. by Wilhelm Gundlach, in *Monumenta Germaniae historica, Epistolae*, vol. 3 (Berlin: Weidmann, 1892), pp. 450–453; trans. by Jo Ann McNamara and John E. Halborg, *Sainted Women of the Dark Ages* (Durham, NC: Duke University Press, 1992), pp. 114–118

Caesarius of Arles, *Letters*, ed. by Germain Morin, *Sancti Caesarii episcopi Arelatensis opera omnia*, vol. 2: Opera varia (Denée: Abbaye de Maredsous, 1942); trans. by William Klingshirn, *Caesarius of Arles: Life, Testament, Letters* (Liverpool: Liverpool University Press, 1994), pp. 78–139

Caesarius of Arles, *Rule for Nuns*, ed. by Adalbert de Vogüé and Joël Courreau, *Regula ad virgines*, in *Césaire d'Arles: œuvres monastiques*, vol. 1: *Œuvres pour les moniales*, Sources chrétiennes, 345 (Paris: Cerf, 1988), pp. 170–273; trans. by Maria Caritas McCarthy, *The Rule for Nuns of St Caesarius of Arles: A Translation with a Critical Introduction* (Washington, DC: Catholic University of America Press, 1960)

Caesarius of Arles, *Sermons*, ed. by Germain Morin, *Sancti Caesarii episcopi Arelatensis opera omnia*, vol. 1.1–2: *Sermones* (Denée: Abbaye de Maredsous, 1937–1942)

Capitularia regum Francorum, ed. by Alfred Edwin Boretius and Viktor Krause, in *Monumenta Germaniae historica, Capitularia regum Francorum*, 2 vols (Hannover: Hahn, 1883–1897)

Concilia Galliae, ed. by Charles Munier, Corpus Christianorum, series Latina, 148–148A, 2 vols (Turnhout: Brepols, 1963); French trans. with intro. and notes by Jean Gaudemet and Brigitte Basdevant, *Les Canons des conciles mérovingiens (vi^e–viie siècles)*, 2 vols (Paris: Cerf, 1989)

Constantius of Lyon, *Life of Germanus, Bishop of Auxerre*, ed. by Bruno Krusch and Wilhelm Levison, *Vita Germani, episcopi Autissiodorensis*, in *Monumenta Germaniae historica, Scriptores rerum Merovingicarum*, vol. 7 (Hanover and Leipzig: Hahn, 1920), pp. 225–283; trans. by Frederick Russell Hoare, *The Western Fathers: Being the Lives of SS Martin of Tours, Ambrose, Augustine of Hippo, Honoratus of Arles and Germanus of Auxerre* (London: Frank Sheed and Maisie Ward, 1954), pp. 284–320

Corippus, *In Praise of Emperor Justin the Younger*, ed. and trans. by Averil Cameron, *In laudem Iustini Augusti minoris libri iv* (London: Athlone Press, 1976)

Cyprian of Toulon, *Life of Caesarius*, ed. by Bruno Krusch, *Vitae Caesarii episcopi Arelatensis: Liber i.*, in *Monumenta Germaniae historica, Scriptores rerum Merovingicarum*, vol. 3 (Hanover: Hahn, 1896), pp. 457–483; trans. by William E. Klingshirn, *Caesarius of Arles: Life, Testament, Letters* (Liverpool: Liverpool University Press, 1994), pp. 9–42

Cyril of Jerusalem, *Lenten Lectures*, ed. by Wilhelm Karl Reischl and Joseph Rupp, *Catecheses*, in *Cyrilli Hierosolymarum Archiepiscopi opera quae supersunt omnia*, 2 vols (Munich: J. J. Lentner, 1848–1860); trans. by Leo P. McCauley and Anthony A. Stephenson, *The Works of St Cyril of Jerusalem*, 2 vols (Washington, DC: Catholic University of America Press, 1969–1970)

Diplomata, chartæ, epistolæ, leges aliaque instrumenta ad res Gallo-Francicas spectantia, ed. by Jean Marie Pardessus, 2 vols (Paris: Ex Typographeo regio, 1843–1849)

Diplomata regum Francorum e stripe Merovingica, ed. by Georg Heinrich Pertz, in *Monumenta Germaniae historica, Diplomata* (Hanover: Hahn, 1872), pp. 1–88

Epistolae Austrasiacae, ed. by Wilhelm Gundlach, *Monumenta Germaniae historica, Epistolae*, vol. 3 (Berlin: Weidmann, 1892), pp. 110–153

Epitaph of Caretena, ed. by Rudolf Peiper, *Epitaphium Caretenes religiosae reginae quae condita est Lugduni in basilica sancti Michaelis*, in *Monumenta Germaniae historica, Auctores antiquissimi*, vol. 6.2 (Berlin: Weidmann, 1883), p. 185

Egeria, *Itinerarium*, ed. by Hélène Péteé, *Éthérie: Journal de voyage*, Sources chrétiennes, 21 (Paris: Cerf, 1948); trans. by George E. Gingras, *Egeria: Diary of a Pilgrimage* (New York: Newman, 1970)

Eusebius of Caesarea, *Ecclesiastical History*, ed. by Eduard Schwartz and Theodor Mommsen, *Eusebius Werke*, vol. 2.1–3: *Die Kirchengeschichte* (Leipzig: Johann Conrad Hinrichs, 1903–1909); trans. by Paul L. Maier, *Eusebius: The Church History* (Grand Rapids, MI: Kregel, 1999)

Flodoard of Reims, *Annals*, ed. by Philippe Lauer, *Les Annales de Flodoard* (Paris: Alphonse Picard et Fils, 1905); trans. by Steven Fanning and Bernard S. Bachrach, *The Annals of Flodoard of Reims, 919–966* (Toronto: University of Toronto Press, 2011)

Florentius of Tricastina, *Life of Rusticula, or Marcia, Abbess of Arles*, ed. by Bruno Krusch, *Vita Rusticulae sive Marciae abbatissae Arelatensis*, in *Monumenta Germaniae historica, Scriptores rerum Merovingicarum*, vol. 4 (Hanover and Leipzig: Hahn, 1902), pp. 337–351; trans. by Jo Ann McNamara and John E. Halborg, *Sainted Women of the Dark Ages* (Durham, NC: Duke University Press, 1992), pp. 112–136

Fortunatus, *Life of Germanus of Paris*, ed. by Bruno Krusch, *Vita sancti Germani*, in *Monumenta Germaniae historica, Auctores antiquissimi*, vol. 4.2 (Berlin: Weidmann, 1885), pp. 11–27

Fortunatus, *Life of Martin*, ed. by Friedrich Leo, *Vita sancti Martini*, in *Monumenta Germaniae historica, Auctores antiquissimi*, vol. 4.1 (Berlin: Weidmann, 1881), pp. 293–370

Fortunatus, *Life of Médard, Bishop of Noyon*, ed. by Bruno Krusch, *Vita sancti Medardi episcopi Noviomensis*, in *Monumenta Germaniae historica, Auctores antiquissimi*, vol. 4.2 (Berlin: Weidmann, 1885), pp. 67–73

Fortunatus, *Life of Radegund*, ed. by Bruno Krusch, *De vitae sanctae Radegundis: Liber I.*, in *Monumenta Germaniae historica, Scriptores rerum Merovingicarum*, vol. 2 (Hanover: Hahn, 1888), pp. 364–377; trans. by Jo Ann McNamara and John E. Halborg, *Sainted Women of the Dark Ages* (Durham, NC: Duke University Press, 1992), pp. 70–86

Fortunatus, *Poems*, ed. and trans. by Michael Roberts, *Venantius Fortunatus: Poems*, Dumbarton Oaks Medieval Library, 46 (Cambridge, MA: Harvard University Press, 2017)

Fredegar, *Chronicles*, ed. by Bruno Krusch, *Chronicarum quae dicuntur Fredegarii scholastici libri IV cum continuationibus*, in *Monumenta Germaniae historica, Scriptores rerum Merovingicarum*, vol. 2 (Hanover: Hahn, 1888), pp. 1–193

Girolamo Lippomano, *Viaggio*, ed. by Niccolò Tommaséo, *Relations des ambassadeurs Vénitiens sur les affaires de France au XVIe siècle*, vol. 2 (Paris: Imprimerie Royale, 1838)

Gregory I (i.e. Gregory the Great), *Register*, ed. by Paul Ewald and Ludwig M. Hartmann, *Registrum Epistolarum*, in *Monumenta Germaniae historica, Epistolae*, vols 1–2

(Berlin: Weidmann, 1891–1899); trans. by John R. C. Martyn, *The Letters of Gregory the Great*, 3 vols (Toronto: Pontifical Institute of Mediaeval Studies, 2004)

Gregory of Tours, *Glory of the Confessors*, ed. by Bruno Krusch, *Liber in gloria confessorum*, in *Monumenta Germaniae historica, Scriptores rerum Merovingicarum*, vol. 1.2 (Hanover: Hahn, 1885; new edn 1969), pp. 744–820 (new edn pp. 284–370); trans. Raymond Van Dam, *Gregory of Tours: Glory of the Confessors*, Translated Texts for Historians, 5 (Liverpool: Liverpool University Press, 1988; repr. 2004)

Gregory of Tours, *Glory of the Martyrs*, ed. by Bruno Krusch, *Liber in gloria martyrum*, in *Monumenta Germaniae historica, Scriptores rerum Merovingicarum*, vol. 1.2 (Hanover: Hahn, 1885; new edn 1969), pp. 484–561 (new edn pp. 34–111); trans. Raymond Van Dam, *Gregory of Tours: Glory of the Martyrs*, Translated Texts for Historians, 4 (Liverpool: Liverpool University Press, 1988; rept. 2004)

Gregory of Tours, *Life of the Fathers*, ed. by Bruno Krusch, *Liber vitae patrum*, in *Monumenta Germaniae historica, Scriptores rerum Merovingicarum*, vol. 1.2 (Hanover: Hahn, 1885; new edn 1969), pp. 661–743 (new edn pp. 211–83); trans. by Edward James, *Gregory of Tours: Life of the Fathers*, 2nd edn, Translated Texts for Historians, 1 (Liverpool: Liverpool University Press, 1991; repr. 2007)

Gregory of Tours, *On the Course of the Stars*, ed. by Bruno Krusch, *De cursu stellarum ratio, qualiter ad officium implendum debeat observari*, ed. by Bruno Krusch, in *Monumenta Germaniae historica, Scriptores rerum Merovingicarum*, vol. 1.2 (Hanover: Hahn, 1885; new edn 1969), pp. 854–872 (new edn pp. 404–422); partial trans. by William C. McDermott, *Monks, Bishops, Pagans: Christian Culture in Gaul and Italy, 500–700* (Philadelphia: University of Pennsylvania Press, 1949; repr. 1979), pp. 207–220

Gregory of Tours, *The Passion and Virtues of St Julian the Martyr*, ed. by Bruno Krusch, *Liber de passione et virtutibus sancti Iuliani martyris*, in *Monumenta Germaniae historica, Scriptores rerum Merovingicarum*, vol. 1.2 (Hanover: Hahn, 1885; new edn 1969), pp. 562–83 (new edn pp. 112–33); trans. by Raymond Van Dam, *Saints and their Miracles in Late Antique Gaul* (Princeton, NJ: Princeton University Press, 1993), pp. 162–195

Gregory of Tours, *The Passion of the Seven Holy Sleepers in Ephesus*, ed. by Bruno Krusch, *Passio sanctorum septem dormientium apud Ephesum*, in *Monumenta Germaniae historica, Scriptores rerum Merovingicarum*, vol. 1.2 (Hanover: Hahn, 1885; new edn 1969), pp. 847–853 (new edn pp. 396–403); trans. by William C. McDermott, *Monks, Bishops, Pagans: Christian Culture in Gaul and Italy, 500–700* (Philadelphia: University of Pennsylvania Press, 1949; repr. 1979), pp. 197–206

Gregory of Tours, *Ten Books of Histories*, ed. by Bruno Krusch and Wilhelm Levison, *Libri historiarum x*, in *Monumenta Germaniae historica, Scriptores rerum Merovingicarum*, vol. 1.1 (Hanover: Hahn, 1951); trans. by O. M Dalton, *The History of the Franks by Gregory of Tours*, vol. 2 (Oxford: Clarendon Press, 1927); trans. by Lewis Thorpe, *Gregory of Tours: The History of the Franks* (London: Penguin Books, 1974); partial trans. by Alexander Callander Murray, *Gregory of Tours: The Merovingians* (Peterborough, CA: Broadview Press, 2006)

Gregory of Tours, *The Virtues of St Martin*, ed. by Bruno Krusch, *Libri i–iv. De virtutibus sancti Martini*, in *Monumenta Germaniae historica, Scriptores rerum Merovingicarum*, vol. 1.2 (Hanover: Hahn, 1885; new edn 1969), pp. 584–660 (new edn pp. 134–210); trans. by Raymond Van Dam, *Saints and their Miracles in Late Antique Gaul* (Princeton, NJ: Princeton University Press, 1993), pp. 199–303

Henry Bradshaw, *Lyfe of saynt Radegunde* (London: Rycharde Pynson, 1525)

Hormisdas, *Exulto in domino*, ed. by Adalbert de Vogüé and Joël Courreau, in *Césaire d'Arles: Œuvres monastiques*, vol. 1: *Œuvres pour les moniales*, Sources chrétiennes, 345 (Paris: Cerf, 1988), pp. 352–359

Inscriptiones latinae christianae veteres, ed. by Ernst Diehl, 3 vols (Berlin: Weidemann, 1925–1931)

Jerome, *Letters*, ed. by Isidor Hilberg, *Epistulae*, 3 vols, Corpus scriptorum ecclesiasticorum Latinorum, 54–56 (Vienna: Österreichische Akademie der Wissenschaften, 1910–1918)

John Lauder, *Journals*, ed. by Donald Crawford, *Journals of Sir John Lauder, Lord Fountainhall, with his Observations on Public Affairs and Other Memoranda, 1665–1676* (Edinburgh: Scottish History Society, 1900)

Jonas of Bobbio, *Life of Columbanus and his Disciples*, ed. by Michele Tosi, *Vita Columbani et discipulorumque eius* (Piacenza: Emiliana Grafica, 1965); trans. by Alexander O'Hara and Ian Wood, *Jonas of Bobbio: Life of Columbanus, Life of John of Réomé, and Life of Vedast* (Liverpool: Liverpool University Press, 2017), pp. 85–239

Liber historiae Francorum, ed. by Bruno Krusch, in *Monumenta Germaniae historica, Scriptores rerum Merovingicarum*, vol. 2 (Hanover: Hahn, 1888), pp. 215–328; trans. by Bernard Bachrach, *Liber historiae Francorum* (Lawrence, KS: Coronado Press, 1973)

Liber pontificalis, ed. by Louis Duchesne, *Le Liber pontificalis*, 2 vols (Paris: E. Thorin, 1888–1892); trans. by Raymond Davis, *The Book of the Pontiffs (Liber Pontificalis)*, 3 vols (Liverpool: Liverpool University Press, 1989–1995)

Life of Bandaridus, Confessor and Bishop of Soissons in Gaul, ed. by Jean-Baptiste Du Sollier, in *Vita s. Bandarido episcopi confessoris Suessione in Gallia*, in *Acta Sanctorum*, 1 August (Antwerp: Jacobus Antonius van Gherwen, 1733), pp. 60–68

Life of Bathild, ed. by Bruno Krusch, *Vita s. Balthildis*, in *Monumenta Germaniae historica, Scriptores rerum Merovingicarum*, vol. 2 (Hanover: Hahn, 1888), pp. 475–508; trans. by Jo Ann McNamara and John E. Halborg, *Sainted Women of the Dark Ages* (Durham, NC: Duke University Press, 1992), pp. 268–278

Life of Caesarius—see Cyprian, *Life of Caesarius* (for what scholarship often describes as book 1), and Messianus and Stephanus, *Life of Caesarius* (for book 2)

Life of Cloud, ed. by Bruno Krusch, *Vita sancti Chlodovaldi*, in *Monumenta Germaniae historica, Scriptores rerum Merovingicarum*, vol. 2 (Hanover: Hahn, 1888), pp. 350–357

Life of Desiderius, Bishop of Vienne, ed. by Bruno Krusch, *Vita Desiderii episcopi Viennensis*, in *Monumenta Germaniae historica, Scriptores rerum Merovingicarum*, vol. 3 (Hanover: Hahn, 1896), pp. 620–648

Life of Geneviève, Virgin of Paris, ed. by Bruno Krusch, *Vita Genovefae virginis Parisiensis*, in *Monumenta Germaniae historica, Scriptores rerum Merovingicarum*, vol. 3 (Hanover: Hahn, 1896), pp. 215–238; trans. by Jo Ann McNamara and John E. Halborg, *Sainted Women of the Dark Ages* (Durham, NC: Duke University Press, 1992), pp. 19–37

Life of Goar, Confessor of the Rhine, ed. by Bruno Krusch, *Vita Goaris, confessoris Rhenani*, in *Monumenta Germaniae historica, Scriptores rerum Merovingicarum*, vol. 4 (Hanover and Leipzig: Hahn, 1902), pp. 402–422

Life of Radegund—see Fortunatus, *Life of Radegund* (for what scholarship often describes as book 1), and Baudonivia, *Life of Radegund* (for book 2)

Life of Sadalberg, Abbess of Laon, ed. by Bruno Krusch, *Vita Sadalberga abbatissae Laudunensis*, in *Monumenta Germaniae historica, Scriptores rerum Merovingicarum*, vol. 5 (Hanover and Leipzig: Hahn, 1910), pp. 40–66; trans. by Jo Ann McNamara and

John E. Halborg, *Sainted Women of the Dark Ages* (Durham, NC: Duke University Press, 1992), pp. 178–194

Life of the Jura Fathers, ed. François Martine, *Vita patrum Jurensium*, in *Vie des pères du Jura* (Paris: Cerf, 1968)

Marius of Avenches, *Chronicle*, ed. by Theodor Mommsen, *Chronica a. cccclv–dlxxxi*, in *Monumenta Germaniae historica, Auctores antiquissimi*, vol. 11 (Berlin: Weidmann, 1894), pp. 225–240

Messianus and Stephanus, *Life of Caesarius*, ed. by Bruno Krusch, *Vitae Caesarii episcopi Arelatensis: Liber* ii., in *Monumenta Germaniae historica, Scriptores rerum Merovingicarum*, vol. 3 (Hanover: Hahn, 1896), pp. 483–501; trans. by William E. Klingshirn, *Caesarius of Arles: Life, Testament, Letters* (Liverpool: Liverpool University Press, 1994), pp. 43–65

Pactus legis salicae, ed. by Karl August Eckhardt, *Monumenta Germaniae historica, Leges nationum Germanicarum*, vol. 4.1 (Hanover: Hahn, 1962); trans. by Katherine Fischer Drew, *The Laws of the Salian Franks* (Philadelphia: University of Pennsylvania Press, 1991), pp. 57–168

Paulinus of Nola, *Letters*, ed. by Matthias Skeb, *Pontius Meropius Paulinus: Epistulae–Briefe*, Fontes Christiani, vol. 25.1–3 (Freiburg im Breisgau: Herder, 1998); trans. by Patrick G. Walsh, *Letters of St Paulinus of Nola*, 2 vols (Westminster, MD: Newman Press, 1966–1967)

Procopius of Caesarea, *History of the Wars*, trans. by H. B. Dewing, 5 vols, Loeb Classical Library, 48, 81, 107, 173, 217 (Cambridge, MA: Harvard University Press, 1912–1928)

Protoevangelium of James, ed. by Constantin von Tischendorf, *Protoevangelium Iacobi*, in *Evangelia apocrypha* (Leipzig: Avenarius & Mendelssohn, 1853), pp. 1–50; trans. by J. K. Elliott, *The Apocryphal New Testament: A Collection of Apocryphal Christian Literature in an English Translation* (Oxford: Clarendon Press, 1993), pp. 57–67

Radegund, *Dominis sanctis*, ed. by Bruno Krusch and Wilhelm Levison, in *Monumenta Germaniae historica, Scriptores rerum Merovingicarum*, vol. 1.1 (Hanover: Hahn, 1951), pp. 470–474; trans. in Appendix 1 of this book; also trans. in Cassandra M. Casias, 'Rebel Nuns and the Bishop Historian: The Competing Voices of Radegund and Gregory', *Studies in Late Antiquity*, 6.1 (2022), pp. 5–34; and in Jane E. Jeffrey, 'Radegund and the Letter of Foundation', in *Women Writing Latin: From Roman Antiquity to Early Modern Europe*, vol. 2: *Medieval Women Writing Latin*, ed. by Laurie J. Churchill, Phyllis R. Brown, and Jane E. Jeffrey (London: Routledge, 2002), pp. 11–23

Rufinus of Aquileia, *Ecclesiastical History*, ed. by Eduard Schwartz and Theodor Mommsen, *Eusebius Werke*, vol. 2.1–3: *Die Kirchengeschichte* (Leipzig: Johann Conrad Hinrichs, 1903–1909); trans. by Philip R. Amidon, *Rufinus of Aquileia: History of the Church* (Washington, DC: Catholic University of America Press, 2016)

Sallust, *The Conspiracy of Catiline*, ed. by Patrick McGushin, *Bellum Catilinae* (Bristol: Bristol Classical Press, 1999); trans. by John Carew Rolfe, *Sallust: The War with Catiline, the War with Jugurtha*, new edn (Cambridge, MA: Harvard University Press, 2013), pp. 20–49

Sidonius Apollinaris, *Letters*, ed. by Christian H. C. Lütjohann and others, *Epistulae et Carmina*, in *Monumenta Germaniae historica, Auctores antiquissimi*, vol. 8 (Berlin: Weidmann, 1887), pp. 1–172; trans. by O. M. Dalton, *The Letters of Sidonius*, 2 vols (Oxford: Clarendon Press, 1915)

Sulpicius Severus, *Life of Martin*, ed. by Jacques Fontaine, *Sulpicius Severus: vie de Saint Martin* (Paris: Cerf, 1967); trans. by Frederick Russell Hoare, *The Western Fathers: Being the Lives of SS Martin of Tours, Ambrose, Augustine of Hippo, Honoratus of Arles and Germanus of Auxerre* (London: Frank Sheed and Maisie Ward, 1954), pp. 10–44

Venantius Fortunatus—entries listed under 'Fortunatus'

Secondary Sources

Adenis-Lamarre, Odile, *La Sainte Croix de Poitiers: 15 siècle d'histoire et de dévotion* (Le Coudray-Macouard: Saint-Léger Éditions, 2019)

Adenis-Lamarre, *Sainte Radegonde, un sainte pour notre temps* (Le Coudray-Macouard: Saint-Léger Éditions, 2018)

Aigrain, René, *Sainte Radegonde vers 520–587*, rev. edn (Poitiers: Editions des Cordeliers, 1952; orig. publ. Paris: V. Lecoffre, 1918)

Aigrain, René, 'Le Voyage de sainte Radegonde à Arles', *Bulletin philologique et historique du Comité des travaux historiques et scientifiques* (1926–1927), 119–127

Alciati, Roberto, 'And the Villa Became a Monastery: Sulpicius Severus' Community of Primuliacum', in *Western Monasticism ante litteram: The Spaces of Monastic Observance in Late Antiquity and the Early Middle Ages*, ed. by Hendrik Dey and Elizabeth Fentress (Turnhout: Brepols, 2011), pp. 85–98

Bailey, Lisa Kaaren, 'Handmaidens of God: Images of Service in the *Lifes* of Merovingian Female Saints', *Journal of Religious History*, 43.3 (2019), 359–379

Bailey, Lisa Kaaren, 'Leadership and Community in Late Antique Poitiers', in *Leadership and Community in Late Antiquity: Essays in Honour of Raymond Van Dam*, ed. by Young Richard Kim and A. E. T. McLaughlin (Turnhout: Brepols, 2020), pp. 47–62

Bailey, Lisa Kaaren, *The Religious Worlds of the Laity in Late Antique Gaul* (London: Bloomsbury, 2016)

Balberg, Mira, and Ellen Muehlberger, 'The Will of Others: Coercion, Captivity, and Choice in Late Antiquity', *Studies in Late Antiquity*, 2.3 (2018), 294–315

Barcellona, Rossana, 'Lo spazio declinato al femminile nei concili gallici fra IV e VI secolo', in *Munera amicitiae: Studi di storia e cultura sulla tarda antichità offerti a Salvatore Pricoco*, ed. by Rossana Barcellona and Teresa Sardella (Soveria Mannelli: Rubbettino, 2003), pp. 25–49

Barlow, Jonathan, 'Gregory of Tours and the Myth of the Trojan Origins of the Franks', *Frühmittelalterliche Studien*, 29.1 (1995), 86–95

Baudouin, Marcel, 'Le Pas de Dieu, à Sainte-Radegonde, de Poitiers', *Bulletin de la Société préhistorique de France*, 8.5 (1911), 320–334

Belting-Ihm, Christa, 'Das Juztinskreuz in der Schatzkammer der Peterskirche zu Rom', *Jahrbuch des Römisch-Germanischen Zentralmuseums Mainz*, 12 (1965), 142–166

Benoit, Fernand, 'Topographie monastique d'Arles au VIᵉ siècle', in *Études mérovingiennes: actes des journées de Poitiers, 1ᵉʳ–3 mai 1952* (Paris: Picard, 1953), pp. 13–17

Bernet, Anne, *Radegonde: Épouse de Clotaire Iᵉʳ* (Paris: Pygmalion, 2007)

Bezzola, Reto R., *Les Origines et la formation de la littérature courtoise en Occident (500–1200)*, 3 vols (Paris: Honoré Champion, 1944–1963)

Bikeeva, Natalia Yurievna, 'Secrecy in the Asceticism of St Radegund according to Venantius Fortunatus's *Vita*', *Terra Sebus: Acta Musei Sabesiensis* (2014), 445–457

Bikeeva, Natalia Yurievna, ''Serente diabulo': The Revolt of the Nuns at Poitiers and Tours in the Late 6th Century', in *Ecclesia et Violentia: Violence against the Church and Violence within the Church in the Middle Ages*, ed. by Radosław Kotecki and Jacek Maciejewski (Newcastle upon Tyne: Cambridge Scholars, 2014), pp. 72–90

Binder, Marcin, 'The Evolution of the Female Diaconate in the Legislation of Gallic Synods in Late Christian Antiquity', *Canon Law*, 27.2 (2017), 79–108

Bjornlie, Shane, 'Gregory of Tours and the *Decem libri Historiarum*: Between Religious Belief and Rhetorical Habit', *Studies in Late Antiquity*, 4.2 (2020), 153–184

Borgia, Stefano, *De cruce Vaticana ex dono Iustini Augusti in parasceve maioris hebdomadae publicae venerationi exhiberi solita commentarius* (Rome: Typographia Sacrae Congregationis de Propaganda Fide, 1779)

Boucet, Jehan, *L'Histoire et chronique de Clotaire, premier de ce nom, VII roy des Fraçoys et monarque des Gaules* (Poitiers: Enguilbert de Marnef, 1517)

Bouchard, Constance B., 'Reconstructing Sanctity and Refiguring Saints in Early Medieval Gaul', in *Studies on Medieval Empathies*, ed. by Karl F. Morrison and Rudolph M. Bell (Turnhout: Brepols, 2013), pp. 91–114

Bratož, Rajko, 'Venanzio Fortunato e lo scisma dei Tre Capitoli', in *Venanzio Fortunato e il suo tempo: Convegno internazionale di studio, Valdobbiadene, Chiesa di S. Gregorio Magno, 29 novembre 2001: Treviso, Casa dei Carraresi 30 novembre–1 dicembre 2001* (Treviso: Fondazione Cassamarca, 2003), pp. 363–401

Brennan, Brian, 'The Career of Venantius Fortunatus', *Traditio*, 41 (1985), 49–78

Brennan, Brian, 'Deathless Marriage and Spiritual Fecundity in Venantius Fortunatus's *De virginitate*', *Traditio*, 51 (1996), 73–97

Brennan, Brian, 'The Disputed Authorship of Fortunatus' Byzantine Poems', *Byzantion*, 66.2 (1996), 335–345

Brennan, Brian, 'Piety and Politics in Nineteenth-Century Poitiers: The Cult of St Radegund', *Journal of Ecclesiastical History*, 47.1 (1996), 65–81

Brennan, Brian, 'The Relic of the True Cross in the Statecraft of Justin II and Sophia in the West', *Byzantion*, 91 (2021), 47–73

Brennan, Brian, 'St Radegund and the Early Development of her Cult of Poitiers', *Journal of Religious History*, 13 (1985), 340–354

Brennan, Brian, 'Venantius Fortunatus: Byzantine Agent?', *Byzantion*, 65 (1995), 7–16

Brennan, Brian, 'Weaving with Words: Venantius Fortunatus's Figurative Acrostics on the Holy Cross', *Traditio*, 74 (2019), 27–52

Brown, Peter, 'Gregory of Tours', in *The World of Gregory of Tours*, ed. by Kathleen Mitchell and Ian Wood (Leiden: Brill, 2002), pp. 1–28

Brown, Peter, *The Rise of Western Christendom: Triumph and Diversity, AD 200–1000*, 2nd edn (Oxford: Blackwell, 2003)

Buchberger, Erica, *Shifting Ethnic Identities in Spain and Gaul, 500–700: From Romans to Goths and Franks* (Amsterdam: Amsterdam University Press, 2017)

Buchner, Rudolf, *Gregor von Tours: Zehn Bücher Geschichten*, 2 vols (Darmstadt: Wissenschaftliche Buchgesellschaft, 1967)

Buckton, David, 'Byzantine Enamels in the Twentieth Century', in *Byzantine Style Religion and Civilization in Honour of Sir Steven Runciman*, ed. by Elizabeth M. Jeffreys (Cambridge: Cambridge University Press, 2006), pp. 25–37

Bullough, Vern, 'On Being Male in the Middle Ages', in *Medieval Masculinities: Regarding Men in the Middle Ages*, ed. by Clare A. Lees (Minneapolis: University of Minnesota Press, 1994), pp. 31–46

Cameron, Averil, 'The Early Religious Policies of Justin II', *Studies in Church History*, 13 (1976), 51–67

Cameron, Averil, 'How Did the Merovingian Kings Wear their Hair?', *Revue belge de philologie et d'histoire*, 43.4 (1965), 1203–1216

Carrasco, Magdalena Elizabeth, 'Spirituality in Context: The Romanesque Illustrated Life of St Radegund of Poitiers (Poitiers, Bibliothèque Municipale, MS 250)', *Art Bulletin*, 72.3 (1990), 415–435

Casias, Cassandra M., 'Rebel Nuns and the Bishop Historian: The Competing Voices of Radegund and Gregory', *Studies in Late Antiquity*, 6.1 (2022), 5–34

Castritius, Helmut, Dieter Geuenich, and Matthias Werner, eds, *Die Frühzeit der Thüringer: Archäologie, Sprache, Geschichte* (Berlin: Walter de Gruyter, 2009)

Charlier, Marj, *The Rebel Nun* (Ashland, OR: Blackstone, 2022)

Cherewatuk, Karen, 'Germanic Echoes in Latin Verse: The Voice of the Lamenting Woman in Radegund's Poetry', *Allegorica*, 14 (1993), 3–21

Cherewatuk, Karen, 'Radegund and the Epistolary Tradition', in *Dear Sister: Medieval Women and the Epistolary Genre*, ed. by Karen Cherewatuk and Ulrike Wiethaus (Philadelphia: University of Pennsylvania Press, 1993), pp. 20–45

Clark, Gillian, *Women in Late Antiquity: Pagan and Christian Lifestyles* (Oxford: Oxford University Press, 1993)

Coates, Simon, 'Regendering Radegund? Fortunatus, Baudonivia and the Problem of Female Sanctity in Merovingian Gaul', *Studies in Church History*, 34 (1998), 37–50

Consolino, Franca Ela, 'Due agiografi per una regina: Radegonda di Turingia fra Fortunato e Baudonivia', *Studi Storici*, 29 (1988), 143–159

Conway, Martin, 'St Radegund's Reliquary at Poitiers', *Antiquaries Journal*, 3.1 (1923), 1–12

Coon, Lynda, 'Merovingian Meditations on Jesus', in *The Oxford Handbook of the Merovingian World*, ed. by Bonnie Effros and Isabel Moreira (Oxford: Oxford University Press, 2020), pp. 1071–1105

Coon, Lynda, *Sacred Fictions: Holy Women and Hagiography in Late Antiquity* (Philadelphia, PA: University of Pennsylvania Press, 1997)

Cooper, Kate, 'The Household and the Desert: Monastic and Biological Communities in the *Lives* of Melania the Younger', in *Household, Women, and Christianities in Late Antiquity and the Middle Ages*, ed. by Anneke B. Mulder-Bakker and Jocelyn Wogan-Browne (Turnhout: Brepols, 2005), pp. 11–36

Cooper, Kate, *The Virgin and the Bride: Idealized Womanhood in Late Antiquity* (Cambridge, MA: Harvard University Press, 1996)

Coralini, Antonella, 'Immagini di Tyche/Fortuna in età romana: l'Italia settentrionale', in *Le Fortune dell'età arcaica nel Lazio ed in Italia e la loro posterità: atti del 3° convegno di studi archeologici sull'antica Preneste, Palestrina, 15/16 ottobre 1994* (Palestrina: Società Tiburtina di Storia e d'Arte, 1997), pp. 219–300

Crawford, Jan, and Marie Anne Mayeski, 'Reclaiming an Ancient Story: Baudonivia's Life of St Radegund', in *Women Saints in World Religions*, ed. by Arvind Sharma (Albany, State University of New York Press, 2000), pp. 71–106

Coudanne, Louise, 'Baudonivie, moniale de Sainte-Croix et biographe de Sainte-Radegonde', in *Études mérovingiennes : actes des journées de Poitiers, 1er–3 mai 1952* (Paris: Picard, 1953), pp. 45–49

Coudanne, Louise, 'Regards sur la vie liturgique à Sainte-Croix de Poitiers', *Bulletin de la Société des Antiquaires de l'Ouest*, 4th series, 14 (1977), 353–379

Coumert, Magali, 'Les "Prologues" de la loi salique: les premiers temps des Francs suivant les copistes carolingiens', in *Autour du règne de Clovis: les grands dans l'Europe du haut Moyen Âge: histoire et archéologie, actes des xxxiie journées internationales d'archéologie* *mérovingienne*, ed. by Michel Kazanski and Patrick Périn (Caen: Association française d'archéologie mérovingienne, 2020), pp. 43–57

Coville, Alfred, *Recherches sur l'histoire de Lyon du ve au ixe siècle (450–800)* (Paris: Picard, 1928)

Curta, Florin, 'Merovingian and Carolingian Gift Giving', *Speculum*, 81.3 (2006), 671–699

Dailey, Erin Thomas, 'Confinement and Exclusion in the Monasteries of Sixth-Century Gaul', *Early Medieval Europe*, 22.3 (2014), 304–335

Dailey, Erin Thomas, 'Gregory of Tours and the Paternity of Chlothar II: Strategies of Legitimation in the Merovingian Kingdoms', *Journal of Late Antiquity*, 7.1 (2014), 3–27

Dailey, Erin Thomas, 'The Horizons of Gregory of Tours', in *Authorship, Worldview, and Identity in Medieval Europe*, ed. by Christian Raffensperger (London: Routledge, 2022), pp. 17–37

Dailey, Erin Thomas, 'Introducing Monastic Space: The Early Years, 250–750', in *Monastic Space through Time*, ed. by E. T. Dailey and Stephen Werronen, special issue, *Bulletin of International Medieval Research*, 19 (Leeds: Institute for Medieval Studies, 2013 [2014]), pp. 5–25

Dailey, Erin Thomas, 'Misremembering Radegund's Foundation of Sainte-Croix', in *Erfahren, Erzählen, Erinnern: Narrative Konstruktionen von Gedächtnis und Generation in Antike und Mittelalter*, ed. by Hartwin Brandt, Benjamin Pohl, W. Maurice Sprague, and Lina K. Hörl (Bamberg: University of Bamberg Press, 2012), pp. 117–140

Dailey, Erin Thomas, *Queens, Consorts, Concubines: Gregory of Tours and Women of the Merovingian Elite*, Mnemosyne Supplements: Late Antique Literature, 381 (Leiden: Brill, 2015)

Danna, Antonella, 'La *Vita sanctae Radegundis* di Venanzio Fortunato fra topica agiografica ed esperienza personale', *Schede medievali: Rassegna dell'Officina di studi medievali*, 57 (2019), 1–14

David, Massimiliano, 'Potere imperiale e devozione cristiana: La Santa Croce a Roma e a Ravenna', in *La Basilica di Santa Croce e le reliquie della passione*, ed. by Roberto Cassanelli and Emilia Stolfi (Milan: Jaca Book, 2012), pp. 41–49

De Blaauw, Sible, 'Jerusalem in Rome and the Cult of the Cross', in *Pratum Romanum: Richard Krautheimer zum 100. Geburtstag*, ed. by Renate L. Colella (Wiesbaden: Ludwig Reichert, 1997), pp. 55–73

De Chergé, Charles, *Guide du voyageur á Poitiers et aux environs*, 3rd edn (Poitiers: Librairie Létang, 1872)

Debus, Karl Heinz, 'Studien zu merowingischen Urkunden und Briefen: Untersuchungen und Texte', *Archiv für Diplomatik, Schriftgeschichte, Siegel- und Wappenkunde*, 13 (1967), 1–109

De Fleury, Edouard, *Histoire de Sainte Radegonde, reine de France au vi^e siècle et patronne de Poitiers* (Poitiers: Henri Oudin, 1847)

De Gaiffier, Baudouin, 'Saint Venance Fortunat, évêque de Poitiers: les témoignages de son culte', *Analecta Bollandiana*, 70 (1952), 262–284

De Jong, Mayke, 'Monastic Prisoners or Opting Out? Political Coercion and Honour in the Frankish Kingdoms', in *Topographies of Power in the Early Middle Ages*, ed. by Mayke de Jong, Frans Theuws, and Carine van Rhijn (Leiden: Brill, 2001), pp. 291–328

Delaruelle, Étienne, 'Sainte Radegonde, son type de sainteté et la chrétienté de son temps', in *Études mérovingiennes: actes des journées de Poitiers, 1er–3 mai 1952* (Paris: Picard, 1953), pp. 65–74

Delehaye, Hippolyte, *Les Origines du culte des martyres* (Brussels: Société des Bollandistes, 1912)

Del Fiat Miola, Maria, 'Permitted and Prohibited Textiles in the *Regula virginum*: Unweaving the Terminology', *Early Medieval Europe*, 26 (2018), 90–102

De Mérindol, Christian, 'Le Culte de sainte Radegonde et la monarchie française à la fin du Moyen Âge', in *Les Religieuses dans le cloître et dans le monde, des origines à nos jours: actes du deuxième colloque international du CERCOR. Poitiers, 29 septembre–2 octobre 1988* (Saint-Étienne: Publications de l'Université de Saint-Étienne, 1994), pp. 789–795

De Monsabert, Pierre, 'Le "Testament" de Sainte Radegonde', *Bulletin philologique et historique du Comité des travaux historiques et scientifiques* (1926–1927), 129–134

De Nie, Giselle, 'Consciousness Fecund through God: From Male Fighter to Spiritual Bride-Mother in Late Antique Female Sanctity', in *Sanctity and Motherhood: Essays on Holy Mothers in the Middle Ages*, ed. by Anneke Moulder-Bakker (New York: Routledge, 1995), pp. 100–161

De Nie, Giselle, 'Fatherly and Motherly Curing in Sixth-Century Gaul: Saint Radegund's *Mysterium*', in *Women and Miracle Stories: A Multidisciplinary Exploration*, ed. by Anna Korte (Leiden: Brill, 2003), pp. 53–87

Dey, Hendrik, 'Bringing Chaos out of Order: New Approaches to the Study of Early Western Monasticism', in *Western Monasticism ante litteram: The Spaces of Monastic Observance in Late Antiquity and the Early Middle Ages*, ed. by Hendrik Dey and Elizabeth Fentress (Turnhout: Brepols, 2011), pp. 19–40

Diem, Albrecht, 'Gregory's Chess Board: Monastic Conflict and Competition in Early Medieval Gaul', in *Compétition et sacré au haut Moyen Âge: entre médiation et exclusion*, ed. by Philippe Depreux, François Bougard, and Régine Le Jan (Turnhout: Brepols, 2015), pp. 165–191

Diem, Albrecht, 'Inventing the Holy Rule: Some Observations on the History of Monastic Normative Observance in the Early Medieval West', in *Western Monasticism ante litteram: The Spaces of Monastic Observance in Late Antiquity and the Early Middle Ages*, ed. by Hendrik Dey and Elizabeth Fentress (Turnhout: Brepols, 2011), pp. 53–84

Diem, Albrecht, 'Merovingian Monasticism: Voices of Dissent', in *The Oxford Handbook of the Merovingian World*, ed. by Bonnie Effros and Isabel Moreira (Oxford: Oxford University Press, 2020), pp. 320–341

Diem, Albrecht, 'Monks, Kings, and the Transformation of Sanctity: Jonas of Bobbio and the End of the Holy Man', *Speculum*, 82 (2007), 521–559

Diem, Albrecht, *The Pursuit of Salvation: Community, Space, and Discipline in Early Medieval Monasticism, with a Critical Edition and Translation of the 'Regula cuiusdam ad virgines'* (Turnhout: Brepols, 2021)

Diem, Albrecht, '... ut si professus fuerit se omnia impleturum, tunc excipiatur: Observations on the Rules for Monks and Nuns of Caesarius and Aurelianus of Arles', *Edition und Erforschung lateinischer patristischer Texte: 150 Jahre CSEL: Festschrift für Kurt Smolak zum 70. Geburtstag*, ed. by Victoria Zimmerl-Panagl, Lukas J. Dorfbauer, and Clemens Weidmann (Berlin: Walter de Gruyter, 2014), pp. 191–224

Diesenberger, Max, 'Hair, Sacrality and Symbolic Capital in the Frankish Kingdoms', in *The Construction of Communities in the Early Middle Ages: Texts, Resources and Artefacts*, ed. by Richard Corrandini, Max Dieseberger, and Helmut Reimitz (Leiden: Brill, 2003), pp. 173–212

Dissertori, Renate, *Berichten Frauen anders? Die heilige Radegunde von Poitiers in den Viten des Venantius Fortunatus und der Baudonivia* (Saarbrücken: Dr Müller, 2008)

Dolbeau, François, 'La Vie en prose de saint Marcel de Die', *Francia*, 11 (1983), 97–129

Drake, H. A., *A Century of Miracles: Christians, Pagans, Jews, and the Supernatural, 312–410* (Oxford: Oxford University Press, 2017)

Drijvers, Jan Willem, *Helena Augusta: The Mother of Constantine the Great and the Legend of her Finding of the True Cross* (Leiden: Brill, 1992)

Drijvers, Jan Willem, 'Promoting Jerusalem: Cyril and the True Cross', in *Portraits of Spiritual Authority: Religious Power in Early Christianity, Byzantium and the Christian Orient*, ed. by Jan Willem Drijvers and John Watt (Leiden: Brill, 1999), pp. 79–95

Duchesne, Louis, *Fastes épiscopaux de l'ancienne Gaule*, 3 vols (Paris: Albert Fontemonig, 1907–1910)

Dumézil, Bruno, *La Reine Brunehaut* (Paris: Fayard, 2008)

Dumézil, Bruno, 'La Royauté mérovingienne et les élections épiscopales au VIᵉ siècle', in *Episcopal Elections in Late Antiquity*, ed. by Johan Leemans, Peter van Nuffelen, Shawn W. J. Keough, and Carla Nicolaye (Berlin: Walter de Gruyter, 2011), pp. 127–144

Edwards, Jennifer C., 'Man Can Be Subject to Woman': Female Monastic Authority in Fifteenth-Century Poitiers', *Gender & History*, 25.1 (2013), 86–106

Edwards, Jennifer C., *Superior Women: Medieval Female Authority in Poitiers' Abbey of Sainte-Croix* (Oxford: Oxford University Press, 2019)

Edwards, Jennifer C., 'Their Cross to Bear: Controversy and the Relic of the True Cross in Poitiers', *Essays in Medieval Studies*, 24 (2007), 65–77

Effros, Bonnie, *Creating Community with Food and Drink in Merovingian Gaul* (Basingstoke: Palgrave Macmillan, 2002)

Effros, Bonnie, 'Images of Sanctity: Contrasting Descriptions of Radegund by Venantius Fortunatus and Gregory of Tours', *UCLA Historical Journal*, 10 (1990), 38–58

Effros, Bonnie, *Merovingian Mortuary Archaeology and the Making of the Early Middle Ages* (Berkeley: University of California Press, 2003)

Effros, Bonnie, 'Monuments and Memory: Repossessing Ancient Remains in Early Medieval Gaul', in *Topographies of Power in the Early Middle Ages*, ed. by Mayke de Jong, Frans Theuws, and Carine van Rhijn (Leiden: Brill, 2001), pp. 93–118

Eidam, Hardy, and Gudrun Noll, eds, *Radegunde: Ein Frauenschicksal zwischen Mord und Askese* (Erfurt: Stadtmuseum–Haus zum Stockfisch, 2006)

Elliott, J. K., *The Apocryphal New Testament: A Collection of Apocryphal Christian Literature in an English Translation* (Oxford: Clarendon Press, 1993)

Elm, Susanna, *Virgins of God: The Making of Asceticism in Late Antiquity* (Oxford: Clarendon Press, 1996)

Esders, Stefan, '"Avenger of All Perjury" in Constantinople, Ravenna and Metz: Saint Polyeuctus, Sigibert I, and the Division of Charibert's Kingdom in 568', in *Western Perspectives on the Mediterranean: Cultural Transfer in Late Antiquity and the Early Middle Ages, 400–800 AD*, ed. by Andreas Fischer and Ian Wood (London: Bloomsbury, 2014), pp. 17–40

Esders, Stefan, *Römische Rechtstradition und merowingisches Königtum: Zum Rechtscharakter politischer Heerschaft in Burgund im 6. und 7. Jahrhundert* (Göttingen: Vandenhoeck & Ruprecht, 1997)

Evans, Michael R., *Inventing Eleanor: The Medieval and Post-Medieval Image of Eleanor of Aquitaine* (London: Bloomsbury, 2014)

Ewig, Eugen, 'Das Bild Constantins des Grossen in den ersten Jahrhunderten des abendländischen Mittelalters', *Historisches Jahrbuch*, 75 (1956), 133–192

Ewig, Eugen, *Die fränkischen Teilungen und Teilreiche* (Wiesbaden: Franz Steiner, 1953)

Ewig, Eugen, 'Die Namengebung bei den ältesten Frankenkönigen und im merowingischen Königshaus', *Francia*, 18 (1991), 21–69

Ewig, Eugen, 'Studien zur merowingischen Dynastie', in *Frühmittelalterlichen Studien*, 8 (1974), 15–59

Eygun, François, 'Circonscription de Poitiers', *Gallia*, 21 (1963), 433–484

Fauquier, Michel, 'La Chronologie radegondienne: un enseignement sur la conception de la vocation à la fin de l'antiquité en Gaule', *Antiquité tardive*, 25 (2017), 315–340

Favreau, Robert, 'Le Culte de sainte Radegonde à Poitiers au Moyen Âge', in *Les Religieuses dans le cloître et dans le monde, des origines à nos jours: actes du deuxième colloque international du CERCOR. Poitiers, 29 septembre–2 octobre 1988* (Saint-Étienne: Publications de l'Université de Saint-Étienne, 1994), pp. 91–109

Favreau, Robert, ed., *Radegonde: de la couronne au cloître* (Poitiers: Association Gilbert de La Porrée, 2005)

Favreau, Robert, ed., *La Vie de sainte Radegonde par Fortunat: Poitiers, Bibliothèque Municipale Manuscrit 250 (136)* (Paris: Éditions du Seuil, 1995)

Favreau, Robert, and Marie-Thérèse Camus, 'Le Chapitre et l'église de sainte Radegonde de Poitiers à Poitiers', in *La Vie de sainte Radegonde par Fortunat: Poitiers, Bibliothèque Municipale Manuscrit 250 (136)*, ed. by Robert Favreau (Paris: Éditions du Seuil, 1995), pp. 189–196

Ferrante, Joan, 'What Really Matters in Medieval Women's Correspondence', in *Medieval Letters between Fiction and Document*, ed. by Christian Høgel and Elisabetta Bartoli (Turnhout: Brepols, 2015), pp. 179–199

Février, Paul-Albert, *Le Développement urbain en Provence de l'époque romaine à la fin du XIVᵉ siècle (archéologie et histoire urbaine)* (Paris: De Boccard, 1964)

Fielding, Ian, *Transformation of Ovid in Late Antiquity* (Cambridge: Cambridge University Press, 2017)

Filleau, Jean, *La Preuve historique des litanies de la grande reyne de France Saincte Radegonde* (Poitiers: Abraham Mounin, 1643)

Filosini, Stefania, 'Tra elegia lieta ed elegia triste: una rilettura del De excidio Thoringiae', *Bollettino di studi Latini*, 50 (2020), 105–126

Fleury, Édouard, *Histoire de sainte Radegonde, reine de France au VIᵉ siècle et patronne de Poitiers* (Poitiers: H. Oudin, 1847)

Flierman, Robert, 'Gregory of Tours and the Merovingian Letter', *Journal of Medieval History*, 47.2 (2021), 119–144

Folz, Robert, *Les Saintes Reines du Moyen Âge en Occident (VIᵉ–XIIIᵉ siècle)* (Brussels: Société des bollandistes, 1992)

Fontaine, Jacques, 'Hagiographie et politique de Sulpice Sévère à Venance Fortunat', *Revue de l'histoire de l'Église de France*, 62 (1976), 113–140

Foucart, Émile-Victor, *Poitiers et ses monuments* (Poitiers: A. Pichot, 1841)

Fouracre, Paul, 'Lights, Power, and the Moral Economy of Early Medieval Europe', *Early Medieval Europe*, 28.3 (2020), 367–387

Fouracre, Paul, 'The Origins of the Carolingian Attempt to Regulate the Cult of Saints', in *The Cult of Saints in Late Antiquity and the Middle Ages: Essays on the Contribution of Peter Brown*, ed. by James Howard-Johnston and Paul Antony Hayward (Oxford: Oxford University Press, 1999), pp. 143–165

Fouracre, Paul, 'Why Were So Many Bishops Killed in Merovingian Francia?', in *Bischofsmord im Mittelalter–Murder of Bishops*, ed. by Natalie Fryde and Dirk Reitz (Göttingen: Vandenhoeck & Ruprecht, 2003), pp. 13–36; reprinted in Paul Fouracre, *Frankish History: Studies in the Construction of Power* (Farnham: Ashgate, 2012), article v

Fowden, Garth, 'Constantine's Porphyry Column: The Earliest Literary Allusion', *Journal of Roman Studies*, 81 (1991), 119–131

Frakes, Jerold C., *The Fate of Fortune in the Early Middle Ages: The Boethian Tradition* (Leiden: Brill, 1988)

Friese, Michael, ed., *Die heilige Radegunde von Thüringen* (Erfurt: Verlagshaus Thüringen, 2001)

Frolow, Anatole, *La Relique de la vraie Croix: recherches sur le développement d'un culte* (Paris: Institut français d'Études byzantines, 1961)

Gäbe, Sabine, 'Radegundis: *sancta regina, ancilla*: Zum Heiligkeitsideal der Radegundisviten von Fortunat und Baudonivia', *Francia*, 16.1 (1989), 1–30

Gaudemet, Jean, *Les Élections dans l'Église latine des origines au xvie siècle* (Paris: Lanore, 1979)

George, Judith W., 'Poet as Politician: Venantius Fortunatus' Panegyric to King Chilperic', *Journal of Medieval History*, 15 (1989), 5–18

George, Judith W., *Venantius Fortunatus: A Latin Poet in Merovingian Gaul* (Oxford: Clarendon Press, 1992)

Gerber, Frédéric, *Poitiers antique: 40 ans d'archéologie préventive* (Poitiers: INRAP/Ville de Poitiers, 2014)

Gerberding, Richard A., *The Rise of the Carolingians and the Liber Historiae Francorum* (Oxford: Clarendon Press, 1987)

Germond, François, *Le Pupitre de Sainte Radegonde: le plus ancien meuble français (vi^e siècle)* (Croissy-sur-Seine: Bricodif, 1990)

Gillette, Gertrude, 'Radegund's Monastery of Poitiers: The Rule and its Observance', in *Papers Presented at the Eleventh International Conference on Patristic Studies Held in Oxford 1991*, ed. by Elizabeth A. Livingstone (Louvain: Peeters, 1993), pp. 381–387

Glenn, Jason, 'Two Lives of Saint Radegund', in *The Middle Ages in Texts and Texture: Reflections on Medieval Sources*, ed. by Jason Glenn (Toronto: University of Toronto Press, 2011), pp. 57–69

Goffart, Walter, 'Byzantine Policy in the West under Tiberius II and Maurice: The Pretenders Hermenegild and Gundovald (579–585)', *Traditio*, 13 (1957), 73–118

Goffart, Walter, 'The Frankish Pretender Gundovald, 582–585: A Crisis of Merovingian Blood', *Francia*, 39 (2012), 1–27

Goffart, Walter, 'From *Historiae* to *Historia Francorum* and Back Again: Aspects of the Textual History of Gregory of Tours', in *Religion, Culture, and Society in the Early Middle Ages: Studies in Honor of Richard E. Sullivan*, ed. by Richard Eugene Sullivan, Thomas F. X. Noble, and John J. Contreni (Kalamazoo, MI: Medieval Institute Publications, 1987), pp. 55–76; reprinted in Walter Goffart, *Rome's Fall and After* (London: Hambledon Press, 1989), pp. 255–274

Goosmann, Erik, 'The Long-Haired Kings of the Franks: "Like so Many Samsons?"', *Early Medieval Europe*, 20.3 (2012), 233–259

Götsch, Kathrin, 'Der Nonnenaufstand von Poitiers: Flächenbrand oder apokalyptisches Zeichen? Zu den merowingischen Klosterfrauen in Gregors Zehn Büchern Geschichte', *Concilium Medii Aevi*, 13 (2010), 1–18

Gradowicz-Pancer, Nira, *Sans peur et sans vergogne: de l'honneur et des femmes aux premiers temps mérovingiens* (Paris: Editions Albin Michel, 2001)

Grahn-Hoek, Heike, 'Gab es vor 531 ein linksniederrheinisches Thüringerreich?', *Zeitschrift des Vereins für Thüringische Geschichte*, 55 (2001), 15–55.

Grierson, Philip, and Mark A. S. Blackburn, *Medieval European Coinage*, vol. 1: *The Early Middle Ages (5th–10th Centuries)* (Cambridge: Cambridge University Press, 1986)

Gryson, Roger, *Le Ministère des femmes dans l'Église ancienne* (Gembloux: Duculot, 1972); trans. by Jean Laporte and Mary Louise Hall, *The Ministry of Women in the Early Church* (Collegeville, MN: Liturgical Press, 1976)

Hahn, Cynthia, 'Collector and Saint: Queen Radegund and Devotion to the Relic of the True Cross', *Word & Image*, 22.3 (2012), 268–274

Hahn, Cynthia, *Portrayed on the Heart: Narrative Effect in Pictoral Lives of Saints from the Tenth through the Thirteenth Century* (Berkeley: University of California Press, 2001)

Halfond, Gregory I., *Bishops and the Politics of Patronage in Merovingian Gaul* (Ithaca, NY: Cornell University Press, 2019)

Halfond, Gregory I., 'Charibert I and the Episcopal Leadership of the Kingdom of Paris (561–567)', *Viator*, 43.2 (2012), 1–28

Halfond, Gregory I., 'Ecclesiastical Politics in the Regnum Chramni: Contextualising Baudonivia's *Vita Radegundis*, ch. 15', *Journal of Ecclesiastical History*, 68.3 (2017), 474–492

Halsall, Guy, 'Female Status and Power in Early Merovingian Central Austrasia', *Early Medieval Europe*, 5.1 (1996), 1–24

Halsall, Guy, 'Material Culture, Sex, Gender, Sexuality, and Transgression in Sixth-Century Gaul', in *Sexuality, Society and the Archaeological Record*, ed. by Lynne Bevan (Glasgow: Cruithne Press, 2001), pp. 130–146; revised in Guy Halsall, *Cemeteries and Society in Merovingian Gaul: Selected Studies in History and Archaeology, 1992–2009* (Leiden: Brill, 2010), pp. 323–356

Halsall, Guy, 'The Preface to Book V of Gregory of Tours' *Histories*: Its Form, Context and Significance', *English Historical Review*, 122 (2007), 297–317

Halsall, Guy, 'Transformations of Romanness: The Northern Gallic Case', in *Transformations of Romanness: Early Medieval Regions and Identities*, ed. by Walter Pohl, Clemens Gantner, Cinzia Grifoni, and Marianne Pollheimer-Mohaupt (Berlin: Walter de Gruyter, 2018), pp. 41–58

Hashimoto, Tatsuyuki, 'Sei-Radegundisu wo meguru futari no denki sakka: Forutwunatwusu to Baudonivia', *Shigaku Kenkyū*, 238 (2002), 21–37

Harper, Kyle, *Slavery in the Late Roman World, AD 275–425* (Cambridge: Cambridge University Press, 2011)

Hartmann, Martina, '*Reginae sumus*: Merowingische Königstöchter und die Frauenklöster im 6. Jahrhundert', *Mitteilungen des Instituts für Österreichische Geschichtsforschung*, 113 (2005), 1–19

Heid, Stefan, 'Die gute Absicht im Schweigen Eusebs über die Kreuzauffindung', *Römische Quartalschrift*, 96 (2001), 37–56

Heijmans, Marc, 'L'Enclos Saint-Césaire à Arles: un chantier controversé', *BUCEMA: Bulletin de centre d'études médévales d'Auxerre*, 3 (2010), 1–14

Heinemeyer, Karl, 'Frankreich und Thüringerreich im 5./6. Jahrhundert', in *Radegunde: Ein Frauenschicksal zwischen Mord und Askese*, ed. by Hardy Eidam and Gudrun Noll (Erfurt: Stadtmuseum–Haus zum Stockfisch, 2006), pp. 14–26

Heinzelmann, Martin, *Bischofsherrschaft in Gallien: Zur Kontinuität römischer Führungsschichten vom 4. bis zum 7. Jahrhundert: soziale, prosopographische und bildungsgeschichtliche Aspekte* (Munich: Artemis, 1976)

Heinzelmann, Martin, *Gregor von Tours (538–594), "Zehn Bücher Geschicht": Historiographie und Gesellschaftskonzept im 6. Jahrhundert* (Darmstadt: Wissenschaftliche Buchgesellschaft, 1994); trans. by Christopher Carroll, *Gregory of Tours: History and Society in the Sixth Century* (Cambridge: Cambridge University Press, 2001)

Heinzelmann, Martin, 'L'Hagiographie mérovingienne: panorama des documents potentiels', in *L'Hagiographie mérovingienne à travers ses réécritures*, ed. by Monique Goullet, Martin Heinzelmann, and Christine Veyrard-Cosme (Ostfildern: Jan Thorbecke, 2010), pp. 27–82

Heinzelmann, Martin, and Joseph-Claude Poulin, *Les Vies anciennes de sainte Geneviève de Paris* (Paris: Honoré Champion, 1986)

Helvétius, Anne Marie, 'L'Organisation des monastères féminins à l'époque mérovingienne', in *Female vita religiosa between Late Antiquity and the High Middle Ages: Structures, Developments, and Spatial Contexts*, ed. by Gert Melville and Anne Müller (Berlin: LIT, 2011), pp. 151–169

Hen, Yitzhak, 'Les Authentiques des reliques de la Terre Sainte en Gaule franque', *Le Moyen Âge*, 105 (1999), 71–90

Hen, Yitzhak, *Culture and Religion in Merovingian Gaul, AD 480–751: Cultures, Beliefs and Traditions* (Leiden: Brill, 1995)

Hen, Yitzhak, 'Paganism and Superstitions in the Time of Gregory of Tours: une question mal posée!', in *The World of Gregory of Tours*, ed. by Kathleen Mitchell and Ian Wood (Leiden: Brill, 2002), pp. 229–240

Hen, Yitzhak, 'The Church in Sixth-Century Gaul', in *A Companion to Gregory of Tours*, ed. by Alexander Callander Murray (Leiden: Brill, 2016), pp. 232–255

Herrin, Judith, 'The Imperial Feminine in Byzantium', *Past & Present*, 169 (2000), 3–35

Hiernard, Jean, 'La Topographie historique de Poitiers dans l'antiquité: bilan et perspectives', *Bulletin de la Société des Antiquaires de l'Ouest et des Musées de Poitiers*, 5 (1987), 163–188

Hillner, Julia, 'Empresses, Queens, and Letters: Finding a "Female Voice" in Late Antiquity', *Gender & History*, 31.2 (2019), 353–382

Hillner, Julia, 'Female Crime and Female Confinement in Late Antiquity', in *Social Control in Late Antiquity: The Violence of Small Worlds*, ed. by Kate Cooper and Jamie Wood (Cambridge: Cambridge University Press, 2020), pp. 15–38

Hillner, Julia, *Helena Augusta: Mother of the Empire* (Oxford: Oxford University Press, 2023)

Hochstetler, Donald, *A Conflict of Traditions: Women in Religion in the Early Middle Ages, 500–840* (Lanham, MD: University Press of America, 1992)

Hochstetler, Donald, 'The Meaning of Monastic Cloister for Women According to Caesarius of Arles', in *Religion, Culture, and Society in the Early Middle Ages: Studies in Honor of Richard E. Sullivan*, ed. by Thomas F. X. Noble and John J. Contreni (Kalamazoo, MI: Medieval Institute Publications, 1987), pp. 27–40

Holum, Kenneth G., 'Hadrian and St Helena: Imperial Travel and the Origins of Christian Holy Land Pilgrimage', in *The Blessings of Pilgrimage*, ed. by Robert G. Ousterhout (Urbana: University of Illinois Press, 1990), pp. 66–81

Hopkins, M. K., 'The Age of Roman Girls at Marriage', *Population Studies*, 18.3 (1965), 309–327

Horden, Peregrine, 'Public Health, Hospitals, and Charity', in *The Oxford Handbook of the Merovingian World*, ed. by Bonnie Effros and Isabel Moreira (Oxford: Oxford University Press, 2020), pp. 299–319

Huber-Rebenich, Gerlinde, 'Die thüringische Prinzessin Radegunde in der zeitgenössischen Überlieferung', in *Die Frühzeit der Thüringer*, ed. by Helmut Castritius, Dieter Geuenich, and Matthias Werner (Berlin: Walter de Gruyter, 2009), pp. 235–252

Hunt, E. D., 'Constantine and Jerusalem', *Journal of Ecclesiastical History*, 48 (1997), 405–424

Jeffrey, Jane E., 'Radegund and the Letter of Foundation', in *Women Writing Latin: From Roman Antiquity to Early Modern Europe*, vol. 2: *Medieval Women Writing Latin*, ed. by Laurie J. Churchill, Phyllis R. Brown, and Jane E. Jeffrey (London: Routledge, 2002), pp. 11–23

Jenks, Martha Gail, *From Queen to Bishop: A Political Biography of Radegund of Poitiers* (Berkeley: University of California Press, 1999)

Joblin, Alain, 'L'Attitude des protestants face aux reliques', in *Les Reliques: objets, cultes, symboles: actes du colloque international de l'Université du Littoral-Côte d'Opale (Boulogne-sur-Mer), 4–6 septembre 1997*, ed. by Edina Bozóky and Anne Marie Helvetius (Turnhout: Brepols, 1999), pp. 123–144

Joerres, Peter, *Chronologische und religionswissenschaftliche Untersuchungen über das Lebender hl. Radegundis und ihrer Verwandten* (Ahrweiler: Plachner, 1897)

Johnsson, Peter H., 'Locks of Difference: The Integral Role of Hair as a Distinguishing Feature in Early Merovingian Gaul', *Ex Post Facto*, 19 (2010), 55–68

Jones, Allen E., *Social Mobility in Late Antique Gaul: Strategies and Opportunities for the Non-Elite* (Cambridge: Cambridge University Press, 2009)

Jones, Lynn, 'Perceptions of Byzantium: Radegund of Poitiers and Relics of the True Cross', in *Byzantine Images and their Afterlives: Essays in Honour of Annemarie Weyl Carr*, ed. by Lynn Jones (Farnham: Ashgate, 2014), pp. 105–124

Joye, Silvie, 'Basine, Radegonde et la Thuringe chez Grégoire de Tours', *Francia*, 32 (2005), 1–18

Joye, Silvie, *La Femme ravie: le mariage par rapt dans les sociétés occidentales du haut Moyen Âge* (Turnhout: Brepols, 2012)

Kampers, Gerd, 'Caretena—Königin und Asketin', *Francia*, 27 (2000), 1–32

Kelley, J. N. D., *Early Christian Creeds*, 3rd edn (London: Longman, 1972; repr. 2008)

Kelley, Justin L., *The Church of the Holy Sepulchre in Text and Archaeology: A Survey and Analysis of Past Excavations and Recent Archaeological Research, with a Collection of Principal Historical Sources* (Oxford: Archaeopress, 2019)

Kitchen, John, *Saints' Lives and the Rhetoric of Gender: Male and Female in Merovingian Hagiography* (Oxford: Oxford University Press, 1998)

Klein, Holger A., 'Constantine, Helena, and the Cult of the True Cross in Constantinople', in *Byzance et les reliques du Christ: xxe congrès international des études Byzantines 19–25 août 2001*, ed. by Jannic Durand and Bernard Flusin (Paris: Association des Amis du Centre d'Histoire et Civilisation de Byzance, 2004), pp. 31–59

Klein, Holger A., 'Sacred Relics and Imperial Ceremonies at the Great Palace of Constantinople', in *Visualisierungen von Herrschaft: Frühmittelalterliche*

Residenzen—Gestalt und Zeremoniell: Internationales Kolloquium 3./4. Juni 2004 in Istanbul, ed. by Franz Alto Bauer (Istanbul: Ege Yayınlar, 2006), pp. 79–99

Kleinmann, Dorothée, *Radegonde, une sainte européenne: vénération et lieux de vénération dans les pays germanophones* (Ludon: PSR Éditions, 2000)

Klingshirn, William E., *Caesarius of Arles: The Making of a Christian Community in Late Antique Gaul* (Cambridge: Cambridge University Press, 1994)

Kneepkens, C. H., 'À propos des débuts de l'histoire de l'église-funéraire Sainte Radegonde de Poitiers', *Cahiers de civilisation médiévale*, 29 (1986), 331–338

Kneepkens, C. H., '*Supra sanctae Radegundis cilicium*: Notes on Baudonivia's *Life of Radegund* (ii, 15)', in *Eulogia: mélanges offerts à Antoon A. R. Bastiaensen à l'occasion de son soixante-cinquième anniversaire*, ed. by Gerhardus Johannes Marinus Bartelink, A. Hilhorst, and C. H. Kneepkens (The Hague: Martinus Nijhoff Publishers, 1991), pp. 163–173

Koebner, Richard, *Venantius Fortunatus: Seine Persönlichkeit und seine Stellung in der geistigen Kultur des Merowinger-Reiches* (Leipzig: Benedictus Gotthelf Teubner, 1915)

Krautheimer, Richard, *Early Christian and Byzantine Architecture* (Harmondsworth: Penguin Books, 1965)

Krautschick, Stefan, 'Radegunde', in *Reallexikon der Germanischen Altertumskunde*, ed. by Herbert Jankuhn, Heinrich Beck, Hans Kuhn, Kurt Ranke, and Reinhard Wenskus 2nd edn, vol. 24 (Berlin: Walter de Gruyter, 2003), pp. 61–63

Kroll, Jerome, and Bernard Bachrach, *The Mystic Mind: The Psychology of Medieval Mystics and Ascetics* (London: Routledge, 2005)

Kreiner, Jamie, *The Social Life of Hagiography in the Merovingian Kingdom* (Cambridge: Cambridge University Press, 2014)

Krusch, Bruno, 'De vita sanctae Radegundis libri duo', in *Monumenta Germaniae historica, Scriptores rerum Merovingicarum*, ed. by Bruno Krusch vol. 2 (Hanover: Hahn, 1888), pp. 358–364

Kuefler, Matthew, *The Manly Eunuch: Masculinity, Gender Ambiguity, and Christian Ideology in Late Antiquity* (Chicago: University of Chicago Press, 2001)

Labande, Edmond-René, 'Radegonde: reine, moniale et pacificatrice', in *La Riche Personnalité de sainte Radegonde: conférences et homélies prononcées à Poitiers à l'occasion du xive Centenaire de sa mort (587–1987)*, ed. by Edmond-René Labande and Pierre Riché (Poitiers: Comité du xive Centenaire, 1988), pp. 23–32

Labande-Mailfert, Yvonne, 'Les Débuts de Sainte-Croix', in *Histoire de l'abbaye Sainte-Croix de Poitiers: quatorze siècles de vie monastique*, ed. by Edmond-René Labande (Poitiers: Société des Antiquaires de l'Ouest, 1986), pp. 25–75

Labande-Mailfert, Yvonne, 'Poitiers: abbaye Sainte-Croix', in *Les Premiers Monuments chrétiens de la France*, vol. 2: *Sud-Ouest et Centre*, ed. by Guy Barruol (Paris: Picard, 1996), pp. 284–289

Lange, Imke, '"Teste Deo, me nihil audisse modo saeculare de cantico": "Volk" und "Elite" als kulturelle Systeme in *De vita s. Radegundis libri duo*', *Medium Aevum Quotidianum*, 36 (1997), 20–38

Leclercq, Jean, 'La Sainte Radegonde de Venance Fortunat et celle de Baudovinie', in *Fructus centesimus: mélanges offerts à Gerard J. M. Bartelink à l'occasion de son soixante-cinquième anniversaire*, ed. by Antoon A. R. Bastiaensen, Antonius Hilhorst, and Corneille Henri Kneepkens (Dordrecht: Kluwer, 1989), pp. 207–216

Le Jan, Régine, *Famille et pouvoir dans le monde franc (viie–xe siècle): essai d'anthropologie sociale* (Paris: Sorbonne, 1995)

Levillain, Léon, 'La Révolte des nonnains de Sainte-Croix à Poitiers', *Mémoires de la Société des antiquaires de l'Ouest*, 3rd series, 2 (1909), xix–lxvi

Liebeschuetz, John Hugo Wolfgang Gideon, *Ambrose of Milan: Political Letters and Speeches* (Liverpool: Liverpool University Press, 2005)

Life of Chlothild, 'Vita sanctae Chrothildis', in *Monumenta Germaniae historica, Scriptores rerum Merovingicarum*, ed. by Bruno Krusch, vol. 2 (Hanover: Hahn, 1888), pp. 342–348; trans. by Jo Ann McNamara and John E. Halborg, *Sainted Women of the Dark Ages* (Durham, NC: Duke University Press, 1992), pp. 40–50

Lemaître, Jean-Loup, ed., *Radegonde, reine, moniale et sainte: son culte en Limousin* (Ussel: Musée du Pays d'Ussel, 2003)

Leonardi, Claudio, 'Fortunato e Baudonivia', in *Aus Kirche und Reich: Studien zu Theologie, Politik und Recht im Mittelalter: Festschrift für Friedrich Kempf zu seinem 75. Geburtstag und fünfzigjährigen Doktorjubiläum*, ed. by Hubert Mordek (Sigmaringen: J. Thorbecke, 1983), pp. 23–32

Levine, Robert, 'Patronage and Erotic Rhetoric in the Sixth Century: The Case of Venantius Fortunatus', in *Words of Love and Love of Words in the Middle Ages and the Renaissance*, ed. by Albrecht Classen (Tempe, AZ: Arizona Center for Medieval and Renaissance Studies, 2008), pp. 75–93

Leyser, Conrad, '"Divine Power Flowed from his Book": Ascetic Language and Episcopal Authority in Gregory of Tours' *Life of the Fathers*', in *The World of Gregory of Tours*, ed. by Kathleen Mitchell and Ian Wood (Leiden: Brill, 2002), pp. 281–294

Lillich, Meredith Parsons, *The Armor of Light: Stained Glass in Western France, 1250–1325* (Berkeley: University of California Press, 1994)

Liverani, Paolo, 'Saint Peter's and the City of Rome between Late Antiquity and the Early Middle Ages', in *Old Saint Peter's, Rome*, ed. by Rosamond McKitterick, John Osborne, Carol M. Richardson, and Joanna Story (Cambridge: Cambridge University Press, 2018), pp. 21–34

Leyerle, Blake, 'Mobility and the Traces of Empire', in *A Companion to Late Antiquity*, ed. by Philip Rousseau (Chichester: John Wiley & Sons, 2009), pp. 110–124

Loseby, Simon T., 'Lost Cities: The End of the *civitas*-system in Frankish Gaul', in *Gallien in Spätantike und Frühmittelalter: Kulturgeschichte einer Region*, ed. by Steffen Diefenbach and Gernot Michael Müller (Berlin: Walter de Gruyter, 2013), pp. 223–252

Marenbon, John, *Boethius* (Oxford: Oxford University Press, 2003)

Markus, R. A., *The End of Ancient Christianity* (Cambridge: Cambridge University Press, 1990)

Marié, Georges, 'Sainte Radegonde et le milieu monastique contemporain', in *Études mérovingiennes: actes des journées de Poitiers, 1er–3 mai 1952* (Paris: Picard, 1953), pp. 210–225

Martindale, J. R., *Prosopography of the Later Roman Empire*, 3 vols in 4 parts (Cambridge: Cambridge University Press, 1971–1992)

Mathisen, Ralph W., 'The Family of Georgius Florentius Gregorius and the Bishops of Tours', *Medievalia et Humanistica: Studies in Medieval and Renaissance Culture*, n.s., 12 (1984), 83–95; reprinted in Ralph W. Mathisen, *Studies in the History, Literature and Society of Late Antiquity* (Amsterdam: Adolf M. Hakkert, 1991), pp. 53–66

Mathisen, Ralph W., 'Roman Identity in Late Antiquity, with Special Attention to Gaul', in *Transformations of Romanness: Early Medieval Regions and Identities*, ed. by Walter Pohl, Clemens Gantner, Cinzia Grifoni, and Marianne Pollheimer-Mohaupt (Berlin: Walter de Gruyter, 2018), pp. 255–274

Mathisen, Ralph W., 'Sidonius's People', in *the Edinburgh Companion to Sidonius Apollinaris*, ed. by Gavin Kelley and Joop van Waarden (Edinburgh: Edinburgh University Press, 2020), pp. 29–165

Mathisen, Ralph W., 'Vouillé, Voulon, and the Location of the Campus Vogladensis', in *The Battle of Vouillé, 507 CE: Where France Began*, ed. by Ralph W. Mathisen and Danuta Shanzer (Berlin: Walter de Gruyter, 2012), pp. 43–62

Matteo, Martelli, 'Alchemical Textiles: Colourful Garments, Recipes and Dyeing Techniques in Graeco-Roman Egypt', in *Greek and Roman Textiles and Dress: An Interdisciplinary Anthology*, ed. by Mary Harlow and Marie-Louise Nosch (Oxford: Oxbow Books, 2014), pp. 111–129

Maurin, Louis, *Topographie chrétienne des cités de la Gaule des origines au milieu de VIIIᵉ siècle*, vol. 10: *Province ecclésiastique de Bordeaux (Aquitania secunda)* (Paris: De Boccard, 1998)

Mayeski, Marie Anne, and Jane Crawford, 'Reclaiming an Ancient Story: Baudonivia's Life of St Radegund (circa 525–587)', in *Women Saints in World Religions*, ed. by Arvind Sharma (Albany: State University of New York Press, 2000), pp. 71–106

McClanan, Anne L., *Representations of Early Byzantine Empresses: Image and Empire* (London: Palgrave Macmillan, 2002)

McGinn, Thomas A. J., 'The Augustan Marriage Legislation and Social Practice: Elite Endogamy versus Male "Marrying Down"', in *Speculum Iuris: Roman Law as a Reflection of Social and Economic Life in Antiquity*, ed. by Jean-Jacques Aubert and Adriaan Johan Boudewijn Sirks (Ann Arbor: University of Michigan Press, 2002), pp. 46–93

McNamara, Jo Ann, 'Chastity as a Third Gender in the History and Hagiography of Gregory of Tours', in *The World of Gregory of Tours*, ed. by Kathleen Mitchell and Ian Wood (Leiden: Brill, 2002), pp. 199–210

McNamara, Jo Ann, '*Imitatio Helenae*: Sainthood as an Attribute of Queenship', in *Saints: Studies in Hagiography*, ed. by Sandro Sticca (Binghamton, NY: Medieval & Renaissance Texts & Studies, 1996), pp. 51–80

McNamara, Jo Ann, and John E. Halborg, *Sainted Women of the Dark Ages* (Durham, NC: Duke University Press, 1992)

Meyer, Jean, 'Mythologies monarchiques d'Ancien Regime et Moyen Âge', in *Media in Francia: recueil de mélanges offert à Karl Ferdinand Werner*, ed. by Georges Duby (Paris: Hérault- Éditions, 1989), pp. 285–302

Meyer, Wilhelm, *Der Gelegenheitsdichter Venantius Fortunatus* (Berlin: Weidmann, 1901)

Mikat, Paul, *Die Inzestgesetzgebung der merowingisch-fränkischen Konzilien (511–626/27)* (Paderborn: Ferdinand Schöningh, 1994)

Mineau, Robert, 'Un évêque de Poitiers au VIᵉ siècle: Marovée', *Bulletins de la Société des Antiquaries de l'Ouest*, 11.1 (1972), 361–383

Moreira, Isabel, 'Provisatrix optima: St Radegund of Poitiers's Relic Petitions to the East', *Journal of Medieval History*, 19 (1993), 285–305

Müller, Mechthild, *Die Kleidung nach Quellen des frühen Mittelalters: Textilien und Mode von Karl dem Großen bis Heinrich III* (Berlin: Walter de Gryuter, 2003)

Muschiol, Gisela, 'Vorbild und Konkurrenz: Martin von Tours und die heiligen Frauen', *Rottenburger Jahrbuch für Kirchengeschichte*, 18 (1999), 77–88

Murray, Alexander, *Suicide in the Middle Ages*, vol. 2: *The Curse on Self-Murder* (Oxford: Oxford University Press, 2000)

Murray, Alexander Callander, 'Chronology and the Composition of the *Histories* of Gregory of Tours', *Journal of Late Antiquity*, 1 (2008), 157–196

Murray, Alexander Callander, 'The Composition of the *Histories* of Gregory of Tours and its Bearing on the Political Narrative', in *A Companion to Gregory of Tours*, ed. by Alexander Callander Murray (Leiden: Brill, 2016), pp. 63–101

Murray, Alexander Callander, '*Post vocantur Merohingii*: Fredegar, Merovech, and "Sacral Kingship" ', in *After Rome's Fall: Narrators and Sources of Early Medieval History: Essays Presented to Walter Goffart*, ed. by Alexander Callander. (Toronto: University of Toronto Press, 1998), pp. 121–152

Natali, Mario, 'Santa Radegonda di Poitiers nelle *Vitae* di Ildeberto di Lavardino e di Henry Bradshaw'. *Studi e materiali di storia delle religioni*, 17 (1993), 247–264

Navalesi, Kent E., 'The Prose Lives of Venantius Fortunatus: Hagiography, Lay Piety, and Pastoral Care in Sixth-Century Gaul' (unpublished PhD dissertation: University of Illinois at Urbana-Champaign, 2020)

Nelson, Janet L., 'Queens as Jezebels: The Careers of Brunhild and Balthild in Merovingian History', *Studies in Church History Subsidia*, 1 (1978), 31–77

Nelson, Janet L., 'Women and the Word in the Earlier Middle Ages', in Janet L. Nelson, *The Frankish World, 750–900* (London: A&C Black, 1996), pp. 199–221

Neumeister, Peter, 'The Ancient Thuringians: Problems of Names and Family Connections', in *The Baiuvarii and Thuringi: An Ethnographic Perspective*, ed. by Janine Fries-Knoblach and Heiko Steuer (Woodbridge: Boydell, 2014), pp. 83–102

Nisard, Charles, 'Des poésies de sainte Radegonde attribuées jusqu'ici à Fortunat', *Revue Historique*, 37.1 (1888), 49–57

Noga-Banai, Galit, 'Architectural Frames for Relics of the True Cross: Two Frankish Test Cases', in *Devotional Cross-Roads: Practicing Love of God in Medieval Jerusalem, Gaul and Saxony*, ed. by Hedwig Röckelein, Galit Noga-Banai, and Lotem Pinchover (Göttingen: Göttingen University Press, 2019), pp. 63–90

Noga-Banai, Galit, 'Relocation to the West: The Relic of the True Cross in Poitiers', *East and West in the Early Middle Ages: The Merovingian Kingdoms in Mediterranean Perspective*, ed. by Stefan Esders, Yaniv Fox, Yitzhak Hen, and Lauri Sarti (Cambridge: Cambridge University Press, 2019), pp. 189–201

Norberg, Dag, 'Le *Pange lingua* de Fortunat pour la croix', *La Maison-Dieu*, 173 (1988), 71–79

O'Faolain, Julia, *Women in the Wall* (New York: Carroll & Graf, 1973)

Orlinski, Shachar F., 'Lost in Translation: A Study of the Unfreedom of Freewomen in Merovingian Francia' (unpublished MA thesis: The Hebrew University of Jerusalem, 2021)

Oswald, Gert, *Lexikon der Heraldik: Von Apfelkreuz bis Zwillingsbalken*, 3rd edn (Battenberg: Regenstauf, 2011)

Ousterhout, Robert, 'Architecture as Relic and the Construction of Sanctity: The Stones of the Holy Sepulchre', *Journal of the Society of Architectural Historians*, 62.1 (2003), 4–23

Pace, Valentino, Guido Sante, and Paolo Radiciotti, *La Crux vaticana o croce di Giustino II: Museo storico artistico del tesoro di S. Pietro* (Vatican City: Edizioni Capitolo Vaticano, 2009)

Papa, Cristina, 'Radegonda e Batilde: modelli di santita regia femminile nel regno merovingio', *Benedictina*, 36.1 (1989), 13–33

Partner, Nancy F., 'No Sex, No Gender', *Speculum*, 68 (1993), 419–443

Patterson, Orlando, *Slavery and Social Death: A Comparative Study* (Cambridge, MA: Harvard University Press, 1982)

Patzold, Steffen, 'Zur Sozialstruktur des Episkopats und zur Ausbildung Bischöflicher Herrschaft in Gallien zwischen Spätantike und Frühmittelalter', in *Reiche und Namen im Frühen Mittelalter*, ed. by Matthias Becher and Stefanie Dick (Munich: Wilhelm Fink, 2010), pp. 121–140

Pejenaute Rubio, Francisco, 'Los milagros de santa Radegunda y dos apéndices', *Archivum*, 60 (2010), 289–340

Pejenaute Rubio, Francisco, 'El prólogo de Venancio Fortunato a la *Vida de santa Radegunda* frente a los de Baudonivia y Hildeberto de Lavardin', *Minerva*, 18 (2004), 171–186

Pejenaute Rubio, Francisco, 'Venancio Fortunato, *Vida de Santa Radegunda*', *Archivum*, 57 (2007), 219–266

Pejenaute Rubio, Francisco, 'La *Vida de Santa Radegunda* escrita por Baudonivia', *Archivum*, 56 (2006), 313–360

Percival, John, 'Villas and Monasteries in Late Roman Gaul', *Journal of Ecclesiastical History*, 48.1 (1997), 1–21

Périn, Patrick, 'À propos de la datation et de l'interprétation de la tombe no 49 de la basilique de Saint-Denis, attribuée à la reine Arégonde, éspouse de Clotaire Iᵉʳ', in *L'Art des invasions en Hongrie et en Wallonie: actes du colloque tenu au Musée royal de Mariemont du 9 au 11 avril 1979* (Morlanwelz: *Musée royal de Mariemont*, 1991), pp. 11–30

Petersen, Joan M., 'The Spirituality and Miracles of St Radegund', in *Monastic Studies: The Continuity of Tradition*, ed. by Judith Loades (Bangor: Headstart History, 1990), pp. 37–47

Peyroux, Catherine, 'The Leper's Kiss', in *Monks and Nuns, Saints and Outcasts: Religion in Medieval Society: Essays in Honor of Lester K. Little*, ed. by Sharon Farmer and Barbara H. Rosenwein (Ithaca, NY: Cornell University Press, 2000), pp. 172–188

Pietri, Luce, *La Ville de Tours du IVᵉ au VIᵉ siècle: naissance d'une cité chrétienne*, Collection de l'École Française de Rome, 69 (Rome: École française de Rome, 1983)

Pisacane, Maria, 'La regalità merovingia tra giochi di parole e astrattismo filosofico-artistico (Ven. Fort. Carm. App. 5)', *Romanobarbarica*, 19 (2006–2009), 157–187

Pischel, Barbara, *Radegunde: Zur europäischen Volkskunde* (Bern: Peter Lang, 1997)

Pizarro, Joaquín Martínez, 'Gregory of Tours and the Literary Imagination: Genre, Narrative Style, Sources, and Models in the *Histories*', in *A Companion to Gregory of Tours*, ed. by Alexander Callander Murray (Leiden: Brill, 2016), pp. 337–374

Platts, Calum, 'Competing Influences: Francia, Rome and the English in the Seventh Century' (unpublished PhD thesis: University of Cambridge, 2021)

Pohl, Walter, 'Christian and Barbarian Identities in the Early Medieval West: Introduction', in *Post-Roman Transitions: Christian and Barbarian Identities in the Early Medieval West*, ed. by Walter Pohl and Gerda Heydemann (Turnhout: Brepols, 2013), pp. 1–46

Pohl, Walter, '*Germania*, Herrschaftssitze östlich des Rheins und nördlich der Donau', in *Sedes regiae (ann. 400–800)*, ed. by Gisela Ripoll López and José María Gurt Esparraguera (Barcelona: Reial Acadèmia de Bones Lletres, 2000), pp. 305–318

Pon, Georges, 'Un corps martyrisé: l'exemple de sainte Radegonde', in *Corps outragés, corps ravagés de l'Antiquité au Moyen Âge*, ed. by Lydie Bodiou, Véronique Mehl, and Myriam Soria-Audebert (Turnhout: Brepols, 2011), pp. 249–260

Puhak, Shelley, *The Dark Queens: The Bloody Rivalry that Forged the Medieval World* (London: Bloomsbury, 2022)

Radle, Gabriel, 'The Veiling of Women in Byzantium: Liturgy, Hair, and Identity in a Medieval Rite of Passage', *Speculum*, 94.4 (2019), 1070–1115

Réal, Isabelle, *Vie des saints, vie de famille: représentation et système de la parenté dans le Royaume mérovingien (481–751) d'après les sources hagiographiques* (Turnhout: Brepols, 2002)

Réau, Louis, *Histoire du vandalisme: les monuments détruits de l'art français*, 2 vols (Paris: Hachette, 1959), vol. 1: *Du haut Moyen Âge au xixe siècle*; vol. 2: *xixe et xxe siècles*

Redellet, Marc, 'Tours et Poitiers: les relations entre Grégoire et Fortunat', in *Grégoire de Tours et l'espace gaulois*, ed. by Nancy Gauthier and Henri Galinié (Tours: Fédération pour l'édition de la Revue archéologique du Centre, 1997), pp. 159–176

Renaud, Jean, *Les Vikings de la Charente à l'assaut de l'Aquitaine* (Cressé: Éditions des Régionalismes & PRNG Éditions, 2015)

Reimitz, Helmut, *History, Frankish Identity, and the Framing of Western Ethnicity, 550–850* (Cambridge: Cambridge University Press, 2015)

Rennie, Kriston R., *The Destruction and Recovery of Monte Cassino, 529–1964* (Amsterdam: Amsterdam University Press, 2021)

Riché, Pierre, *Education and Culture in the Barbarian West: From the Sixth through the Eighth Century*, trans. by John J. Contreni (Columbia, SC: University of South Carolina Press, 1976)

Riché, Pierre, 'La vita s. Rusticulae: note d'hagiographie mérovingienne', *Analecta Bollandiana*, 72 (1954), 369–377

Ringrose, Kathryn M., *The Perfect Servant: Eunuchs and the Social Construction of Gender in Byzantium* (Chicago: University of Chicago Press, 2004)

Roberts, Michael, *The Humblest Sparrow: The Poetry of Venantius Fortunatus* (Ann Arbor: University of Michigan Press, 2009)

Roberts, Michael, 'Venantius Fortunatus and Gregory of Tours: Poetry and Patronage', in *A Companion to Gregory of Tours*, ed. by Alexander C. Murray (Leiden: Brill, 2015), pp. 35–59

Roberts, Michael, 'Venantius Fortunatus's Elegy on the Death of Galswintha (*Carm.* 6.5)', in *Society and Culture in Late Antique Gaul: Revisiting the Sources*, ed. by Ralph W. Mathisen and Danuta Shanzer (Farnham: Ashgate, 2001), pp. 298–312

Roberts, Michael, 'Venantius Fortunatus's *Life of Saint Martin*', *Traditio*, 57 (2002), 129–187

Rosenwein, Barbara, 'Inaccessible Cloisters: Gregory of Tours and Episcopal Exemption', in *The World of Gregory of Tours*, ed. by Kathleen Mitchell and Ian Wood (Leiden: Brill, 2002), pp. 181–198

Rossiter, Jeremy, 'Convivium and Villa in Late Antiquity', in *Dining in a Classical Context: An Investigation of the Role of the Feast as a Cultural Focus for the Classical World*, ed. by William J. Slater (Ann Arbor: University of Michigan Press, 1991), pp. 199–214

Rotman, Tamar, *Hagiography, Historiography, and Identity in Sixth-Century Gaul: Rethinking Gregory of Tours* (Amsterdam: Amsterdam University Press, 2022)

Rouche, Michel, 'Le Célibat consacré de sainte Radegonde', in *La Riche Personnalité de sainte Radegonde: conférences et homélies prononcées à l'occasion du xive centenaire de sa mort (587–1987)*, ed. by Edmond-René Labande and Pierre Riché (Poitiers: Comité du xive Centenaire, 1988), pp. 77–98; reprinted in Michel Rouche, *Le Choc des cultures: Romanité, Germanité, Chrétienté, durant le haut Moyen Âge*, ed.

by Jean Heuclin (Villeneuve d'Ascq: Presses Universitaires du Septentrion, 2003), pp. 283–298

Rouche, Michel, 'Fortunat et Baudonivie: deux biographes pour une seule sainte', in *La Vie de sainte Radegonde par Fortunat: Poitiers, Bibliothèque Municipale Manuscrit 250 (136)*, ed. by Robert Favreau (Paris: Éditions du Seuil, 1995), pp. 239–249

Rouche, Michel, 'Radegonde, une mort programmée', in *Moines et moniales face à la mort: actes du colloque de Lille, 2–4 octobre 1992* (Lille: Villetaneuse, 1992), pp. 13–17; reprinted in Michel Rouche, *Le Choc des cultures: Romanité, Germanité, Chrétienté, durant le haut Moyen Âge*, ed. by Jean Heuclin (Villeneuve d'Ascq: Presses Universitaires du Septentrion, 2003), pp. 299–305

Rousselle, Aline, *Porneia: de la maîtrise du corps à la privation sensorielle IIe–IVe siècle de l'ère chrétienne* (Paris: Presses Universitaires de France, 1983); trans. by Felicia Pheasant, *Porneia: On Desire and the Body in Antiquity* (Cambridge: Blackwell, 1988)

Rousseau, Philip, *Pachomius: The Making of a Community in Fourth-Century Egypt* (Berkeley: University of California Press, 1985)

Rousseau, Philip, 'The Pious Household and the Virgin Chorus: Reflections on Gregory of Nyssa's *Life of Macrina*', *Journal of Early Christian Studies*, 13.2 (2005), 165–186

Rudge, Lindsay, 'Dedicated Women and Dedicated Spaces: Caesarius of Arles and the Foundation of St John', in *Western Monasticism ante litteram: The Spaces of Monastic Observance in Late Antiquity and the Early Middle Ages*, ed. by Hendrik Dey and Elizabeth Fentress (Turnhout: Brepols, 2011), pp. 99–116

Rütjes, Sarah, *Der Klosterstreit in Poitiers: Untersucht anhand der hagiographischen Quellen von Gregor von Tours 'Decem libri historiarum'* (Norderstedt: Grin, 2009)

Salzman, Michele R., *The Making of a Christian Aristocracy* (Cambridge, MA: Harvard University Press, 2002)

Scheibelreiter, Georg, 'Königstöchter im Kloster: Radegund († 587) und der Nonnenaufstand von Poitiers (589)', *Mitteilungen des Instituts für Österreichische Geschichtsforschung*, 87.1 (1979), 1–37

Scheibelreiter, Georg, 'Der Untergang des Thüringerreiches: Aus der Sicht des Frühmittelalters', in *Die Frühzeit der Thüringer*, ed. by Helmut Castritius, Dieter Geuenich, and Matthias Werner (Berlin: Walter de Gruyter, 2009), pp. 171–199

Schimpff, Volker, 'Pagan? Arianisch? Katholisch? Zu welcher Religion bekannte sich das altthüringische Königshaus?', *Concilium Medii Aevi*, 16 (2013), 97–184

Schmidt, Berthold, 'Das Königreich der Thüringer und seine Eingliederung in das Frankenreich', in *Die Franken: Wegbereiter Europas*, 2 vols (Mainz: Philip von Zabern, 1996), vol. 1, pp. 285–297

Schmidt, Berthold, 'Die Thüringer', in *Die Germanen: Geschichte und Kultur der germanischen Stämme in Mitteleuropa*, vol. 2: *Die Stämme und Stammesverbände in der Zeit vom 3. Jahrhundert bis zur Herausbildung der politischen Vorherrschaft der Franken*, ed. by Bruno Krüger (Berlin, Akademie Verlag, 1986), pp. 502–548

Schulenburg, Jane, 'Female Religious as Collectors of Relics: Finding Sacrality and Power in the "Ordinary"', in *Where Heaven and Earth Meet: Essays on Medieval Europe in Honor of Daniel F. Callahan*, ed. by Michael Frassetto, Mathew Gabriele, and John D. Hosler (Leiden: Brill, 2014), pp. 152–177

Shanzer, Danuta, 'Dating the Baptism of Clovis: The Bishop of Vienne vs. the Bishop of Tours', *Early Medieval Europe*, 7.1 (1998), 29–57

Shanzer, Danuta, 'Marriage and Kinship among the Burgundians' (forthcoming)

Shanzer, Danuta, and Ian Wood, *Avitus of Vienne: Letters and Selected Prose* (Liverpool: Liverpool University Press, 2002)

Sidéris, George, 'Eunuchs of Light: Power, Imperial Ceremonial, and Positive Representations of Eunuchs in Byzantium (4th–12th centuries AD), in *Eunuchs in Antiquity and Beyond*, ed. by Shaun Tougher (London: Classical Press of Wales and Duckworth, 2002), pp. 161–176

Singer, Rachel, 'Gregory's Forgotten Rebel: The Portrayal of Basina by Gregory of Tours and its Implications', *Early Medieval Europe*, 30.2 (2022), 185–208

Skubiszewski, Pitor, 'La Staurothèque de Poitiers', *Cahiers de civilisation médiévale x^e–xiie siècles*, 35 (1992), 65–75

Smit, Peter-Ben, 'Man or Human? A Note on the Translation of Άνθρωπος in Mark 10.1–9 and Masculinity Studies', *Bible Translator*, 69 (2018), 19–39

Smith, Julia M. H., ' "Carrying the Cares of State": Gender Perspectives on Merovingian "Staatlichkeit" ', in *Der frühmittelalterliche Staat—europäische Perspektiven*, ed. by Walter Pohl and Veronika Wieser (Vienna: Österreichische Akademie der Wissenschaften, 2009), pp. 227–240

Smith, Julia M. H., '*Radegundis peccatrix*: Authorizations of Virginity in Late Antique Gaul', in *Transformations of Late Antiquity: Essays for Peter Brown*, ed. by Philip Rousseau and Manolis Papoutsakis (Farnham: Ashgate, 2009), pp. 303–326

Smith, Julia M. H., 'Rulers and Relics c. 750–c. 950: Treasure on Earth, Treasure in Heaven', *Past & Present*, 206 (2010), 73–96

Smith, Julia M. H., 'Women at the Tomb: Access to Relic Shrines in the Early Middle Ages', in *The World of Gregory of Tours*, ed. by Kathleen Mitchell and Ian Wood (Leiden: Brill, 2002), pp. 163–180; translated from Julia M. H. Smith, 'L'Accès des femmes aux saintes reliques durant le haut Moyen Âge', *Médiévales*, 40 (2001), pp. 81–98

Stafford, Pauline, 'Queens and Treasure in the Early Middle Ages', in *Treasure in the Middle Ages*, ed. by Elizabeth Tyler (York: York Medieval Press, 2000), pp. 61–82

Stafford, Pauline, *Queens, Concubines and Dowagers: The King's Wife in the Early Middle Ages* (Athens: University of Georgia Press, 1983)

Steuer, Heiko, 'Die Herrschaftssitze der Thüringer', in *Die Frühzeit der Thüringer*, ed. by Helmut Castritius, Dieter Geuenich, and Matthias Werner (Berlin: Walter de Gruyter, 2009), pp. 201–234

Stevenson, Jane, *Women Latin Poets: Language, Gender, and Authority from Antiquity to the Eighteenth Century* (Oxford: Oxford University Press, 2005)

Szövérffy, Joseph, 'Venantius Fortunatus and the Earliest Hymns to the Holy Cross', *Classical Folio*, 20 (1966), 107–122

Tardi, Dominique, *Fortunat: étude sur un dernier représentant de la poésie latine dans la Gaule mérovingienne* (Paris: Boivin, 1927)

Tatum, Sarah, 'Auctoritas as Sanctitas: Balthild's Depiction as "Queen-Saint" in the *Vita Balthildis*', *European Review of History*, 16.6 (2009), 809–834

Thiellet, Claire, *Femmes, reines et saintes, v^e–xie siècles* (Paris: Sorbonne Université Presses, 2004)

Thomas, Emma Jane, 'The "Second Jezebel": Representations of the Sixth-Century Queen Brunhild' (unpublished PhD thesis: University of Glasgow, 2012)

Thraede, Klaus, *Grundzüge griechisch-römischer Brieftopik* (Munich: C. H. Beck, 1970)

Trenkmann, Ulrike, *Thüringen im Merowingerreich: Zur chronologischen und kulturgeschichtlichen Aussagekraft von Gräberfeldern des 6.–8. Jahrhunderts* (Langenweißbach: Beier & Beran, 2021)

Troncarelli, Fabio, *Tradizioni perdute: la 'Consolazione Philosophiae' nell'alto medioevo* (Padua: Antenor, 1981)

Tougher, Shaun, *The Eunuch in Byzantine History and Society* (London: Routledge, 2008)

Tyrell, V. Alice, *Merovingian Letters and Letter Writers* (Turnhout: Brepols, 2019)

Uytfanghe, Marc van, 'L'Audience de l'hagiographie au vi^e siècle en Gaul', in *Scribere sanctorum gesta: recueil d'études d'hagiographie médiévale offert à Guy Philippart*, ed. by Etienne Renard, Michel Trigalet, Xavier Hermand, and Paul Bertrand (Turnhout: Brepols, 2005), pp. 157–177

Uytfanghe, Marc van, 'L'Hagiographie et son public à l'époque mérovingienne', in *Papers Presented to the Seventh International Conference on Patristic Studies Held in Oxford 1975*, ed. by Elizabeth A. Livingstone, 2 vols (Berlin: Akademie-Verlag, 1983), vol. 2, pp. 54–62

Van Dam, Raymond, *Saints and their Miracles in Late Antique Gaul* (Princeton, NJ: Princeton University Press, 1993)

Van der Does, J. C., *Prinsessen uit het Huis van Oranje* (Puttern: C. J. Terwee, 1938)

Van Nuffelen, Peter, 'Gélase de Césarée, un compilateur du cinquième siècle', *Byzantinische Zeitschrift*, 95 (2002), 621–639

Veneskey, Laura, 'Jerusalem Refracted: Geographies of the True Cross in Late Antiquity', in *Natural Materials of the Hold Land and the Visual Translation of Place, 500–1500*, ed. by Renana Bartal, Neta B. Bodner, and Bianca Kühnel (London: Routledge, 2017), pp. 64–75

Verdon, Jean, 'Le Monachisme féminin à l'époque mérovingienne: le témoignage de Grégoire de Tours', in *Les Religieuses dans le cloître et dans le monde, des origines à nos jours: actes du deuxième colloque international du CERCOR. Poitiers, 29 septembre–2 octobre 1988* (Poitiers: Publications de l'Université de Saint-Étienne, 1994), pp. 29–44

Vezin, Jean, 'Étude paléographique et codicologique du manuscrit de la *Vita Radegundis*', in *La Vie de sainte Radegonde par Fortunat: Poitiers, Bibliothèque Municipale Manuscrit 250 (136)*, ed. by Robert Favreau (Paris: Éditions du Seuil, 1995), pp. 115–126

Vieillard-Troiekouroff, May, *Les Monuments religieux de la Gaule d'après les œuvres de Grégoire de Tours* (Paris: Honoré Champion, 1976)

Vihervalli, Ulriika, 'Wartime Rape in Late Antiquity: Consecrated Virgins and Victim Bias in the Fifth-Century West', *Early Medieval Europe*, 30.1(2022), 3–19

Von Moos, Peter, *Hildebert von Lavardin, 1056–1133: Humanitas an der Schwelle des höffischen Zeitalters* (Stuttgart: Anton Hiersemann, 1965)

Wallace-Hadrill, J. M., 'Fredegar and the History of France', *Bulletin of the John Rylands Library*, 40.2 (1958), 527–550

Wasyl, Anna Maria, 'An Aggrieved Heroine in Merovingian Gaul: Venantius Fortunatus, Radegund's Lament on the Destruction of Thuringia, and Echoing Ovid's *Heroides*', *Bollettino di studi latini*, 45.1 (2015), 64–75

Weaver, Rebecca Harden, 'The Legacy of Caesarius of Arles in Baudonivia's Biography of Radegund', *Studia Patristica*, 33 (1997), 475–480

Wehlau, Ruth, 'Literal and Symbolic: The Language of Asceticism in Two Lives of St Radegund', *Florilegium*, 19 (2002), 75–89

Weidemann, Margarete, 'Urkunde und Vita der hl. Bilhildis aus Mainz', *Francia*, 21.1 (1994), 17–84

Wemple, Suzanne F., 'Female Spirituality and Mysticism in Frankish Monasteries: Radegund, Balthild and Aldegund', in *Medieval Religious Women, 2: Peaceweavers*, ed.

by Lillian Thomas Shank and John A. Nichols (Kalamazoo. MI: Cistercian Publications, 1987), pp. 39–53

Wemple, Suzanne F., *Women in Frankish Society: Marriage and the Cloister, 500–900* (Philadelphia: University of Pennsylvania Press, 1981)

Weston, Lisa, 'Elegiac Desire and Female Community in Baudonivia's *Life of Saint Radegund*', in *Same-Sex Love and Desire among Women in the Middle Ages*, ed. by Francesca Sautman and Pamela Sheingorn (New York: Palgrave, 2001), pp. 85–99

Whatley, E. Gordon, 'An Early Literary Quotation from the *Inventio s. Crucis*: A Note on Baudonivia's *Vita s. Radegundis* (BHL 7049)', *Analecta Bollandiana*, 111.1–2 (1993), 81–91

Whitby, Michael, 'Images for Emperors in Late Antiquity: A Search for New Constantine', in *New Constantines: The Rhythm of Imperial Renewal in Byzantium, 4th–13th Centuries: Papers from the Twenty-Sixth Spring Symposium of Byzantine Studies, St Andrews, March 1992*, ed. by Paul Magdalino (Ashgate: Variorum, 1994), pp. 83–94

Widdowson, Marc, 'Merovingian Partitions: A "Genealogical Charter"?', *Early Medieval Europe*, 17.1 (2009), 1–22

Williard, Hope Deejune, 'Friendship in the Works of Venantius Fortunatus' (unpublished PhD thesis: University of Leeds, 2016)

Winkelmann, Friedhelm, 'Die Beurteilung des Eusebius von Cäsarea und seiner *Vita Constantini* im griechischen Osten', in *Byzantinistische Beiträge: Gründungstagung der Arbeitsgemeinschaft Byzantinistik in der Sektion Mittelalter der Deutschen Historiker-Gesellschaft vom 18. bis 21.4.1961 in Weimar*, ed. by Johannes Irmscher (Berlin: Akademie, 1964), pp. 91–119

Wilkinson, John, *Jerusalem Pilgrims before the Crusades* (Warminster: Aris & Philips, 1977)

Wittern, Susanne, 'Frauen zwischen asketischem Ideal und weltlichem Leben: Zur Darstellung des christlichen Handelns der merowingischen Königinnen Radegunde und Balthilde in den hagiographischen Lebensbeschreibungen des 6. und 7. Jahrhunderts', *Frauen in der Geschichte VII: Interdisziplinäre Studien zur Geschichte der Frauen im Frühmittelalter: Methode—Probleme—Ergebnisse*, ed. by Werner Affeldt and Annette Kuhn (Düsseldorf: Schwann, 1986), pp. 272–294

Wood, Ian, 'Assimilation von Romanen und Burgundern im Rhone-Raum', in *Die Burgunder: Ethnogenese und Assimilation eines Volkes: Dokumentation des 6. wissenschaftlichen Symposiums der Nibelungenliedgesellschaft Worms e.V. und der Stadt Worms vom 21. bis 24. September 2006*, ed. by Volker Gallé (Worms: Worms Verlag, 2008), pp. 215–236

Wood, Ian, 'Deconstructing the Merovingian Family', in *The Construction of Communities in the Early Middle Ages: Texts, Resources, and Artefacts*, ed. by Richard Corradini, Max Diesenberger, and Helmut Reimitz (Leiden: Brill, 2003), pp. 149–172

Wood, Ian, 'Defining the Franks: Frankish Origins in Early Medieval Historiography', in *Concepts of National Identity in the Middle Ages*, ed. by Simon Forde, Leslie Johnson, and Alan V. Murray (Leeds: University of Leeds, 1995), pp. 47–58; reprinted in *From Roman Provinces to Medieval Kingdoms*, ed. by Thomas F. X. Noble (London: Routledge, 2006), pp. 91–98

Wood, Ian, 'The Development of the Visigothic Court in the Hagiography of the Fifth and Sixth Centuries', in *Rome and Byzantium in the Visigothic Kingdom: Beyond Imitatio Imperii*, ed. by Damián Fernández, Molly Lester, and Jamie Wood (Amsterdam: Amsterdam University Press, 2023)

Wood, Ian, 'The Franks and Papal Theology, 550–660', in *The Crisis of the Oikoumene: The Three Chapters and the Failed Quest for Unity in the Sixth-Century Mediterranean*, ed. by Celia Chazelle and Catherine Cubitt (Turnhout: Brepols, 2007), pp. 223–242

Wood, Ian, 'Fredegar's Fables', in *Historiographie im frühen Mittelalter*, ed. by Anton Scharer and Georg Scheibelreiter, Veröffentlichungen des Instituts für Österreichische Geschichtsforderung, 32 (Vienna: Oldenbourg, 1994), pp. 359–366

Wood, Ian, 'The Frontiers of Western Europe: Developments East of the Rhine in the Sixth Century', in *The Sixth Century: Production, Distribution and Demand*, ed. by Richard Hodges and William Marwin Bowsky, The Transformation of the Roman World, 3 (Leiden: Brill, 1998), pp. 231–253

Wood, Ian, *Gregory of Tours* (Bangor: Headstart History, 1994)

Wood, Ian, 'Gregory of Tours and Clovis', *Revue belge de philologie et d'histoire*, 63 (1985), 249–272

Wood, Ian, 'Hair and Beards in the Early Medieval West', *Al-Masāq*, 30.1 (2018), 107–116

Wood, Ian, 'Incest, Law and the Bible in Sixth-Century Gaul', *Early Medieval Europe*, 7.3 (1998), 291–303

Wood, Ian, *The Merovingian Kingdoms, 450–751* (Harlow: Pearson, 1994)

Wood, Ian, 'Pagan Religion and Superstitions East of the Rhine from the Fifth to the Ninth Century', in *After Empire: Towards an Ethnology of Europe's Barbarians: Papers Presented at the First Conference on 'Studies in Historical Archaeoethology' Organised by the Center for Interdisciplinary Research on Social Stress, Which Was Held in San Marino from 26th August to 1st September 1993*, ed. by Giorgio Ausenda (Woodbridge: Boydell, 1995), pp. 253–279

Wood, Ian, 'Religion in Pre-Carolingian Thuringia and Bavaria', in *The Baiuvarii and Thuringi: An Ethnographic Perspective*, ed. by Janine Fries-Knoblach and Heiko Steuer, with John Hines (Woodbridge: Boydell, 2014), pp. 317–329

Wood, Ian, 'Royal Succession and Legitimation in the Roman West, 419–536', in *Staat im frühen Mittelalter*, ed. by Stuart Airlie, Walter Pohl, and Helmut Reimitz (Vienna: Österreichische Akademie der Wissenschaften, 2006), pp. 59–72

Wood, Ian, 'The Secret Histories of Gregory of Tours', in *Revue belge de philologie et d'histoire*, 71.2 (1993), 253–270

Wood, Ian, 'Topographies of Holy Power in Sixth-Century Gaul', in *Topographies of Power in the Early Middle Ages*, ed. by Mayke de Jong, Frans Theuws, and Carine van Rhijn (Leiden: Brill, 2001), pp. 137–154

Index